HEALTH & SAFETY IN PRACTICE

Health and Safety Law

Jeremy Stranks
MSc, FIEH, FIOSH, RSP

PITMAN
PUBLISHING

PITMAN PUBLISHING
128 Long Acre, London WC2 9AN

A Division of Pearson Professional Limited

First published in Great Britain 1994

British Library Cataloguing in Publication Data
A CIP catalogue record for this book can be obtained from the British Library.

ISBN 0 273 60733 2

10 9 8 7 6 5 4 3 2

Typeset by Northern Phototypesetting Co. Ltd., Bolton
Printed and bound in Great Britain by
Bell & Bain Ltd., Glasgow

The Publishers' policy is to use paper manufactured from sustainable forests

Contents

Preface

Health and safety law involves both common and statute law. The statute law in this area goes back over nearly two centuries, starting with the Health and Morals of Apprentices Act 1802. This legislation was largely introduced to combat the appalling working conditions in the cotton industry and to limit the hours worked by apprentices. As technology moved forwards, a succession of protective legislation followed in its wake: the Factory Act 1833, the Workshop Regulation Acts 1867 and 1901, the Factories Acts 1937 and 1961 and the Health and Safety at Work, etc. Act 1974. These statutes were accompanied by regulations covering a wide range of health and safety-related issues. More recently, in the last decade, considerable developments have taken place in health and safety legislation, largely as a result of the various EC Directives. Moreover, there has been a significant change in approach. No longer can employers merely comply with the minimum prescribed standards. They must now manage health and safety at work effectively.

This book has been written with the syllabus requirements of the National Diploma and Certificate examinations of the National Examination Board in Occupational Safety and Health (NEBOSH) in mind. It is also intended to provide practical guidance to health and safety practitioners, managers, safety representatives and others with a direct or indirect involvement in occupational health and safety. The depth of treatment of different aspects of the law is directly related to the relative significance of these aspects.

Jeremy Stranks
1994

List of abbreviations

AC	Appeal cases
ACOP	Approved Code of Practice
AER	All England Reports
BATNEEC	Best available technique not entailing excessive costs
BPEO	Best practicable environmental option
CEN	European Committee for Standardization
CENELEC	European Committee for Electrotechnical Standardization
CGPR	Construction (General Provisions) Regulations 1961
CHIPR	Chemicals (Hazard Information and Packaging) Reguations 1993
CIMAHR	Control of Industrial Major Accidents Hazards Regulations 1984
CJA	Criminal Justices Act 1991
COSHHR	Control of Substances Hazardous to Health Regulations 1988
CPLR	Classification, Packaging and Labelling of Dangerous Substances Regulations 1984
CWPR	Construction (Working Places) Regulations 1966
DWI	Disposable weekly income
EC	European Community
ECJ	European Court of Justice
EEC	European Economic Community
EMA	Employment Medical Adviser
EPA	Environmental Protection Act 1990
FA	Factories Act 1961
FPA	Fire Precautions Act 1971
FSSPSA	Fire Safety and Safety of Places of Sport Act 1987
GMO	Genetically modified organism
HFL	Highly flammable liquid
HSC	Health and Safety Commission
HMIP	Her Majesty's Inspectorate of Pollution
HSE	Health and Safety Executive
HSWA	Health and Safety at Work, etc. Act 1974
IPC	Integrated Pollution Control
IRLR	Industrial Relations Law Reports
LA	Local Authority
LPG	Liquefied petroleum gas
LT	*Law Times* Reports
MEL	Maximum Exposure Limit
MEP	Member of the European Parliament
MHSWR	Management of Health and Safety at Work Regulations 1992
MQA	Mines and Quarries Act 1954
OES	Occupational Exposure Standard
OLA	Occupiers Liability Acts 1957 and 1984

RIDDOR	Reporting of Injuries, Diseases and Dangerous Occurrences Regulations 1985
RPE	Respiratory protective equipment
RSA	Radioactive Substances Act 1960
SC	Sessions cases
SI	Statutory instrument
SLT	*Scots Law Times* Reports
SRSCR	Safety Representatives and Safety Committees Regulations 1977
TGC	Transportable gas container

1

Elements of health and safety law

SOURCES OF LAW

Health and safety law is derived from a number of sources. The three principal sources of English law are legislation, or statute law, common law, from which most case law is derived, and contract law.

Statute law

Statute law consists of Acts of Parliament, such as the Health and Safety at Work, etc. Act 1974 (HSWA), which is an enabling Act, together with a large number of statutory instruments (SIs) made under the Acts of Parliament. Statutory instruments are generally known as 'subordinate legislation', or, 'delegated legislation'. Subordinate legislation relating to workplace health and safety consists of statutory instruments proposed by the Health and Safety Commission (HSC), after consultation with industry and local authorities and other relevant bodies, to the Secretary of State for Employment and, subsequently, laid before Parliament. Statutory instruments take the form of regulations, such as the Management of Health and Safety at Work Regulations 1992 (MHSWR), the Control of Substances Hazardous to Health Regulations 1989 (COSHHR) and Electricity at Work Regulations 1989. Since 1974, when the HSWA was introduced, all regulations concerning workplace health, safety and welfare have been passed in furtherance of HSWA.

Common law

Common law is an area of law that has developed since the eleventh century and is based on the decisions of the courts whereby *precedents* are established. Common law is, thus, the body of case law that is universally, or commonly, applied as a result of the judgments of the courts. Each judgment contains the judge's enunciation of the facts, a statement of the law applying to the case and their *ratio decendi*, or legal reasoning, for the finding that has been arrived at. These various judgments are recorded in the series of *Law*

Reports and have developed into the body of decided case law we now have and continue to develop. Common law is, then, accumulated case law, recorded for the most part in law reports, underpinned by the doctrine of precedent, under which a court is bound to follow earlier decisions of courts of its own level and those of superior courts.

Contract law

A contract is an agreement between two parties and, to be legally binding, must have certain basic features.

First, it must be certain in its wording. A contract consists of an *offer* made by one party that must be accepted unconditionally by the other. Second, there must be *consideration* that flows from one party to another, that is, the legal ingredient that changes an informal agreement into a legally binding contract, such as goods for money, work for pay. Third, there must be *intention,* whereby the parties concerned must intend to enter into this legally binding agreement. Finally, both parties must have the legal *capacity* to make such a contract. Legally, capacity usually means that parties concerned be sane, sober and over the age of 18.

Criminal and civil law

A *crime* is an offence against the state. In such a case, a person who commits a crime, which is a breach of criminal law, is *prosecuted* and brought before a court. The burden of proving a criminal charge *beyond reasonable doubt* rests with the prosecution. If found guilty of the crime, the court will impose some form of *punishment,* such as a fine or jail sentence, or both. While it is not the function of a criminal court to compensate, compensation may be ordered by a court to be given to an individual to cover personal injury and damage to property. However, a compensation order is not possible for the dependants of a deceased person in consequence of that person's death. Criminal cases are heard in the magistrates' courts and in the Crown Court. The more serious cases, which pass to the Crown Court, are heard before a judge and jury.

A *civil action,* on the other hand, generally involves individuals. In such actions, a plaintiff *sues* a defendant for a remedy (or remedies) that is beneficial to the plaintiff. In most cases this is *damages,* a form of financial compensation. (Many accident claims, for instance, pass through the civil courts, with damages being awarded to the injured person.) In a substantial number of cases, the plaintiff will agree to settle out of court. The civil courts are the County Courts and the High Court. A civil case must be proved on the *balance of probabilities,* which is a lesser standard than that of 'beyond reasonable doubt' required in a criminal case.

Criminal and civil liability

Criminal liability refers to the responsibilities under statute and the penalties that can be imposed by criminal courts, such as fines, imprisonment and remedial orders. The criminal courts in question are the magistrates' courts, which handle the bulk of health and safety offences as these tend to be the less serious offences, and the Crown Courts, which deal with the more serious ones (see The court hierarchy in England and Wales later in this chapter). Appeals can be made to the High Court and beyond, to the Court of Appeal, and, assuming leave is given, to the House of Lords. Subject to certain criteria, a case may pass to the European Court of Justice.

Criminal law is based on a system of enforcement. Its statutory provisions are enforced by the State's enforcement agencies, such as the police. Health and safety law is enforced mainly by the Health and Safety Executive (HSE), local authorities and fire authorities. In contrast to civil liability in tort, criminal liability cannot be insured against by employers, directors or employees. However, it is lawful to insure against court costs and the legal expenses of counsel in connection with a prosecution for health and safety offences.

Civil liability refers to the 'penalty' that can be imposed by a civil court. The civil courts are the County Court, High Court, Court of Appeal (civil division) or House of Lords. In general terms, the first two courts are courts of first instance, that is, they try cases for the first time, whereas the latter two courts are courts of appeal. Civil liability consists of awards of damages for injury, disease and/or death at work:

- in circumstances disclosing a breach of common law and/or statutory duty (normally negligence (see Chapter 2) on the part of an employer/factory occupier)
- arising out of and in the course of employment.

The damages that can be recovered following an injury-causing accident, contracting of an occupational disease or death fall into two categories:

- *general damages* – these relate to losses incurred after the hearing of the action, namely actual and probable (not merely 'possible') loss of future earnings following the accident)
- *special damages* – these relate to quantifiable losses incurred before the hearing of the case, and mainly consist of:
  - medical expenses incurred before the hearing of the case
  - loss of earnings incurred before the hearing of the case.

In the case of fatal injury, compensation for death negligently caused is payable under the Fatal Accidents Act 1976. Moreover, a fixed lump sum is payable under the Administration of Justices Act 1982 in respect of bereavement.

As far as assessment of future probable earnings under the heading of 'general damages' is concerned, such future earnings are assessed net (that is, as if tax had been deducted). Moreover, where, as is likely, an injured employee is in receipt of social security benefits, the Social Security (Consequential Provisions) Act 1975 provides that half of the value of certain social security benefits, including particularly sickness benefit and disablement benefit, must be deducted from the subsequently awarded damages.

THE COURT HIERARCHY IN ENGLAND AND WALES

There are two distinct systems, the courts dealing with criminal or civil actions respectively. Some courts have both criminal and civil jurisdiction, however.

The Magistrates' Courts

This is the lowest of the courts and deals mainly with criminal matters. Magistrates determine and sentence for many of the less serious offences. They also hold preliminary examinations into other offences to see if the prosecution can show a prima-facie case, as a result of which the accused may be committed for trial at a higher court.

The Crown Courts

Serious criminal charges (and some not so serious, but where the accused has the right to jury trial) are heard on indictment in the Crown Court. This court also hears appeals from magistrates' courts.

The County Courts

Each of these courts deal with civil matters only.

The High Court of Justice

More important civil matters – because of the sums involved or their legal complexity – will start in the High Court of Justice. The High Court has three divisions:

- Queen's Bench, which deals with contract and torts
- Chancery, which deals with matters relating to, for instance, land, wills, partnerships and companies
- Family.

In addition, the Queen's Bench division hears appeals on matters of law:

- from the magistrates' courts and from the Crown Court on the procedure called 'case stated'
- from some tribunals, for example the finding of an industrial tribunal on an enforcement notice under the HSWA.

The Queen's Bench division also has some supervisory functions over the

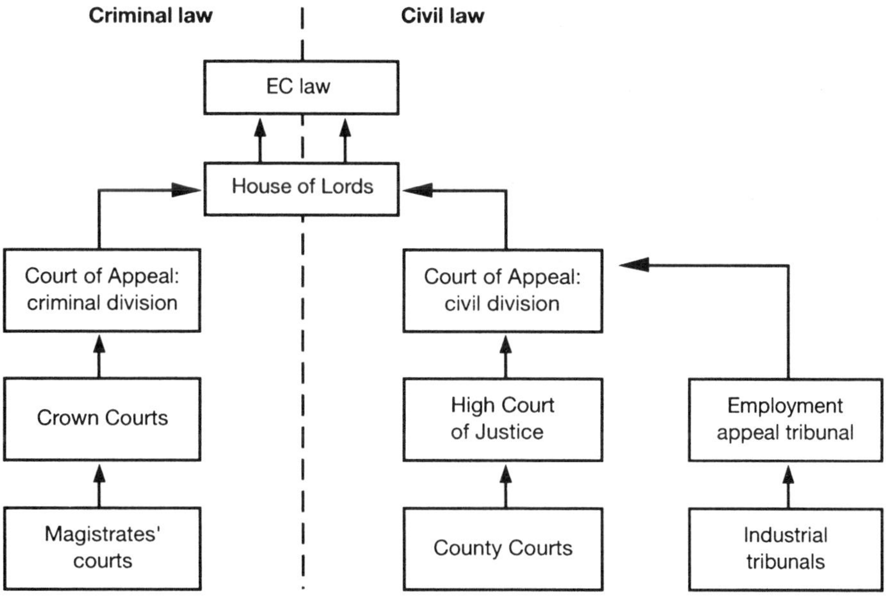

● **FIG 1.1 The court structure and hierarchy in England and Wales**

1

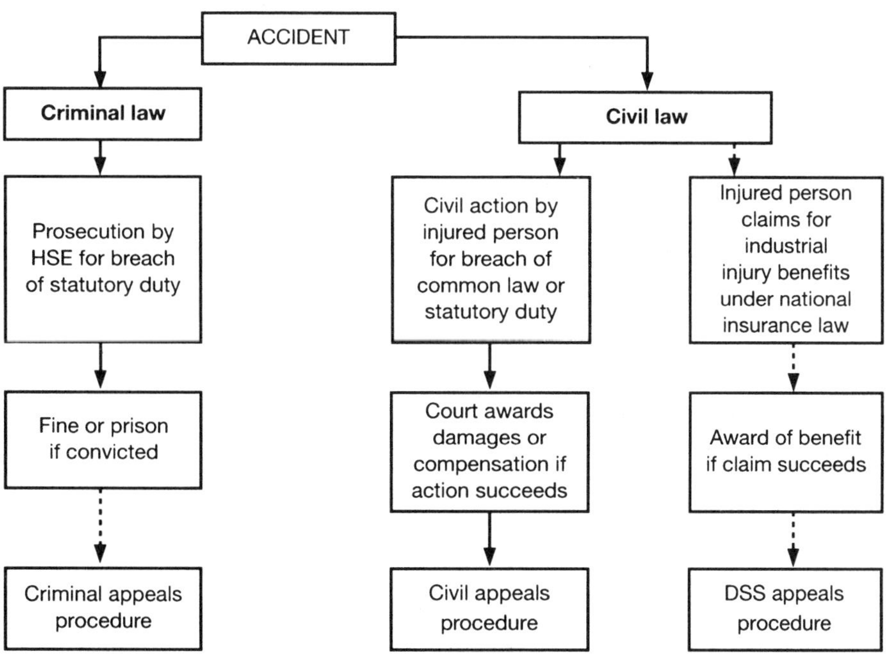

● **FIG 1.2 The routes that could be taken through the legal system following an accident at work**

lower courts and tribunals if they exceed their powers or fail to undertake their functions properly, or at all.

The High Court, the Crown Courts and the Court of Appeal are known collectively as the Supreme Court of Judicature.

The Court of Appeal

The Court of Appeal has two divisions:

- the civil division, which hears appeals from the County Courts and the High Court
- the criminal division, which hears appeals from the Crown Courts.

The House of Lords

Further appeal (in practice, this is on important matters of law only) is made to the House of Lords from the Court of Appeal and, in restricted circumstances, from the High Court.

European Court of Justice

This is the supreme law court, whose decisions on the interpretation of European Community law are sacrosanct. Such decisions are enforceable through the network of courts and tribunals in all member states.

Cases can only be brought before this court by organizations or individuals representing organizations.

For a summary of the positions of these courts in the judicial hierarchy and which hear criminal and which civil cases, see Figure 1.1

TRIBUNALS

Industrial tribunals were first established under the Industrial Training Act 1964 to deal with appeals against industrial training levies by employers. They now cover a wide range of other industrial matters, including industrial relations issues, unfair dismissal, equal pay and sex discrimination.

Composition

Each tribunal consists of a legally qualified chairperson appointed by the Lord Chancellor and two lay members – one from management and one from a trade union – selected from panels maintained by the Department of Employment following nominations from employers' organizations and trade unions.

Decisions

When all three members of a tribunal are sitting, the majority view prevails.

Complaints relating to health and safety issues

Industrial tribunals deal with the following employment/health and safety issues:

- appeals against improvement and prohibition notices
- time off for the training of safety representatives (Safety Representatives and Safety Committees Regulations 1977 (SRSCR), regulation 11(1)(a))
- failure of an employer to pay a safety representative for time off for undertaking their functions and training (SRSCR regulation 11(1) (b))
- failure of an employer to make a medical suspension payment (Employment Protection (Consolidation) Act 1978, section 22)
- dismissal, actual or constructive, following a breach of health and safety law, regulation and/or term of employment contract.

THE EUROPEAN DIMENSION

The European Community (EC)

The EC is administered by the following four bodies.

- *The Commission* – The Commission performs a civil service-like function in the EC and is headed by a body of commissioners from the various member states. It is empowered to take action against any member state not complying with EC legislation. The Commission is also empowered to make proposals for future EC legislation to the Council of Ministers (see Figure 1.3). These normally take the form of *Directives*.
- *The Council of Ministers* – This is the final decision-making body in the EC, that is, the EC Government. The governments of member states are represented on this body.
- *The European Parliament* – This consists of members, (MEPs) who represent constituencies in their own member states. The Parliament's principal role is one of discussion of EC proposals, and it must be consulted on all proposed legislation.
- *The European Court of Justice (ECJ)* – This is the supreme law court, the decisions of which regarding the interpretation of EC law are sacrosanct. EC law is enforced through a network of courts and tribunals in all member states. Cases can only be brought before this Court by organizations or individuals representing organizations.

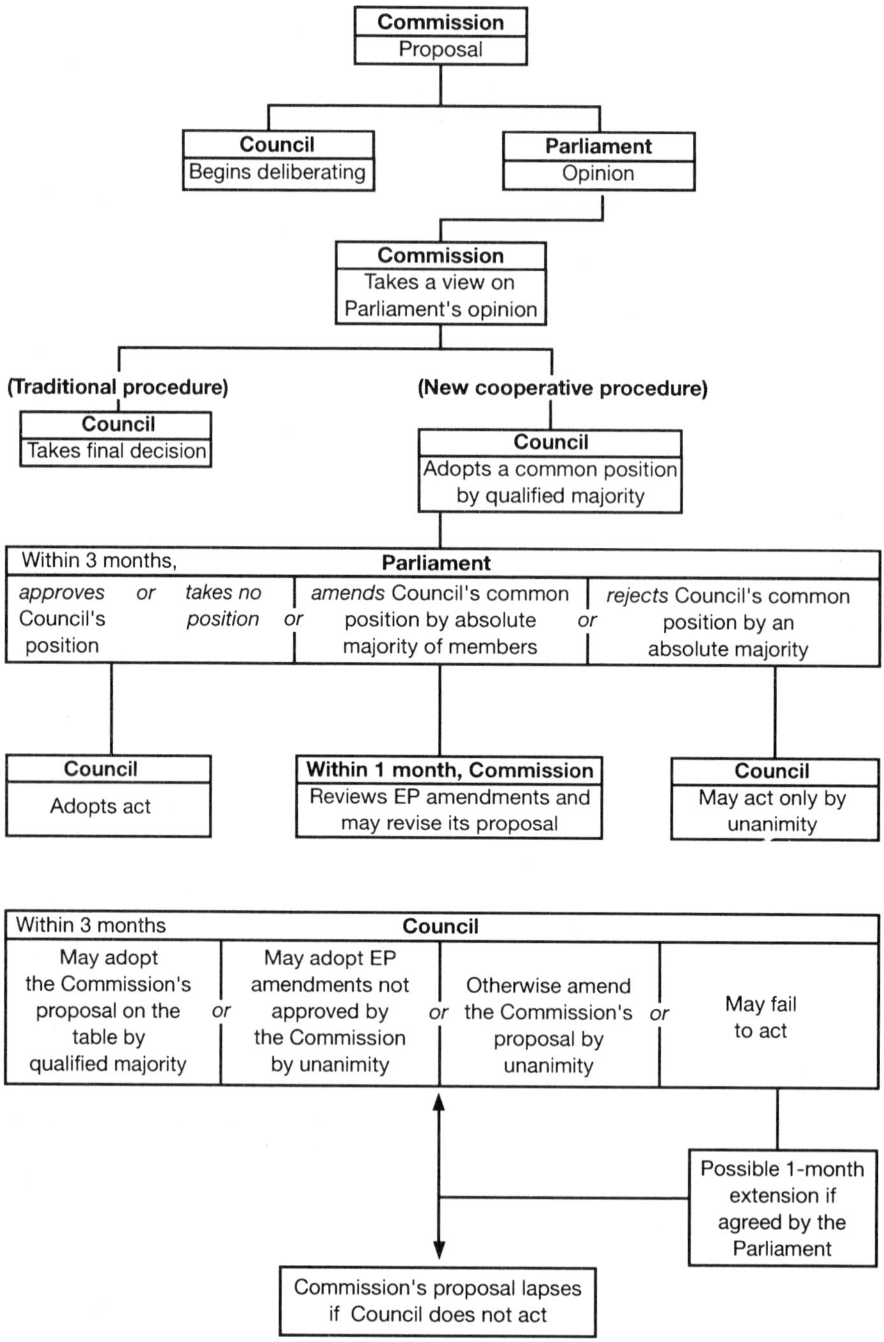

● **FIG 1.3 The legislative process of the EC**

EC standards

Under the Treaty of Rome, the Council of the European Commission can issue Directives. Directives usually provide for 'harmonization' of the laws of the member states, including those covering occupational health and safety. The process commences when representatives of the member states meet to agree the content of draft Directives. Once agreed, drafts are presented to the European Parliament for ratification. Directives impose a duty on each member state to:

- make legislation to conform to the Directive
- enforce such legislation.

Directives are legally binding on all governments, which must introduce national legislation or use certain administrative procedures. *Framework Directives* set out overall objectives, which are subsequently dealt with individually by *Daughter Directives.*

The Single European Act

This Act fundamentally identified the need to eliminate technical barriers to trade, one of which was the varying legal standards for health and safety requirements throughout the Community. It introduced the *new approach* to technical harmonization and standards, the development of the *essential safety requirements* philosophy and of harmonization Directives that establish these essential safety requirements. The Act further recognized the need to encourage improvements in the working environment.

Agreement on European standards

The 'new approach' depends heavily on the availability of European standards. These are usually prepared by the European standards bodies – which are the European Committee for Standardization (CEN) and the European Committee for Electrotechnical Standardization (CENELEC) – as a result of mandates being agreed with the European Commission. CEN and CENELEC are based in Brussels and bring together the national standards bodies of the Community and European Free Trade Association (EFTA). The British Standards Institute is the UK member.

Setting standards in CEN and CENELEC is essentially a process of consensus among the national members (see Figure 1.4). Once an acceptable text has been developed in the relevant committee, it is circulated to all national members for comment. The committee then reviews the comments and the draft standard is circulated to national members for adoption by weighted majority voting.

Alternatively, particularly if the proposal is to adopt an existing international standard as a European standard, a questionnaire procedure can be used to secure endorsement for a text. This can avoid the need to convene any meeting.

All national members have agreed to adopt the resulting European standards as their national standards (in the case of the United Kingdom, as British Standards) and to withdraw any existing and conflicting national standards.

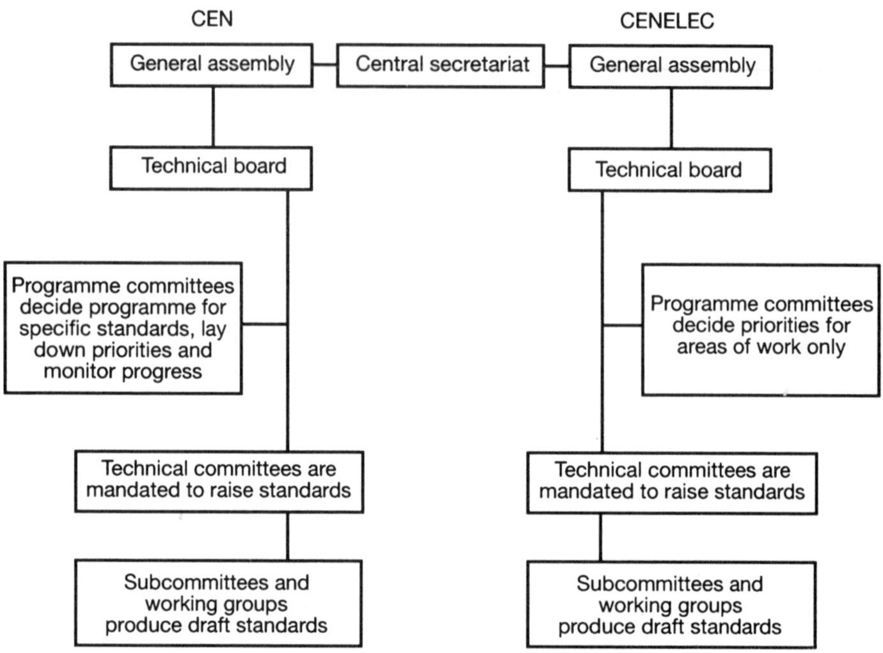

• FIG 1.4 The procedure followed for developing harmonized standards in Europe

2

Civil liability

INTRODUCTION

The two main areas of civil liability at common law are *contract* and *tort*. This chapter examines the duties that the law of tort has placed on employers. Contract law has generally not been concerned with liability for injuries, disease or death.

AN EMPLOYER'S LIABILITY IN TORT

A tort is a 'civil wrong'. The three principal torts are those of *negligence*, *trespass* and *nuisance*. The rule of common law is that everyone owes a duty to everyone else to take *reasonable care* so as not to cause them foreseeable injury. Where an employee suffers injury or disease at work, he may be in a position to sue his employer within the tort of negligence or breach of statutory duty.

The common duty of care

The position at common law is that employers must take reasonable care to protect their employees from the risks of foreseeable injury, disease or death at work. The effect of this requirement is that if an employer knows of a health and safety risk to employees, or ought, in the light of knowledge current at that time, to have known of the existence of a hazard, he will be liable if an employee is injured or killed or suffers illness as a result of the risk, or if the employer failed to take reasonable care to avoid this happening.

An employer's duties under common law were identified in general terms by the House of Lords in *Wilsons & Clyde Coal Co. Ltd* v. *English* (1938) AC57 2AER 628. The common law requires that all employers provide and maintain:

- a safe place of work with safe means of access and egress
- safe appliances and equipment and plant for doing the work
- a safe system for doing the work
- competent and safety-conscious personnel.

These duties apply even though an employee may be working away on a third party's premises, or where an employee has been hired out to another employer, but where the control of the task he is performing still lies with the permanent employer. The test of whether or not an employee has been temporarily 'employed' by another employer is one of 'control'.

Vicarious liability

The doctrine of vicarious liability is based on the fact that if an employee, while acting in the course of his employment, negligently injures another employee or the employee of a contractor working on the premises, or even a member of the public, the *employer*, rather than the employee, will be liable for that injury. As most accidents at work are caused in this way, rather than as a result of personal negligence on the part of the employer, vicarious liability is the ground on which most civil claims for injury-type accidents are won.

Vicarious liability rests on the employer simply as a result of the fact that he is the employer and is deemed to have ultimate control over the employee in what is known as a master and servant relationship. This liability *must* be insured against under the Employers' Liability (Compulsory Insurance) Act 1969, and, indeed, employers cannot contract out of this liability as it is prohibited by the Law Reform (Personal Injuries) Act 1948 and the Unfair Contract Terms Act 1977.

The key to liability is that the accident causing the injury, disease or death arises, first, out of and, second, in the course of employment. This does not, however, normally include the time travelling to and from work (though it would if the mode of transport for such travelling was within the employer's control or was provided by them or in arrangement with them).

Notwithstanding vicarious liability, the employee can be sued instead of, or as well as, an employer where the employee has been negligent (see *Lister* v. *Romford Ice & Cold Storage Co. Ltd* (1957) and Chapter 5).

The tort of negligence

'Negligence' can be defined as 'careless conduct injuring another'. The duties of employers at common law listed above are part of the general law of negligence and, as such, are specific aspects of the duty to take reasonable care. *Negligence* has been defined at common law as:

- the existence of a duty of care owed by the defendant to the plaintiff
- breach of that duty
- damage, loss or injury resulting from or caused by that breach (see *Lochgelly Iron & Coal Co. Ltd* v. *M'Mullan* (1934) ACI)

These three circumstances must be established by an injured employee before they will be entitled to bring a civil claim for damages. (Cases illustrating these three aspects of negligence are covered in Chapter 5.)

Employers' defences

There are two defences available to an employer sued for a breach of duties at common law, namely:

- voluntary assumption of risk (*volenti non fit injuria*)
- contributory negligence.

The first of these is a complete defence and means that no damages will be payable. The second is a partial defence and means that the injured employee's damages will be reduced to the extent to which they are adjudged to be blamed for their injuries.

Volenti non fit injuria

The English translation of this term is 'to one who is willing, no harm is done'. It applies to a situation where an employee, being fully aware of the risks that he is taking in not complying with safety instructions, duties and so on, after being exhorted and supervised, and having received training and instruction in the dangers involved in not following safety procedures and statutory duties, suffers injury, disease and/or death as a result of not complying with them. Here, it is open to an employer to argue that the employee, in effect, agreed to run the risk of the injury, disease and/or death involved in such action. If this defence is successfully pleaded, the employer will be required to pay no damages.

This defence has not generally been successful in cases brought by injured employees, as there is a presumption that employment and the dangers sometimes inherent in it are not voluntarily accepted by workers, but, rather, that employment is an economic necessity. This has been the position since the decision of *Smith* v. *Baker & Sons* (1891) AC 325, where the appellant, who was employed to drill rocks, was injured by stones falling from a crane operated by a fellow employee. Although the appellant knew of the risk he was running from the falling stones, it was held by the House of Lords that he had not agreed to run the risk of being injured.

An exception to this general position occurred in the case of *ICI Ltd* v. *Shatwell* (1964) 2 AER 999. Here, two brothers, the respondents, were employees of the appellant, and were employed as skilled shotfirers in rock blasting, for which they were highly paid. A statutory duty was placed on the two employees personally to take specific safety precautions when shotfiring was about to commence. The two employees had been thoroughly briefed regarding the dangers of the work and the risks involved, for example, premature explosion. They knew of the statutory prohibition in question. Nevertheless, they decided to test although a cable was too short to reach the shelter, rather than wait a few minutes until a workmate could go to get another cable. One brother handed the other brother two wires and the latter applied them to the galvanometer terminals. An explosion resulted, injuring both employees. On an appeal to the House of Lords, it was held that the employer was *not* liable for the following reasons:

- the employer was not in breach of statutory duty, that is, the breach of statutory duty was committed by the employees
- the two employees were highly skilled operators, part of a well-paid team, who were well aware of the risks.

The 'double-barrelled' action

Because an injured employee is entitled to sue his employer for damages for injury resulting from a breach of both a duty at common law and a statutory duty, this has led to the emergence of the 'double-barrelled' action against employers. In such cases, an injured employee sues separately, though simultaneously, for breach of both duties on the part of the employer. This development can be traced back to the decision in *Kilgollan* v. *Cooke & Co. Ltd* (1956) 2 AER 294, a case that involved the fencing requirements of the FA 1937.

It should be noted, however, that section 47 of the HSWA provides that:

- a breach of any of the general duties in sections 2–8 will *not* give rise to civil liability, but
- breach of any duty contained in regulations made under the Act *will* give rise to civil liability, unless the regulations state otherwise.

The tort of nuisance

Halsbury's Laws of England states that 'nuisances are divisible into common law and statutory nuisances'. 'A common law nuisance is one which apart from statute, violates the principles which the common law lays down for the protection of the public and of individuals in the exercise and enjoyment of their rights.' A 'nuisance' has also been defined as 'an act not warranted by law, or an omission to discharge a legal duty, which act or omission obstructs or causes inconvenience or damage to the public in the exercise of rights common to all Her Majesty's subjects'.

Nuisances at common law may be private nuisances or public nuisances. A *private nuisance* can take many forms, but in all cases, they constitute some form of act, or failure to act, on the part of an individual or group that results in obstruction, inconvenience or damage to another individual or group. An action for private nuisance lies where there has been interference with the enjoyment of land. Such interference need not be intentional, however. Private nuisances are associated with, for example, the keeping of animals – say, dogs barking – the emission of smoke and gases from the burning of refuse and the longstanding problem of noise nuisance from neighbours. Such interference must be sufficiently significant and unreasonable, that is without thought for a neighbour or other person who could be affected, for such a case to be successful.

Actions in respect of private nuisances may be brought by a person injured by the nuisance and they may make a claim for damages and/or obtain an injunction. In appropriate cases, they may abate the nuisance themselves, for example, by lopping overhanging trees.

Public nuisances, on the other hand, have a direct effect on the public at large. Typical examples include obstruction of a public right of way or footpath, failure to make secure an excavation in a public car park and hosing down of brickwork whereby spray falls on members of the public in close proximity.

In cases of public nuisances, the person primarily responsible for the initiation of any action is the Attorney General, who has complete discretion in the matter. The Attorney General may, however, permit an individual or a local authority to use their name to bring a *relator* action if they are satisfied that it is justified.

However, a private individual may bring an action in their own name if they have suffered some direct and substantial injury, different in kind from that suffered by the rest of the public, or if the act is also a private nuisance against their land.

The tort of trespass

Trespass implies the intentional invasion of somebody's person, land or goods. An action for trespass involves a civil claim for damages resulting from false imprisonment, unlawful entry on to the land of another, assault and battery.

AN OCCUPIER'S LIABILITY

While health and safety law is largely concerned with the relationships between employers and employees, consideration must also be given to the duties of those people and organizations, such as local authorities and companies, who occupy land and premises. Their land and premises are visited by people for a variety of purposes, such as to undertake work, provide goods and services, settle accounts and so on. The HSWA, section 4, requires those people *in control* of premises to take reasonable care towards such others, and failure to comply with this duty can lead to prosecution and a fine on conviction.

Furthermore, anyone who is injured while visiting or working on land or premises may be in a position to sue the occupier for damages, even though that injured person may not be their employee. Lord Gardner in the case of *Commissioner for Railways* v. *McDermott* (1967) 1 AC 169 explained the position thus: 'occupation of premises is a ground of liability and is not a ground of exemption from liability. It is a ground of liability because it gives some control over and knowledge of the state of the premises, and it is natural and right that the occupier should have some degree of responsibility for the safety of persons entering his premises with his permission . . . there is 'proximity' between the occupier and such persons and they are his 'neighbours'. Thus arises a duty of care . . . .

The Occupier's Liability Acts 1957 and 1984

Occupier's liability is a branch of civil law concerned with the duties of occupiers of premises to all those who may enter on to those premises. The legislation covering this area of civil liability is the Occupier's Liability Act (OLA) 1957 and, specifically in the case of trespassers, the OLA 1984.

The OLA 1957

Previously, common law had given some form of protection to lawful visitors to premises that was based on proof of negligence against the occupier. The level of protection was related to whether or not the visitor was an invitee or licensee. This distinction is now obsolete and there is now one, common duty on the part of an occupier under the OLA – namely *a common duty of care* – to all lawful visitors. This common duty of care is defined as 'a duty to take such care as in all the circumstances of the case is reasonable to see that the visitor will be reasonably safe in using the premises for the purposes for which he is invited or permitted by the occupier to be there'.

Section 1 of the OLA defines the duty owed by the occupiers of premises to all persons lawfully on the premises in respect of 'dangers due to the state of the premises or to things done or omitted to be done on them'. Such liability is not confined to buildings and has been held to include, for instance, that of the main contractors retaining general control over a tunnel being constructed (see *Bunker* v. *Charles Brand & Son Ltd* (1969) 2 AER 59).

The OLA regulates the nature of the duty imposed in consequence of a person's occupation of premises (section 1(2)). The duties are not personal duties, but, rather, are based on the occupation of premises and extend to 'a person occupying, or having control over, any fixed or moveable structure, including any vessel, vehicle or aircraft' (section 1(3)).

Visitors

Visitors to premises are classed as both invitees and licensees. Protection is afforded to *all* lawful visitors, whether they enter for the occupier's benefit, such as customers or clients, or for their own benefit, for instance, a police officer, though not to persons exercising a public or private right of way over premises (section 2(6)).

Warning notices

Under the OLA 1957, occupiers have a duty to erect notices warning visitors of any imminent danger, such as an uncovered pit or obstruction. However, section 2(4) states that a warning notice does not, in itself, absolve the occupier from liability, unless, in all the circumstances, it was sufficient to enable the visitor to be reasonably safe. Moreover, while an occupier, under the provisions of the OLA, could have excused his liability by a suitable, prominent and carefully worded notice, the chance of such avoidance is not permitted as a result of the Unfair Contract Terms Act 1977 (UCTA). This Act states that it is not permissible to exclude liability for death or injury due to negligence by a contract or by a notice, including a notice displayed in accordance with section 2(4) of the OLA.

Trespassers

A trespasser is defined in common law as a person who:

- goes on to premises without invitation or permission
- although invited or permitted to be on premises, goes to a part of the premises to which the invitation or permission does not extend
- remains on premises after the invitation or permission to be there has expired
- deposits goods on premises when not authorized to do so.

The OLA 1984

The common law was, for many years, biased against trespassers. However, the OLA 1984 took a more humane approach. Section 1 of this Act imposes a duty on an occupier in respect of trespassers, namely 'persons who may have lawful authority to be in the vicinity or not', who may be at risk of injury on the occupier's premises. This duty can be discharged by issuing some form of warning, such as the display of hazard warning notices, but such warnings must be very explicit. For example, it is insufficient to display a notice that merely states 'Eye hazard' where there may be a risk to visitors from welding activities. A suitable notice in such a circumstance might read,

RISK OF EYE INJURY FROM WELDING ACTIVITIES. NO PERSON IS ALLOWED TO ENTER THIS AREA UNLESS WEARING APPROVED EYE PROTECTION.

It is not good enough, however, to merely *display* such a notice. The requirements of such notices must be actively *enforced* by management. Thus, the old maxim 'A notice without more is no defence in law' applies in this case. Generally, the displaying of a notice, the clarity, legibility and explicitness of such a notice, and evidence of regular reminding of people of the message outlined in the notice, may count to a certain extent as part of the defence when sued for injury by a simple trespasser under the OLA 1984.

Individual risk taking

Under the OLA 1984, there is no duty on the part of occupier's to persons who willingly accept risks (section 2(5)). Also, the fact that an occupier has taken precautions to prevent persons going into their premises or on to their land where some form of danger exists, does not mean that the occupier has reason to believe that someone would be likely to come into the vicinity of the danger, thereby owing a duty to the trespasser under the OLA 1984 (section 1 (4)).

Children

Children generally, from a legal viewpoint, have always been deemed to be less responsible than adults. The OLA 1957 is quite specific on this matter.

Section 2(3)(a) requires an occupier to be prepared for children to be less careful than adults. Where, for instance, there is something or a situation on the premises that is a lure or an attraction to a child, such as an old motor car, a pond or scaffolding, this can constitute a 'trap' as far as a child is concerned. Should a child be injured as a result of this 'trap', the occupier could then be liable. Much will depend on the location of the premises, for instance, whether or not it is close to houses or a school or isolated, such as a farmyard deep in the countryside but, in all cases, occupiers must consider the potential for child trespassers and take appropriate precautions.

Structural defects

An occupier's liability for injury to a visitor resulting from structural defects, such as a defective roof or a hole in the road, only applies to those defects of which the occupier had prior knowledge or had reason to believe existed. This duty was extended to trespassers under section 1 of the OLA 1984.

Contractors and their employees

The relationship between occupiers and contractors has always been a tenuous one. Section 2(3)(b) of the OLA 1957 states that an occupier may expect that a person, in exercising their calling, such as a bricklayer, painter or window cleaner, will appreciate and guard against any risks ordinarily incident to it, say, the risk of falling, so far as the occupier gives them leave to do so. This means that the risks associated with the system of work on a third party's premises are the responsibility of the contractor's employer, not the occupier. (It should be appreciated, however, that while the above may be the case in civil law, the situation of criminal law, namely the duties of an employer towards a non-employee under section 3 of the HSWA, is quite different – see General duties of employers and the self-employed to people other than their employees, Chapter 3.)

Where work is being done on premises by a contractor, the occupier is not liable if they:

- took care to select a competent contractor
- satisfied themselves that the work was being properly done by the contractor (OLA, section 2(4)(b)).

However, in many cases, an occupier may not be competent or knowledgeable enough to ascertain whether or not the work *is* being 'properly done'. For instance, an occupier may feel that an unsafe system of work adopted by a contractor's employee, such as cleaning windows to the fourth floor offices without using any form of protection, such as a suspended scaffold or safety line, is standard practice among window cleaners! In such cases, an occupier might need to be advised by a surveyor, architect or consultant health and safety specialist in order to be satisfied that the work is being done properly.

THE EMPLOYER'S LIABILITY (DEFECTIVE EQUIPMENT) ACT 1969

As a result of the Employer's Liability (Defective Equipment) Act 1969, employers have been strictly liable for injuries to employees caused by defective equipment, where the defect is wholly or in part the result of manufacture, that is by a third party.

This Act was passed largely to reverse the effect of the case of *Davie* v. *New Merton Board Mills Ltd* (1956) 1 AER 379. This case involved a worker who had been blinded in one eye when a drift that he was using broke and a piece flew out, hitting him in the eye. The employers argued that they had acquired the drifts from a well-known and reputable supplier. On this basis, the House of Lords ruled that the company had exercised reasonable care.

The Act provides that an injury suffered by an employee is to be attributable to negligence by the employer in the following situations:

- where an employee suffers personal injury (including death) in the course of employment in consequence of a defect in equipment
- the equipment was provided by the employer for use in the employer's business
- the defect is attributable, wholly or in part, to the fault of a third party, whether identified or not, such as a manufacturer, supplier, distributor, importer.

Employers therefore, are, liable for defects in manufacture and supply and should protect themselves against this by way of contractual indemnity against the manufacturer or importer.

DEFENCES AVAILABLE IN CIVIL LIABILITY CLAIMS

When presented with a civil claim, an occupier or employer may make a denial of liability based on the following:

- that the duty alleged to have been breached by the defendant was never owed in the first place
- that the nature of the duty was different to that pleaded by the defendant
- that the duty was complied with
- that the breach of duty did not lead to the damage in question
- that the plaintiff was guilty of contributory negligence that resulted wholly in the damage.

A further aspect of any defence could be the fact that the conduct of the plaintiff, which constituted contributory negligence in this case, caused and/or resulted in the damages they suffered and that a proportion of the damages should be reduced accordingly. Moreover, in certain situations, it may be possible to show that the accident was the fault of some other party.

Where another party is blamed in the defence, the usual result is that they are joined as co-defendant by the plaintiff, and they sue both.

Res ipsa loquitur

This term means 'the thing speaks for itself'. It is a term that commonly arises in civil actions, implying that the defendant was negligent or careless, or that if they had taken proper precautions or ordered their work correctly, the damage would not have arisen. In other words, the negligence is self-evident. On this basis, it is for the defendant to prove the absence of fault rather than for the plaintiff to prove fault on the part of an employer or occupier.

In the case of *Ward* v. *Tesco Stores Ltd* (1976) 1 AER 219, the appellant slipped while shopping on some yogurt that had been spilled on the floor, was injured and sued the respondent for negligence. It was held that it was the duty of the respondents to keep the floors clean and free from spillages and that it was for the respondents to show that the accident had not arisen from a lack of reasonable care on their part. In the absence of a satisfactory explanation as to how the yogurt was spilled on the floor, the inference was that the spillage had occurred because the respondents had failed to exercise reasonable care.

Res ipsa loquitur applies, therefore, in the following circumstances:

- the thing or event causing the accident must be under the control of the employer, or under their management/control
- the injury-causing accident must be one that does not happen in the ordinary course of events
- the accident would not have happened if management had been exercising reasonable care
- absence of explanation, on the part of the defendant, to indicate that they had used reasonable care.

A defendant can set aside the presumption against them by:

- proving that reasonable care *was* taken
- providing an alternative explanation for the accident that is equally probable and does not involve negligence on their part
- providing a complete analysis of the facts, that is, by stating the specific facts of the case and inviting full consideration of liability.

3

Statute law

A QUICK GUIDE TO STATUTES, REGULATIONS, APPROVED CODES OF PRACTICE AND GUIDANCE NOTES

Statutes

These, as we have seen, are Acts of Parliament, such as the Factories Act 1961, the Offices, Shops and Railway Premises Act 1963 and the Health and Safety at Work Act 1974.

Regulations

Most statutes give the Minister(s) power to make regulations (subordinate or delegated legislation) without referring the matter to Parliament. The regulations may be drafted by the HSE and submitted through the HSC to the Secretary of State or Minister, such as the Control of Substances Hazardous to Health Regulations 1988, the Noise at Work Regulations 1989, the Safety Representatives and Safety Committees Regulations 1977 and the Management of Health and Safety at Work Regulations 1992.

There is a general requirement for the HSC and HSE to keep interested parties informed of, and adequately advised on, such matters.

Approved Codes of Practice (ACOPs)

The need to provide elaboration on the implementation of regulations is recognized in section 16 of the HSWA, which gives the HSC power to prepare and approve codes of practice on matters contained not only in regulations, but in sections 2 to 7 of the Act. Before approving a Code, the HSE, acting for the HSC, must consult with any interested body.

An ACOP is a quasi-legal document and, although non-compliance does not constitute a breach, if the contravention of the Act or regulations is alleged, the fact that the ACOP was not followed would be accepted in court as evidence of failure to do all that was reasonably practicable. A defence would be to prove that works of equivalent nature had been carried out or something equally good or better had been done.

Examples of ACOPs are Control of Asbestos at Work, Control of Substances Hazardous to Health, Protection of Persons against Ionising Radiation Arising From Any Work Activity and Safety of Pressure Systems.

HSE Guidance Notes

The HSE issues Guidance Notes in some cases to supplement the information in ACOPs. Such Guidance Notes have no legal status and are purely of an advisory nature.

HSE Guidance Notes fall into six categories:

- general safety (GS)
- chemical safety (CS)
- environmental hygiene (EH)
- medical series (MS)
- plant and machinery (PM)
- health and safety (Guidance) (HS(G)).

Examples of HSE Guidance Notes are:

EH40	Occupational Exposure Limits
MS20	Pre-employment Health Screening
HS(G)37	Introduction to Local Exhaust Ventilation
PM41	Application of Photoelectric Safety Systems to Machinery
GS20	Fire Precautions in Pressurised Workings.

THE PARLIAMENTARY PROCESS

Statutes

One of the principal functions of Parliament is the enactment of *statutes*, or, *Acts of Parliament*.

Most statutes commence their lives as *bills* and most government-introduced bills start the Parliamentary process in the House of Commons (though some bills of a non-controversial nature may start in the House of Lords). The process in the House of Commons commences with a formal *first reading*. This is followed by a *second reading*, at which stage, there is discussion of the general principles and the bill's main purpose. Following the second reading, the bill goes to the *committee stage* for detailed consideration by an appointed committee, comprising both Members of Parliament and specialists. After due consideration, the committee reports back to the House with recommendations for amendments. Such amendments are considered by the House and they, in turn, may make amendments at this stage and/or return the bill to the committee for further consideration. After this *report stage*, the bill receives a *third reading* where only verbal alterations are made.

The bill is then passed to the House of Lords where it goes through a similar process. The House of Lords either passes the bill or amends it. In the case of an amendment it is returned to the House of Commons for further consideration.

After a bill has been passed by both Houses, it receives the *Royal Assent*, which is always granted, and then becomes an *Act of Parliament*.

Regulations

A statute generally confers power on a Minister or Secretary of State to make *statutory instruments*, which may indicate more detailed rules or requirements for implementing the overall objectives of the statute. Most statutory instruments take the form of *regulations* and come within the area of law known as *delegated or subordinate legislation*.

The HSWA is an *enabling Act*. This means that, in the case of health and safety regulations, the Secretary of State for Employment has powers conferred under the HSWA (section 15, Schedule 3 and section 80) to make regulations on a wide variety of issues, but within the general objectives and aims of the parent Act. Examples of regulations made under the HSWA are the:

- Electricity at Work Regulations 1989
- Health and Safety (First Aid) Regulations 1981
- Management of Health and Safety at Work Regulations 1992.

Regulations may:

- repeal or modify existing statutory provisions
- exclude or modify the provisions of sections 2–9 of the HSWA or existing provisions in relation to any specified class
- make a specified authority, such as a local authority, responsible for enforcement
- impose approval requirements
- refer to specified documents to operate as references
- give exemptions
- specify the class of person who may be guilty of an offence, for example, employers
- apply to a particular case only.

THE PRINCIPAL STATUTES IN FORCE BEFORE THE HEALTH AND SAFETY AT WORK, ETC. ACT 1974

Prior to the HSWA, the principal health and safety legislation was contained in the Factories Act 1961, the Offices, Shops and Railway Premises Act 1963 and the Mines and Quarries Act 1954. Much of this legislation, including regulations made under these Acts, was repealed by subsequent statutes and regulations made under the HSWA, for instance the Fire Precautions Act 1971 and the Pressure Systems and Transportable Gas Containers Regulations 1989, the Workplace (Health, Safety and Welfare) Regulations 1992, the Provision and Use of Work Equipment Regulations 1992, and the Personal Protective Equipment at Work Regulations 1992 respectively (see also Chapter 4)

THE FACTORIES ACT 1961

This Act is a *consolidating Act* as it brings together earlier separate pieces of legislation relating to health, safety and welfare in factories. It incorporates both general and specific provisions relating to working conditions, machinery safety, structural safety and the welfare of people working in factories.

Whilst much of the Factories Act 1961 (FA) has been repealed or revoked by the Workplace (Health, Safety and Welfare) Regulations 1992 (WHSWR) and the Provision and Use of Work Equipment Regulations 1992 (PUWER), the following remaining provisions are of importance.

- *Section 20: Cleaning of machinery by young people* This section requires that no young person shall clean any part of a prime mover or of any transmission machinery while the prime mover or transmission machinery is in motion, and shall not clean any part of any machine if the cleaning thereof would expose the young person to risk of injury from any moving part either of that machine or of any adjacent machinery.
- *Section 21: Training and supervision of young people working at dangerous machines* This section prohibits young people from working at any prescribed dangerous machine unless they have been fully instructed as to the dangers arising in connection with it and the precautions to be observed, and:

  - have received sufficient training in work at the machine
  - are under adequate supervision by a person who has thorough knowledge and experience of the machine.

- *Section 22: Hoists and lifts (general)* This section lays down general safety provisions relating to hoists and lifts. Hoists and lifts must be of good design and construction, properly maintained and thoroughly examined by a competent person at least once every six months. A report of the result of every such examination in the prescribed form and containing the prescribed particulars shall be signed by the person making the examination and shall, within 28 days be entered in or attached to the general register.

  Every hoistway or liftway shall be efficiently protected by a substantial enclosure fitted with gates, and the enclosure shall be such as to prevent, when the gates are shut, any person falling down the way or coming into contact with any moving part of the hoist or lift. Any such gate shall be fitted with efficient interlocking or other devices so secure that the gate cannot be opened except when the cage or platform is at the landing and that the cage or platform cannot be moved away from the landing until the gate is closed. Every hoist or lift and every such enclosure shall be so constructed as to prevent any part of any person or any goods carried in the hoist or lift from being trapped between any part of the hoist or lift and any fixed structure or between the counterbalance weight and any other moving part of the hoist or lift. The maximum working load that the hoist or lift can carry safely shall be marked conspicuously on every hoist or lift.

- *Section 23*: *Hoists and lifts used for carrying people* The following additional requirements apply to hoists and lifts used for carrying people, whether together with goods or otherwise:

  – efficient automatic devices shall be provided and maintained to prevent the cage or platform overrunning
  – every cage shall, on each side on which access is afforded to a landing, be fitted with a gate and, in connection with every such gate, efficient devices shall be provided so secure that, when persons or goods are in the cage, the cage cannot be raised or lowered unless the gate is closed, and will come to rest when the gate is opened.

- *Section 26*: *Chains, ropes and lifting tackle* The following provisions must be complied with as respects every chain, rope or lifting tackle used for the purpose of raising or lowering people, goods or materials:

  – no chain, rope or lifting tackle shall be used unless it is of *good construction, sound material, adequate strength and free from patent defect*
  – a table showing the safe working loads of every kind and every size of chain, rope or lifting tackle in use, and, in the case of a multiple sling, the safe working load at different angles of the legs shall be posted in the store in which the chains, ropes or lifting tackle are kept, and in prominent positions on the premises, and no chain, rope or lifting tackle not shown in the table shall be used
  – no chain, rope or lifting tackle shall be used for any load exceeding its safe working load shown by the table above or as marked on it
  – all chains, ropes and lifting tackle in use shall be thoroughly examined by a competent person at least once in every period of six months or such greater intervals as the Minister may prescribe
  – no chain, rope or lifting tackle, except a fibre rope or fibre rope sling, shall be taken into use in any factory for the first time in that factory unless it has been tested and thoroughly examined by a competent person and a certificate of the test and examination has been obtained and is kept available for inspection
  – every chain and every lifting tackle except a rope sling shall, unless of a class or description exempted by certificate of the chief inspector on the ground that it is made of such material or so constructed that it cannot be subjected to heat treatment without risk of damage or that it has been

subjected to some form of heat treatment (other than annealing) approved by them, be annealed at least once in every 14 months or, in the case of chains or slings of 1.5-centimetres bar or smaller, or chains used in connection with molten metal or molten slag, in every six months, except that chains and lifting tackle not in regular use need be annealed only when necessary

– a register containing the prescribed particulars shall be kept in respect of all such chains, ropes or lifting tackle, except fibre slings.

By 'lifting tackle' is meant chain slings, rope slings, rings, hooks, shackles and swivels.

- *Section 27: Cranes and other lifting machines* All parts and working gear, whether fixed or movable, including the anchoring or fixing appliances, of every lifting machine shall be *of good construction, sound material, adequate strength and free from patent defect,* and shall be properly maintained.

  All such parts and gear shall be thoroughly examined by a competent person at least once in every period of 14 months and a register shall be kept containing the prescribed particulars of every such examination; and where the examination shows that the lifting machine cannot continue to be used with safety unless certain repairs are carried out immediately or within a specified time, the person making the report of the examination shall, within 28 days of the completion of the examination, send a copy of the report to the inspector for the district.

  All rails on which a travelling crane moves and every track on which the carriage of a transporter or runway moves shall be of the proper size and adequate strength and have an even running surface; and any such rails of track shall be properly laid, adequately supported or suspended and properly maintained.

  There shall be plainly marked on every lifting machine its safe working load or loads, except in the case of a jib crane, which is so constructed that the safe working load may be varied by the raising or lowering of the jib. For this there shall be either an automatic indicator of safe working loads or a table indicating the safe working loads at corresponding inclinations of the jib or corresponding radii of the load shall be attached to it.

  No lifting machine shall, except for the purpose of a test, be loaded beyond the safe working load as marked or indicated above.

  No lifting machine shall be taken into use in any factory for the first time unless it has been tested and all such parts and working gear of the machine as are specified above have been thoroughly examined by a competent person and a certificate of the test and examination specifying the safe working load or loads of the machine and signed by the person making the test and examination has been obtained and is kept available for inspection.

  If any person is employed or working on or near the wheel-track of an overhead travelling crane in any place where they would be liable to be struck by the crane, effective measures shall be taken by warning the driver of the crane or otherwise to ensure that the crane does not approach within 6 metres of that place.

If anyone is employed or is working in a way otherwise than mentioned above, but in a place above floor level where they would be liable to be struck by an overhead travelling crane, or by any load carried by such a crane, effective measures shall be taken to warn them of the approach of the crane, unless their work is so connected or so dependent on the movements of the crane as to make a warning unnecessary.

In this section, 'lifting machine' means a crane, crab, winch, teagle, pulley block, gin wheel, transporter or runway.

- *Section 30: Dangerous fumes and lack of oxygen* This section is principally concerned with the hazards that may exist in confined spaces and the precautions necessary, such as the operation of a permit to work a system. A 'confined space' is defined as including any chamber, tank, vat, pit, pipe, flue or similar confined space and the following precautions must be taken:

  - where there is no adequate means of egress from the confined space, a manhole must be provided of a minimum size
  - a responsible person must certify that the space is safe to enter for a specified length of time without the need for breathing apparatus
  - where the confined space is not certified as being safe, no one must enter or remain in the confined space unless they are wearing breathing apparatus, have authority to enter from a responsible person and, where practicable, are wearing belts with a rope securely attached and a person, keeping watch outside and capable of pulling them out, is holding the free end of the rope
  - there must be sufficient trained people to use the breathing apparatus during the operation
  - there is provided and kept readily available a sufficient supply of approved breathing apparatus, of belts and ropes, and of suitable reviving apparatus and oxygen, and the apparatus, belts and ropes shall be maintained and thoroughly examined at least once a month or at such other intervals as may be prescribed, by a competent person, and a report of every such examination, signed by the person making the examination and containing the prescribed particulars, shall be kept available for inspection
  - a sufficient number of people employed shall be trained and practised in the use of the apparatus mentioned above and in reviving those who have stopped breathing
  - no person shall enter or remain in any confined space in which the proportion of oxygen in the air is liable to have been substantially reduced unless either:

    (i) they are wearing suitable breathing apparatus or

    (ii) the space has been and remains adequately ventilated and a res-

ponsible person has tested and certified it as safe for entry without breathing apparatus
  - no work shall be permitted in any boiler furnace or boiler flue unless it has been sufficiently cooled by ventilation or otherwise to make work safe for the persons employed.

- *Section 31: Precautions with respect to explosive or inflammable dust, gas, vapour or substance* Where, in connection with any grinding, sieving or other process giving rise to dust, there may escape dust of such a character and to such an extent as to be liable to explode on ignition, all practicable steps shall be taken to prevent such an explosion by enclosure of the plant used in the process, and by removal or prevention of accumulation of dust that may escape in spite of the enclosure, and by exclusion or effective enclosure of possible sources of ignition.

  Where there is present in any plant used in any such process as aforesaid dust of such character and to such an extent as to be liable to explode on ignition, then, unless the plant is so constructed as to withstand the pressure likely to be produced by any such explosion, all practicable steps shall be taken to restrict the spread and effects of such an explosion by the provision in connection with the plant, of chokes, baffles and vents, or other equally effective appliances.

  Where any part of a plant contains any explosive or inflammable gas or vapour under pressure greater than atmospheric pressure, that part shall not be opened, except in accordance with the following provisions:

  - before the fastening of any joint of any pipe connected with the part of the plant or the fastening of the cover of any opening into the plant is loosened, any flow of the gas or vapour into the part or into any such pipe shall be effectively stopped by a stop-valve or otherwise
  - before any such fastening is removed, all practicable steps shall be taken to reduce the pressure of the gas or vapour in the pipe or part of the plant to atmospheric pressure

  and if any such fastening has been loosened or removed, no explosive or inflammable gas or vapour shall be allowed to enter the pipe or part of the plant until the fastening has been secured or, as the case may be, securely replaced, but nothing in this subsection applies to a plant installed in the open air.

  No plant tank or vessel that contains, or has contained, any explosive or flammable substance shall be subjected:

  - to any welding, brazing or soldering operation
  - to any cutting operation that involves the application of heat
  - to any operation involving the application of heat for the purpose of taking apart or removing the plant, tank or vessel or any part of it until all practicable steps have been taken to remove the substance and any fumes arising from it, or to render them non-explosive or non-inflammable. If any plant, tank or vessel *has* been subjected to any such

operation, no explosive or inflammable substance shall be allowed to enter the plant, tank or vessel until the metal has cooled sufficiently to prevent any risk of igniting the substance.

- *Section 34*: *Steam boilers (restrictions on entry)* No person shall enter or be in any steam boiler that is one of a range of two or more steam boilers unless:
  - all inlets through which steam or hot water might otherwise enter the boiler from any other part of the range are disconnected from that part
  - all valves or taps controlling the entry of steam or hot water are closed and securely locked, and, where the boiler has a blow-off pipe in common with one or more other boilers or delivering into a common blow-off vessel or sump, the blow-off valve or tap on each boiler is so constructed that it can only be opened by a key that cannot be removed until the valve or tap is closed and is the only key in use for that set of blow-off valves or taps.
- *Section 63*: *Removal of dust or fumes* In every factory in which, in connection with any process carried on, there is given off any dust or fume or other impurity of such a character and to such an extent as to be likely to be injurious or offensive to the people employed, or any substantial quantity of dust of any kind, all practicable measures shall be taken to protect these people against inhalation of the dust or fume or other impurity and to prevent its accumulating in any workroom and, in particular, where the nature of the process makes it practicable, exhaust appliances shall be provided and maintained, as near as possible to the point of origin of the dust or fume or other impurity, so as to prevent it entering the air of any workroom.

  No stationary internal combustion engine shall be used unless:
  - provision is made for conducting the exhaust gases from the engine into the open air
  - the engine (except when used for the purpose of being tested) is so partitioned from any workroom or part of a workroom in which people are employed, other than those attending to the engine, as to prevent any injurious fumes from the engine entering the air of the room or part of the room.

Children and young people

A 'child' is a person under compulsory school-leaving age, which, at present, is under 16 years, while a 'young person' is someone who has ceased to be a 'child', but who is not yet 18 years old.

YTS trainees

Under the Health and Safety (Youth Training Scheme) Regulations 1983, all young people on youth training schemes are covered, as regards their health and safety, in the same way as other employees over the age of 18.

Restrictions and prohibitions on the employment of young people

Under the FA 1961, specific requirements are laid down as regards:

- *conditions and hours of work,* that is, they should work a maximum of 9 hours per day, 48 hours in any week, or for young people under 16 years old, 44 hours a week
- *periods of employment* must not exceed 11 hours in one day, not begin before 7 am, nor end later than 8 pm, or 1 pm on Saturdays
- *continuous employment,* that is, a young person must not be employed for more than four and a half hours without an interval of at least half an hour for a meal break, and there must be a minimum ten-minute rest break per four and a half hours work period
- *meals and rest breaks,* that is, young people must not work during meal or rest periods
- *holidays,* that is, young people must not work on Sundays or public holidays as a rule, but subject to certain provisions
- *shift work,* that is, arrangements must be made with the HSE for all young people employed in factories to work on a shift system and then only within certain defined limits
- *work involving machinery,* that is, as mentioned above, no young person must work with specified machines unless fully instructed in the dangers of, and precautions to be taken with, them
- *restrictions on employment in specific processes,* for example, blasting operations.

THE OFFICES, SHOPS AND RAILWAY PREMISES ACT 1963

The WHSWR 1992 and PUWER 1992 revoked substantial parts of the Offices, Shops and Railway Premises Act 1963 (OSRPA). The following remaining provisions are of importance.

- *Section 18*: *Exposure of young persons to danger in cleaning machinery* No young person, that is someone under the age of 18, must clean any machinery if, by so doing, they expose themselves to risk of injury from it or any adjacent machinery
- *Section 19*: *Training and supervision for working at dangerous machines* No one shall work at any machine that is prescribed as dangerous, unless they have been fully instructed of the dangers arising in connection with it and the precautions to be observed and either have sufficient training in work at the machine or are under the supervision of a person who has thorough knowledge and experience of the machine.
- *Section 49*: *Notification* Before work commences in offices or shops, the employer must notify the enforcing authority (local authority) on Form OSR1.

Fire safety legislation

The Fire Precautions Act (FPA) 1971, as amended by the Fire Safety and Safety of Places of Sport Act (FSSPSA) 1987, applies to all premises actually in use – industrial, commercial or public – and is enforced by the various fire authorities. Where premises incorporate intrinsically hazardous substances, such as the storage of flammable substances and explosives, control is exercised by the HSE. Fire safety legislation is principally concerned with ensuring the provision of:

- means of escape in the event of fire
- the means for fighting fire

and this is implemented by means of a process of fire certification.

The FPA required that a fire certificate be issued for certain classes of factory and commercial premises, based on the concept of *designated use*. The FSSPSA, in effect, deregulated many premises that formerly required certification under the FPA, including:

- factories, offices and shops where:
  - more than 20 people are employed at any one time
  - more than ten people are employed at any one time elsewhere than on the ground floor
  - buildings containing two or more factory and/or office premises, where the aggregate of people employed in all of them at any one time is more than 20
  - buildings containing two or more factory and/or office premises, where the aggregate of people employed at any one time in all of them, elsewhere than on the ground floor, is more than 10
  - factories where explosive or highly flammable materials are stored, or used in or under the premises, unless, in the opinion of the fire authority, there was no serious risk to employees from fire
- hotels and boarding houses where there is sleeping accommodation provided for guest or staff:
  - for six or more people
  - at basement level
  - above the first floor.

The effect of this deregulation was to exempt certain low-risk premises from the certification requirements. Thus, the FSSPSA empowers local fire authorities to grant exemptions in respect of certain medium-risk and low-risk premises that were previously 'designated use' premises. The exemption certificate must, however, specify the maximum number of persons who can safely be in or on the premises at any one time. Furthermore, the exemption can be withdrawn by the fire authority without prior inspection and by service of notice of withdrawal, where the degree of risk associated with the premises increases.

Fire Precautions Act 1971

- *Section 5: Application for fire certificates* Premises will require a fire certificate where they have not been granted an exemption under the FSSPSA. An application for a fire certificate should normally be made to the local fire authority on Form FP1, by the occupier in the case of factories, offices and shops. In certain cases, however, it must be made by the owner, thus:

  - premises consisting of part of a building, all parts of which are owned by the same people, that is, multioccupied buildings in single ownership
  - premises consisting of part of a building, the different parts being owned by different people, that is, multioccupied buildings with plural ownership.

An application must specify the premises concerned, the use to be covered and, if required by the fire authority, be supported within a specified time by plans of the premises. Before a fire certificate is issued, inspection of the premises is essential under the FPA. Where, following an inspection, the fire authority does not consider the premises safe against fire, they will normally require the occupier to carry out improvements before issuing a certificate.

- *Section 6: Fire certificates* A fire certificate specifies:

  - the particular use or uses of the premises that it covers
  - the means of escape in case of fire, indicated in a plan of the premises
  - the means for securing that the means of escape can be safely and effectively used at all relevant times
  - the means for fighting fire for use by persons in the premises
  - the means for giving warnings in the case of fire
  - particulars as to explosive or highly flammable liquids stored and used on the premises.

  The fire certificate may also impose requirements relating to:

  - the maintenance of the means of escape and keeping it free from obstruction
  - the maintenance of other fire precautions outlined in the certificate
  - the training of employees as to action in the event of fire and the maintenance of suitable records of such training
  - limiting the number of people who, at any one time, may be on the premises
  - any other relevant fire precautions.

  A fire certificate, or a copy of same, must be kept in the building concerned.

- *Section 8: Inspection of premises* So long as a fire certificate is in force for any premises, the fire authority may cause inspections to be made from time to time to ascertain whether or not the requirements of the certificate are being maintained or are becoming inadequate.

Before carrying out any structural alterations or any material internal alterations to premises requiring a fire certificate, it is necessary, first, to notify the fire authority, or in the case of 'special premises', the HSE, of the proposed changes. Similar requirements apply in cases of proposed alterations to equipment or furniture on the premises. Following notification, the premises will be inspected before the alteration work can go ahead. Failure to follow this procedure is an offence under the FPA.

Fire Safety and Safety of Places of Sport Act 1987

Legal requirements relating to the fire certification of premises, as contained in the FPA, were modified by the FSSPSA. One of the main general purposes of the FSSPSA was to concentrate effort on premises where there is a high risk of fire, at the same time reducing the need for certification in the case of low-risk premises. The FSSPSA is, therefore, a deregulating measure. It empowers fire authorities to grant exemptions in respect of low-risk premises that were previously 'designated use' premises under the FPA and required a fire certificate. An occupier does not have to formally apply for such exemption. It may be granted either on application for a fire certificate or while a fire certificate is in force. Generally, however, premises would *not* be exempted unless they had been inspected within the previous 12 months. The consequence of this is that if an exemption is granted:

- on application for a fire certificate, it disposes of the application
- while the certificate is in force, the certificate no longer has any effect.

The exemption certificate *must*, however, specify the maximum number of people who can safely be in or on the premises at any one time. Depending on the relative degree of fire risk, the exemption can be withdrawn by the fire authority without prior inspection, on notice being given to the occupier of such a withdrawal.

The following sections of the FSSPSA are important.

- *Section 5: Means of escape in case of fire* Although low- or medium-risk premises may be exempt from certification under the FSSPSA, occupiers must still provide a means of escape and fire fighting equipment. 'Escape' is defined in the Act as 'escape from premises to some place of safety beyond the building, which constitutes or comprises the premises, and any area enclosed by it or within it; accordingly, conditions or requirements can be imposed as respects any place or thing by means of which a person escapes from premises to a place of safety'.
- *Section 8: Alterations to exempted premises* An occupier who intends to carry out any material alterations to a premises while an exemption order is in force must first notify the fire authority of the proposed alterations. Failure to notify is an offence under the Act.

  Notification is particularly necessary in cases where:

  – the proposed extension of, and/or structural alteration to premises may affect the means of escape

  - any alteration to the interior of the premises, in furniture or equipment, may affect the means of escape
  - the proposed storage of explosive or highly flammable material in or on the premises in quantities/aggregate quantities is greater than that specified by the current certificate
  - it is proposed that a greater number of people be on the premises than specified by the certificate.

Enforcement provisions of the FSSPSA

- *Section 9: Improvement notices* Where a fire authority is of the opinion that an occupier has not fulfilled their duty with regard to the provision of:

  - means of escape in case of fire
  - means for fighting fire

  the authority may serve on the occupier an *improvement notice*, detailing the steps that should be taken in the way of improvements, alterations and other measures to remedy this breach of the Act. The occupier must normally undertake remedial work within 21 days, unless they submit an appeal against the notice. Such an appeal must be lodged within 21 days from the date of service of the notice, and it has the effect of suspending the operation of the notice. Where such an appeal fails, the occupier must undertake the remedial work specified in the improvement notice. Failure to do so can result in a fine on summary conviction and, on conviction, an indictment, an indefinite fine or imprisonment for up to two years, or both.
- *Section 10: Prohibition notices* Where there is considered to be a *serious* risk of injury to employees and visitors from fire on the premises, the fire authority can serve a *prohibition notice* on the occupier, requiring that remedial work be carried out in the interests of fire safety or, alternatively, have the premises closed down. The power to serve prohibition notices applies to all former 'designated use' premises, but not places of public religious worship or single private dwellings.

  A prohibition notice may be served on premises:

  - providing sleeping accommodation, such as hotels
  - providing treatment/care, such as nursing homes
  - for the purposes of entertainment, recreation or instruction, or for a club, society or association
  - for teaching, training or research
  - providing access to members of the public, whether for payment or otherwise
  - places of work

  A prohibition notice is most likely to be served where means of escape are inadequate or non-existent or where there is a need to improve means of escape. As with a prohibition notice under the HSWA, such a notice can be served with immediate effect or deferred. An appeal does not suspend the operation of a prohibition notice.

Places of sport

The FSSPSA extends the existing Safety of Sports Grounds Act (SSGA) 1975, which only applied to sports stadia, that is, sports grounds where the accommodation for spectators wholly or substantially surrounds the activity taking place, to all forms of sports ground.

The legal situation relating to sports grounds under the FSSPSA is as follows:

- a *general safety certificate* is required for any sports ground
- the SSGA is extended to any sports ground that the Secretary of State considers appropriate
- the validity of safety certificates no longer requires the provision at a sports ground of a police presence, unless consent has been given by a chief constable or chief police officer
- there is provision for the service of *prohibition notices* in the case of serious risk of injury to spectators, prohibiting or restricting the admission of spectators in general or on specified occasions.

Prohibition notices

A prohibition notice may specify steps that must be taken to reduce risk, particularly from a fire, to a reasonable level, including structural alterations (irrespective of whether or not this may contravene the terms of a safety certificate for the ground issued by the local authority, or for any stand at the ground; see the next section, Safety certificates). Where a prohibition notice requires the provision of a police force, such requirements cannot be specified without the consent of the chief constable or chief police officer.

Under section 23 of the FSSPSA, a prohibition notice may be served on any of the following people:

- the holder of a general safety certificate
- the holder of a *specific safety certificate*, that is, a safety certificate for a specific sporting activity or occasion
- where no safety certificate is in operation, the management of the sports ground
- in the case of a specific sporting activity for which no safety certificate is in operation, the organizers of the activity
- where a general safety certificate is in operation for a stand at a ground, the holder of this certificate
- where a specific safety certificate is in operation for a stand, the holder of the certificate.

Under section 25 of the FSSPSA, sports grounds *must* be inspected at least *once* a year.

Safety certificates

Where a sports ground provides covered accommodation in stands for spectators, a safety certificate, issued by the local authority, is required for each stand providing covered accommodation for 500 or more spectators, that is, a *regulated stand*. In certain cases, safety certificates may be required for stands accommodating smaller numbers.

Records

Section 27 of the Act gives the local authority power to require the keeping of the following records in the case of stands at sports grounds:

- the number of spectators in covered accommodation
- procedures relating to the maintenance of safety in the stand.

Sports grounds with regulated stands must be inspected periodically.

Offences under the FSSPSA

The principal criminal offences under the Act are committed in respect of regulated stands when:

- spectators are admitted to a regulated stand at a sports ground on an occasion when a safety certificate should be, but is not, in operation
- any term or condition of a safety certificate for a regulated stand at a sports ground is contravened.

Both the management of the sports ground and, in the second case, the holder of the certificate, are guilty of an offence (section 36).

Under section 36 of the FSSPSA, a number of defences are available, namely:

- that either:
  - the spectators were admitted when no safety certificate was in operation
  - the contravention of the safety certificate occurred without their consent
- that they took all reasonable precautions and exercised all due care to avoid the offence being committed either by themselves or by people under their control.

Where a person or corporate body is charged with an offence under section 36, that is they had no safety certificate for a regulated stand, the defendant may plead that they did not know that the stand had been designated as being a regulated stand.

The Mines and Quarries Act 1954

The Mines and Quarries Act (MQA) 1954 replaced all the former legislation relating to safety in mines and quarries and should be read in conjunction with the more general provisions of the HSWA. Part III of the Act deals with

'Safety, Health and Welfare in Mines' and is enforced by mines and quarries inspectors of the HSE.

Under section 180, a 'mine' is defined as being 'an excavation or system of excavations made for the purpose of, or in connection with, the getting, wholly or substantially by means involving the employment of persons below ground, of minerals (whether in the natural state or in solution or suspension) or products of minerals'.

The term mine also includes the surface workings: 'so much of the surface (including buildings, structures and works thereon) surrounding or adjacent to the shafts or outlets of the mine as is occupied together with the mine for the purpose of, or in connection with, the working of the mine, the treatment, preparation for sale, consumption or use, storage or removal from the mine of the minerals or products thereof gotten from the mine or the removal from the mine of the refuse thereof' (section 180 (3)).

Premises on the surface do *not* form part of a mine, however, if 'a manufacturing process is carried on otherwise than for the purpose of the working of the mine . . . or the preparation for sale of minerals gotten therefrom'.

Also included in the term mine are refuse dumps and railway lines serving them, together with conveyor or aerial ropeways provided for the removal of minerals or refuse.

There is a similar definition of the term 'quarry' and its associated workings. Broadly, a 'quarry' is defined as a 'system of excavations for minerals which is not a mine'.

The principal duties under the MQA rest with owners of mines and quarries. They have a general duty to ensure that the mine or quarry is managed according to the requirements of the MQA and various regulations and orders made under it. Considerable emphasis is placed on the individual responsibilities and accountabilities for the safety of certain qualified people, that is, a sole manager, under manager, deputies, engineers, surveyors, technicians and other competent people. Their responsibilities must be clearly identified in writing. They must ensure adequate inspection of the mine and its equipment and the thorough supervision of all its operations.

The principal requirements under Part III of the MQA and regulations made under it are outlined below.

Mines

Specific provisions must be made at each mine for:

- the maintenance of plans of the workings of the mine
- securing safe access to and egress from the mine, including appropriate communication between shafts, control over the actual numbers of workers present and safe operation of winding and hauling apparatus
- arrangements for securing shafts and entrances to disused workings
- the safe operation of winding and rope haulage apparatus and conveyors
- the construction and maintenance of roadways, including the operation of specific rules relating to transport and the provision and use of refuge holes

- systematic support for the roof and sides of workings
- the provision and maintenance of adequate ventilation
- the provision and maintenance of adequate lighting generally and of hand lamps
- control over contraband items
- the safe use of electricity and electrical apparatus, blasting materials and devices
- specific fire precautions and rescue procedures
- control over dust
- prevention of external dangers to workings
- specific provisions relating to machinery and apparatus (including the construction and maintenance of these and restrictions and loading of cranes)
- specific provisions relating to buildings and structures.

Other provisions cover training and discipline of operators and specific requirements relating to welfare arrangements (sanitary accommodation, washing and showering facilities and so on).

Quarries

Specific provisions must be made by the manager at each quarry to ensure that:

- all parts and working gear, including anchoring of all machinery and apparatus, are of good construction, suitable material, adequate strength, free from patent defect and properly maintained
- flywheels and other dangerous exposed parts of machinery are securely fenced, the fencing being properly maintained and kept in position
- all vessels containing or producing air, gas or steam at a pressure greater than atmospheric pressure are so constructed, installed, maintained and used as to obviate any risk from fire, bursting, explosion or collapse or the production of noxious gases
- the safe working load is plainly marked on every crane and winch and that this safe load is not exceeded
- all buildings and structures are kept in a safe condition
- safe means of access is provided and maintained
- fencing is provided where a person may fall more than 3 metres unless there is a secure foothold and, where necessary, a secure handhold
- adequate supplies of wholesome drinking water are provided and maintained at suitable points
- safety devices are provided to prevent vehicles that run on rails from running away
- no ropeway is used unless it meets the requirements of the Quarries (Ropeways and Vehicles) Regulations 1958
- artificial lighting is provided and maintained where natural light is insufficient

- steps are taken to protect employees from inhaling dust
- precautions are taken to avoid danger from falls.

No person shall be employed in a quarry unless they are adequately instructed or trained or are under the instruction and supervision of a person who is competent to instruct or supervise that work.

A person who contravenes tipping rules or directions made by the manager in order to comply with the Act shall be guilty of an offence.

A person who:

- negligently or wilfully does anything likely to endanger the safety or health of themselves or others
- wilfully omits to do anything necessary to ensuring safety
- without permission, removes, alters or tampers with anything provided for safety or health

shall be guilty of an offence.

No quarry shall be worked unless there is a sole manager, or managers with jurisdiction for particular parts, who shall closely and effectively supervise all operations in progress.

Where anyone in charge of part of a quarry is of the opinion that a danger exists, they must clear everyone from it, inform their immediate superiors and then ascertain what measures are necessary to render it safe.

Specific provisions for both mines and quarries

Arrangements must be made for:

- undertaking inspections on behalf of the workers
- restricting the employment of women and young people
- keeping records, returns and information
- the fencing off of abandoned or disused mines or quarries.

THE HEALTH AND SAFETY AT WORK, ETC. ACT 1974

This Act covers all people at work, except domestic workers in private employment, whether they be employers, employees or the self-employed. It is aimed at people and their activities, rather than premises and processes.

The legislation includes provisions for both the protection of people at work and the prevention of risks of the health and safety of the general public that may arise from work activities.

The objectives of HSWA

These are:

- to secure the health, safety and welfare of all people at work
- to protect others from the risks arising from workplace activities

- to control the obtaining, keeping and use of explosive or highly flammable substances
- to control emissions into the atmosphere of noxious or offensive substances.

Specific duties

- *Section 2: General duties of employers to their employees* It is the duty of every employer, so far as is reasonably practicable, to ensure the health, safety and welfare at work of all their employees. More particularly, this includes:

  - the provision and maintenance of plant and systems of work that are, so far as is reasonably practicable, safe and without risk to health
  - arrangements for ensuring, so far as is reasonably practicable, safety and absence of risk to health in connection with the use, handling, storage and transport of articles and substances
  - the provision of such information, instruction training and supervision as is necessary to ensure, so far as is reasonably practicable, the health and safety at work of employees
  - so far as is reasonably practicable as regards any place of work under the employer's control, the maintenance of it in a condition that is safe and without risk to health and the provision and maintenance of means of access to and egress from it that are safe and without such risk
  - the provision and maintenance of a working environment for their employees that is, so far as is reasonably practicable, safe, without risk to health, and adequate as regards facilities and arrangements for their welfare at work.

  Employers must prepare and, as often as is necessary, revise a written Statement of Health and Safety Policy, and bring the Statement and any revision of it to the notice of all their employees.

  Every employer must also consult appointed safety representatives with a view to making and maintaining arrangements that will enable them and their employees to cooperate effectively in promoting and developing measures to ensure the health and safety at work of the employees, and in checking the effectiveness of such measures.
- *Section 3: General duties of employers and the self-employed to people other than their employees* Every employer must conduct their undertaking in such a way as to ensure, so far as is reasonably practicable, that people not in their employ who may be affected by the business are not exposed to risks to *their* health or safety. (Similar duties are imposed on the self-employed.)

  Every employer and self-employed person must give to others (those not in their employ) who may be affected by the way in which they conduct their business the prescribed information about such aspects of the way in which they work that might affect their health and safety.

- *Section 4: General duties of people concerned with premises to people other than their employees* This section has the effect of imposing duties in relation to those who:

  - are not their employees, but
  - use non-domestic premises made available to them as a place of work.

  Every person who has, to any extent, control of premises must ensure, so far as is reasonably practicable, that the premises, all means of access to it or egress from it, and any plant or substances on the premises or provided for use there, is or are safe and without risk to health.
- *Section 5: The general duty of people in control of certain premises in relation to harmful emissions into the atmosphere* Any person having control of any premises of a class prescribed for the purposes of section 1(1)(d) must use the best practicable means for preventing the emission into the atmosphere from the premises of noxious or offensive substances and for rendering harmless and inoffensive such substances as may be emitted.
- *Section 6: General duties of manufacturers and so on regarding articles and substances for use at work* Any person who designs, manufactures, imports or supplies any article for use at work:

  - must ensure, so far as is reasonably practicable, that the article is so designed and constructed as to be safe and without risk to health when properly used
  - must carry out or arrange for the carrying out of such testing and examination as may be necessary to comply with the above duty
  - must provide adequate information about the use for which it is designed and has been tested to ensure that, when put to that use, it will be safe and without risk to health.

  Any person who undertakes the design or manufacture of any article for use at work must carry out or arrange for the carrying out of any necessary research with a view to the discovery and, so far as is reasonably practicable, the elimination or minimizing of any risk to health or safety that the design or article may pose.

  Any person who erects or installs any article for use at work must ensure, so far as is reasonably practicable, that nothing about the way it is erected or installed makes it unsafe or a risk to health when properly used.

  Any person who manufactures, imports or supplies any substance for use at work:

  - must ensure, so far as is reasonably practicable, that the substance is safe and without risk to health when properly used
  - must carry out or arrange for the carrying out of such testing and examination as may be necessary
  - must take such steps as are necessary to ensure adequate information about the results of any relevant tests is available in connection with the use of the substance at work.

- *Section 7: General duties of employees at work* It is the duty of every employee while at work:
  - to take reasonable care for the health and safety of themselves and of others who may be affected by their acts or omissions at work
  - as regards any duty or requirement imposed on their employer, to cooperate with them so far as is necessary to enable that duty or requirement to be performed or complied with.
- *Section 8: The duty not to interfere with or misuse things supplied pursuant to certain provisions* No one shall intentionally or recklessly interfere with or misuse anything provided in the interests of health, safety or welfare in order to satisfy any of the relevant statutory provisions.
- *Section 9: The duty not to charge employees for things done or provided pursuant to certain specific requirements* No employer shall levy or permit to be levied on any employee of theirs any charge in respect of anything done or provided in order to comply with any specific requirement of the relevant statutory provisions.

THE SOCIAL SECURITY ACT 1975

Under this legislation:

- employees must notify their employer of any accident resulting in personal injury in respect of which benefit may be payable (notification may be given by a third party if the employee is incapacitated
- employees must enter the appropriate particulars of all accidents in an accident book (Form BI 510), which may be done by another person if the employee is incapacitated; such an entry is deemed to satisfy the requirements given in the first point above
- employers must investigate all accidents of which notice is given by employees and any variations between the findings of this investigation and the particulars given in the notification must be recorded
- employers must, on request, furnish the Department of Social Security with such information as may be required relating to accidents in respect of which benefit may be payable, such as Forms 2508 and 2508A.
- employers must provide and keep readily available an accident book in an approved form in which the appropriate details of all accidents can be recorded (Form BI 510) and such books, when completed, should be retained for three years after the date of the last entry
- for the purposes of the above, the appropriate particulars should include:
  - name and address of the injured person
  - date and time of the accident
  - the place where the accident happened
  - the cause and nature of the injury
  - the name and address of any third party giving the notice.

THE CONSUMER PROTECTION ACT 1987

This Act implements in the UK the provisions of the EC Directive of 25 July 1985 on the approximation of the laws, regulations and administrative provisions of the member states concerning liability for defective products.

The Act also:

- consolidates, with amendments, the Consumer Safety Act 1978 and the Consumer Safety (Amendment) Act 1986
- makes provision with respect to the giving of price indications
- amends Part I of the HSWA and sections 31 and 80 of the Explosives Act 1975
- repeals the Trade Descriptions Act 1972 and the Fabrics (Misdescription) Act 1913.

Part I, which deals with product liability, is significant from a health and safety viewpoint.

Part I: Product liability

Some important definitions

Within the context of Part I, a number of definitions are of significance. For example, *producer* in relation to a product means the following:

- the person who manufactured it
- in the case of a substance that has not been manufactured, but has been won or abstracted, the person who won or abstracted it
- in the case of a product that has not been manufactured, won or abstracted, for which the essential characteristics are attributable to an industrial process having been carried out, such as in relation to agricultural produce, the person who carried out that process.

Product means any goods or electricity and (subject to the proviso below) includes products that are used in another product, whether by virtue of being a component part or raw material for it or otherwise. The proviso is that a person who supplies any product in which products are used whether by virtue of being component parts or raw materials or otherwise, shall not be treated by reason only of their supply of that product, but as supplying any of the products so comprised.

Liability for defective products (section 2)

Where any damage is caused wholly or partly as a result of there being a defect in a product, all of the following people shall be liable for the damage:

- the producer of the product
- any person who, by putting their name on the product or using a trade mark or other distinguishing mark in relation to the product, has held themselves out to be the producer of the product

- any person who has imported the product into a member state from a place other than one of the member states in order, in the course of a business of theirs to supply it to another.

Where any damage is caused wholly or partly as a result of a defect in a product, any person who supplied the product (whether to the person who suffered damage, to the producer of any product in which the product in question is a part or to any other person) shall be liable for the damage if:

- the person who suffered the damage requests the supplier to identify one or more of the people (whether still in existence or not) detailed in the list above in relation to the product
- this request is made within a reasonable period after the damage occurs and at a time when it is not reasonably practicable for the person making the request to identify all these people
- the supplier fails within a reasonable period after receiving the request, either to comply with the request or to identify the person who supplied the product to them.

The meaning of 'defect' (section 3)

Subject to the following provisions, there is a defect in a product if the safety of the product is not of the kind one would generally be entitled to expect. For those purposes *safety*, in relation to a product, shall include safety with respect to products used in that product and safety in the context of any risks of damage to property, as well as in the context of risks of death or personal injury.

In determining what people are generally entitled to expect in relation to a product, all the circumstances shall be taken into account, including:

- the manner in which, and the purposes for which, the product has been marketed, its get-up, the use of any mark in relation to the product and any instructions for, or warnings with respect to doing or refraining from doing anything with or in relation to the product
- what might reasonably be expected to be done with or in relation to the product
- the time when the product was supplied by its producer to another

and nothing in this section requires a defect to be inferred, on its own, from the fact that the safety of a product that is supplied after that time is greater than the safety of the product in question.

Defences (section 4)

In any civil proceedings against any person ('the person proceeded against') in respect of a defect in a product, it shall be a defence if they can show that:

- the defect is attributable to compliance with any requirement imposed by or under any enactment or with any Community obligation
- that the person proceeded against did not at any time supply the product

to another
- that the following conditions are satisfied:
  - that the only supply of the product to another by the person proceeded against was otherwise than in the course of a business of that person's
  - that section 2 above does not apply to that person or applies to them by virtue only of things done otherwise than with a view to profit
- that the defect did not exist in the product at the relevant time
- that the *state of scientific or technical knowledge* at the relevant time was not such that a producer of products of the kind in question might have been expected to have discovered the defect in the products while they were under their control ('state of the art' defence)
- that the defect:
  - constituted a defect in a product ('the subsequent product') of which the product in question was a part
  - was wholly attributable either to the design of the subsequent products or to compliance by the producer of the product in question with instructions given to them by the producer of the subsequent product.

Damage giving rise to liability (section 5)

Subject to the following provisions, by the word *damage* is meant death or personal injury or any loss of or damage to any property (including land).

A person shall *not* be liable under section 2 for any defect in a product, for the loss or damage to the product itself or for the loss or damage to the whole or part of any product if it has been supplied as part of another product.

A person shall not be liable under section 2 for any loss of or damage to any property that, at the time it is lost or damaged, is not:

- ordinarily intended for private use, occupation or consumption
- intended by the person suffering the loss or damage mainly for their own private use, occupation or consumption.

No damages shall be awarded to any person under Part I regarding any loss of or damage to any property if the amount that would be so awarded apart from this subsection and any liability for interest, does not exceed £275.

In determining, for the purposes of this Part, *who* has suffered any loss or damage to property and *when* any such loss occurred, the loss or damage shall be regarded as having occurred at the earliest time at which a person with an interest in the property had *knowledge* of the material facts regarding any loss or damage.

For the purposes of the above subsection, the *material facts* regarding any loss of or damage to any property are those that relate to the kind of loss or damage that would lead a reasonable person with an interest in the property to consider the matter sufficiently serious as to justify their instituting proceedings for damages against a defendant who did not dispute liability and was able to satisfy a judgment.

By a person's *knowledge* is meant knowledge that the person might reasonably have been expected to acquire:

- from the facts observable or ascertainable by this person
- from facts ascertainable by the person with the help of appropriate expert advice that it is reasonable to seek

but a person shall not be taken (by virtue of this subsection) to have knowledge of a fact ascertainable by them only with the help of expert advice *unless* they have failed to take all reasonable steps to obtain (and, where appropriate, act on) that advice.

Prohibition on exclusion from liability (section 7)

The liability of a person by virtue of this Part to a person who has suffered damage caused wholly or partly as a result of a defect in a product, or to a dependant or relative of such a person, shall not be limited or excluded by any contract term, by any notice or by any other provisions. By 'notice' is meant notice in writing.

Part II: Consumer safety

Part II deals with a *general safety requirement*, that making it an offence to supply unsafe consumer goods. This provision supplements certain provisions of the Consumer Safety Act 1978 providing coverage where there are no specific safety regulations under that Act.

Note that although the general safety requirement of Part II is restricted to consumer goods, section 6 of the HSWA applies in respect of the safety of articles and substances used at work. Also, Part I of the Act is not restricted to consumer goods – it can apply to anything described as a product.

THE ENVIRONMENTAL PROTECTION ACT 1990

This Act brought in fundamental changes regarding the control of pollution and the protection of the environment. It repealed completely the Alkali, etc. Works Regulations Act 1906 and the Public Health (Recurring Nuisances) Act 1969, and certain sections of the well-established environmental protection legislation, such as the Public Health Acts 1936 and 1961, Control of Pollution Act 1954 and the Clean Air Act 1956. The Act covers eight specific aspects, namely:

- integrated pollution control and air pollution control by local authorities (Part I)
- waste on land (Part II)
- statutory nuisance and clean air (Part III)
- litter (Part IV)
- amendments to the Radioactive Substances Act 1960 (Part V)

- genetically modified organisms (Part VI)
- nature conservation (Part VII)
- miscellaneous provisions, for instance relating to the control of stray dogs and stubble burning (Part VIII).

Part I: Integrated pollution control and air pollution control by local authorities

A number of terms are of significance in the interpretation of this Part of the Act:

- *environment* consists of all, or any, of the mediums of the air, water and land (and the medium of air includes the air within buildings and other natural or man-made structures above or below ground)
- *pollution of the environment* means pollution of the environment due to the release (into any environmental medium), from any process, of substances that are capable of causing harm to human beings or any other living organisms supported by the environment
- *harm* means harm to the health of living organisms or other interference with the ecological systems of which they form part and, in the case of humans includes offence caused to any of their senses or their property (*harmless* has a corresponding meaning)
- *process* means any activities carried out in Great Britain, whether on premises or by means of mobile plant, that are capable of causing pollution of the environment, and *prescribed process* means a process prescribed under section 2(1)
- *authorization* means an authorization for a process (whether on premises or by means of mobile plant) granted under section 6; and a reference to the conditions of an authorization is a reference to the conditions subject to which, at any time, the authorization has effect
- a substance is *released* into any environmental medium whenever it is released directly into that medium, whether or not it is released into it within or outside Great Britain, and release includes:
  - in relation to air, any emission of the substance into the air
  - in relation to water, any entry (including any discharge) of the substance into water
  - in relation to land, any deposit, keeping or disposal of the substance in or on land.

This Part of the Act identifies industrial processes that are scheduled for control either by Her Majesty's Inspectorate of Pollution (HMIP) or by local authorities (LAs). Industrial processes are split into a two-part schedule for the purposes of enforcement.

Category A processes are subject to *integrated pollution control* (IPC) by HMIP. IPC applies the principle of *best practicable environmental option* (BPEO), and Category A processes have controls applied to all waste streams. BPEO is not defined in the Act, but was considered at length by the Royal Commission on Environmental Protection, whose definition is as follows:

> A BPEO is the outcome of a systematic consultative and decision making procedure which emphasises the protection and conservation of the environment across land, air and water. The BPEO procedure establishes, for a given set of objectives, the option that proves the most benefit or least damage to the environment as a whole, at acceptable cost, in the long term as well as in the short term.

IPC covers waste streams in to the air, water and land. The general approach is to minimize these waste streams to ensure that the BPEO for the process is applied. Authorizations and controls are applied to all emissions (section 7). Fundamentally, the approach hinges on a prior authorization procedure. Authorizations for industrial processes can have stringent conditions applied to them and these conditions apply the concept of the use of *best available techniques not entailing excessive costs* (BATNEEC). The principal objective of this concept is that of minimizing pollution, or predicted pollution, of the environment as a whole from an industrial process. In other words, having regard to the BPEO (section 7(2)) the BATNEEC concept specifies the objectives to be considered in the conditions of authorization as:

- ensuring that, in carrying out a prescribed process, the best available techniques not entailing excessive cost will be used:
  - for preventing the release of substances prescribed for any environmental medium into that medium or, where this is not practicable by such means, for reducing the release of such substances to a minimum and for rendering harmless any such substances that are so released
  - for rendering harmless any other substances that might cause harm if released into any environmental medium
- compliance with any directions that the Secretary of State has given for the implementation of any obligations in the United Kingdom under the Community Treaties or international law relating to environmental protection
- compliance with any limits or requirements and achievements of any quality standards or quality objectives prescribed by the Secretary of State under any of the relevant enactments
- compliance with any requirements applicable to the granting of authorizations specified by or under a plan made by the Secretary of State.

Those processes identified as Category B industrial processes are subject to a similar prior authorization procedure administered by the LA's environmental health department for discharges into the air only. Processes discharging substances in to water are regulated by the National Rivers Authority's (NRA) discharge consent procedure and discharges into land are conrolled by the Waste Regulation Authority (WRA), using controls detailed in Part II of the Act. Liaison between central and local government inspectorates is maintained through HMIP.

Under Part I of the Act, enforcing authorities must establish and maintain public information registers that contain details of the authorizations given for, and conditions applied to, processes.

Enforcement arrangements

Section 13 of the EPA states that where the enforcing authority is of the opinion that the person carrying on a prescribed process under an authorization is contravening any condition of that authorization, or is likely to contravene any such conditions, the authority may serve an *enforcement notice.*

An enforcement notice shall:

- state that the authority is of the said opinion
- specify the matters constituting the contravention or the matters making it likely that the contravention will arise, as the case may be
- specify the steps that must be taken to remedy the contravention or to remedy the matters that make it likely that the contravention will arise, whichever is relevant in the circumstances
- specify the period within which these steps must be taken.

Section 14 of the EPA makes provision for the service of *prohibition notices*. If the enforcing authority is of the opinion, as respects the carrying out of a prescribed process under an authorization, that to continue to carry it out or to do so in a particular manner, involves *an imminent risk of serious pollution of the environment*, the authority shall serve a prohibition notice on the person carrying out the process.

A prohibition notice may be served *whether or not* the manner of carrying out the process in question contravenes a condition of the authorization and may relate to any aspects of the process, whether these are regulated by conditions of the authorization or not.

A prohibition notice shall:

- state the authority's opinion
- specify the risk involved in the process
- specify the steps that must be taken to remove it and the period of time in which they must be taken
- direct that the authorization shall, until the notice is withdrawn, wholly or to the extent specified in the notice, cease to authorize the carrying out of the process.

Also, where the direction applies to only part of the process, it may impose conditions to be observed in the carrying out of the part that is authorized to continue to be carried out.

Section 17 provides inspectors appointed under the EPA with considerable powers regarding premises on which a prescribed process is, or is believed to be, carried out and to those on which a prescribed process has been carried out, the condition of which is believed to pose a risk of serious pollution of the environment. Such powers include those of being able to:

- enter premises at any reasonable time if there is reason to believe that a prescribed process is or has been carried out that is or will give rise to a risk of serious pollution
- take a constable where obstruction on entry is anticipated, plus any necessary equipment or materials
- make such examinations and investigations as may be necessary
- direct that premises, or any part of the premises, remain undisturbed
- take measurements and photographs and make such recordings as are considered necessary
- take samples of articles and substances, and of air, water or land
- cause any article or substance that has caused, or is likely to cause, pollution to be dismantled or subjected to any process or test
- take possession of and detain any above article or substance for the purpose of examination, to ensure it is not tampered with before examination and is available for use as evidence
- require any person to answer questions as the inspector thinks fit and sign a declaration that their answers are the truth
- require the production of written or computerized records and take copies of these
- require that any person provide the facilities and assistance necessary to enable them to exercise their powers
- any other power conferred on them by the regulations.

Part II: Waste on land

The EPA imposes a duty of care on anyone who imports, carries, keeps, treats or disposes of waste. Such people must take all reasonable steps to ensure that the waste is collected, transported, treated and disposed of by licensed operators, that is, those issued with a *waste management licence.*

Public registers must be maintained by the authorities that detail the conditions of the licences issued and details of any enforcement actions taken. This Part should be read in conjunction with the system for IPC that is enforced by HMIP on prescribed Category A process industries.

Part III: Statutory nuisances and clean air

Section 79 deals with statutory nuisances and inspections. The following matters constitute *statutory nuisance:*

- any *premises* that are in such a state as to be prejudicial to health or cause a nuisance
- *smoke* emitted from premises that is prejudicial to health or causes a nuisance
- *fumes or gases* emitted from premises that are prejudicial to health or cause a nuisance
- any *dust, steam, smell or other effluent* arising on industrial, trade or busi-

ness premises that are prejudicial to health or cause a nuisance
- any *accumulation or deposit* that is prejudicial to health or causes a nuisance
- any *animal* kept in a place or manner that is prejudicial to health or causes a nuisance
- *noise* emitted from premises that is prejudicial to health or causes a nuisance
- *any other matter* that is declared by any enactment to be a statutory nuisance.

It shall be the duty of every LA to ensure that its area is inspected from time to time to detect any statutory nuisances that ought to be dealt with under section 80 (Summary proceedings for statutory nuisances) and, where a complaint of a statutory nuisance is made to it by a person living within its area, to take such steps as are reasonably practicable to investigate the complaint. Where a LA is satisfied that a statutory nuisance exists, or is likely to occur or recur, that is in the area of the authority, the LA shall serve an *abatement notice,* imposing all or any of the following requirements:

- requiring the abatement of the nuisance or prohibiting or restricting its occurrence or recurrence
- requiring the execution of any works, and the taking of other steps, that may be necessary for any of these purposes

and the notice shall specify the time or times within which the requirements of the notice are to be complied with. Such a notice shall be served:

- except in the next two cases below, on the person responsible for the nuisance
- where the nuisance arises from any defect of a structural character, on the owner of the premises
- where the person responsible for the nuisance cannot be found or the nuisance has not yet occurred, on the owner or occupier of the premises.

A person served with an abatement notice may appeal to a magistrates' court within 21 days, beginning with the date on which they were served with the notice. If a person is served an abatement notice and, without reasonable cause, contravenes or fails to comply with any requirement or prohibition imposed by the notice, they shall be guilty of an offence.

Failure to comply with an abatement notice can result in the defendant being subjected to a fine not exceeding level 5 on the standard scale, together with a further fine of an amount equal to one-tenth of that level for each day the offence continues after the defendant has been convicted. A person who commits an offence on industrial, trade or business premises, however, shall be liable to a fine not exceeding £20 000 (see Table 3.1 for these penalties and others under the EPA). It is a defence to prove that *best practicable means* were used to prevent, or to counteract the effects of, the nuisance.

Table 3.1 Penalties under the Environmental Protection Act 1990

Part	*Contravention*	*Penalties*
Part I	Operating without an authorization	Summary conviction – £20 000 fine
Integrated pollution control	Failing to comply with or contravening an enforcement or prohibition notice	Indictment: fine, 2 years imprisonment or both both
	Failing to comply with a court order	Summary conviction – £20 000 fine
	Failing to supply required information	Indictment: fine, 2 years or both
Part III	Obstructing or preventing an inspector from carrying out their duties	£2 000 fine
Statutory nuisances		On conviction for nuisance £2 000
		Daily penalty £200
		On conviction for nuisance arising from industrial trade or business premises – £20 000
		Daily penalty – £2 000
Part IV	Leaving litter	On summary conviction – £1 000
Litter		Fixed penalty ticket scheme – £10

Section 81 gives the LA power, where an abatement notice has not been complied with, and whether or not they have already taken proceedings, to abate the nuisance themselves and do whatever may be necessary to execute the notice. Any expenses reasonably incurred may be recovered by them from the person whose actions of failure to act have caused the nuisance or be apportioned among several persons accordingly. This section also gives power to a LA, where proceedings for an offence would afford an inadequate remedy in the case of any statutory nuisance, to take proceedings in the High Court for the purpose of securing the abatement, prohibition or restriction of the nuisance, and the proceedings shall be maintainable notwithstanding the LA having suffered no damage from the nuisance.

A person who is aggrieved by the existence of a statutory nuisance need not necessarily pursue the matter through their local authority. Under section 82, a magistrates' court may act on a complaint made by any person on the ground that they are aggrieved by the existence of a statutory nuisance. If the court is satisfied that the alleged nuisance exists, or that, although abated, it is likely to recur on the same premises, the court shall make an order for either or both of the following:

- requiring the defendant to abate the nuisance (an abatement order) within a time specified in the order and to execute any works necessary to achieve this purpose
- prohibiting a recurrence of the nuisance (a prohibition order) and requiring the defendant, within a time specified in the order, to execute any works necessary to prevent the recurrence

and may also impose on the defendant a fine not exceeding level 5 on the standard scale.

If the court is satisfied that the alleged nuisance exists and is such that, in the opinion of the court, it renders the premises unfit for human habitation, an order (as above) may prohibit the use of the premises for human habitation until the premises are, to the satisfaction of the court, rendered fit for this purpose.

See Figure 3.1 for a summary of the procedure in such cases.

Part IV: Litter and so on

The EPA brought in new procedures regarding the control of litter. Section 87 created the offence of 'leaving litter' and section 88 brought in fixed penalty notices for leaving litter. Section 99 also gives LAs the power to deal with abandoned shopping and luggage trolleys.

Part V: Amendment to the Radioactive Substances Act 1960

Part V of the Act makes a number of amendments to the Radioactive Substances Act (RSA) 1960, the principal amendments being:

- provision for the appointment of inspectors
- provision for a scheme of fees and charges payable for registration and authorization under the RSA
- new powers of enforcement, that is enforcement notices
- withdrawal of the exemption in favour of the UK Atomic Energy Authority from certain requirements of the RSA
- applications of the RSA to the Crown.

Part VI: Genetically modified organisms (GMOs)

This purpose of this Part is to prevent or minimize any damage to the

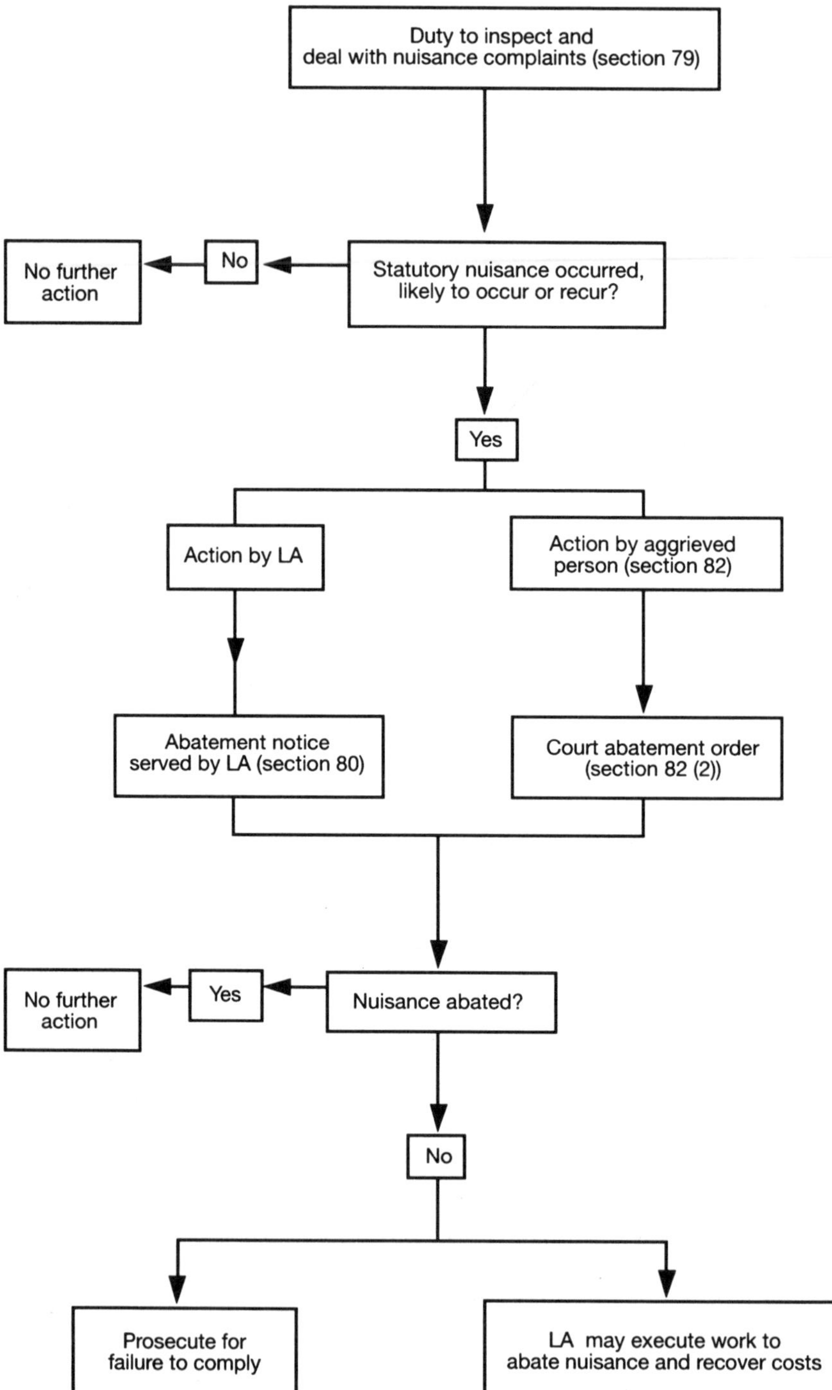

• **FIG 3.1 Statutory nuisance procedure under the Environmental Protection Act**

environment that may arise from the escape or release from human control of GMOs. The following definitions are important here.

- the term *organism* means any acellular, unicellular or multicellular entity (in any form), other than humans or human embryos, and, unless the context otherwise requires, the term also includes any article or substance consisting of biological matter – *biological matter* meaning anything (other than an entity mentioned above) that consists of or includes:
  - tissue or cells (including gametes or propagules) or subcellular entities, of any kind, capable of replication or of transferring genetic material
  - genes or other genetic material, in any form, that are so capable

  and it is immaterial (in determining if something is or is not an organism or biological matter) whether it is the product of natural or artificial processes of reproduction and, in the case of biological matter, whether it has ever been part of a *whole* organism
- an organism is *genetically modified* if any of the genes or other genetic material in the organism:
  - have been modified by means of an artificial technique prescribed in regulations by the Secretary of State
  - are inherited or otherwise derived, through any number of replications, from genes or other genetic material (from any source) that were so modified.
- the *techniques* that may be prescribed for the above purposes include:
  - any technique for the modification of any genes or other genetic material by the recombination, insertion or deletion of, or of any component parts of, that material from its previously occurring state
  - any other technique for modifying genes or other genetic material that, in the opinion of the Secretary of State, would produce organisms which should, for the purposes of this Part, be treated as having been genetically modified,

  but do not include techniques that involve no more than, or no more than the assistance of, naturally occurring processes of reproduction (including selective breeding techniques or *in vitro* fertilization).

Section 108 of the Act requires that no person shall import or acquire, release or market any GMOs unless, before so doing, they:

- have carried out an assessment of the risks of damage to the environment that would be caused as a result of such an act
- in prescribed cases and circumstances, have given notice of this intention and prescribed information to the Secretary of State.

General duties relating to the importation, acquisition, keeping, release or marketing of GMOs are detailed in section 109. Section 110 empowers the Secretary of State to serve a prohibition notice on any person there is reason to believe is:

- is proposing to import or acquit, release or market GMOs
- is keeping any such organisms

if the Secretary of State is of the opinion that doing any such act to those organisms or continuing to keep them would involve a risk of causing damage to the environment.

A system of *consents*, however, is operated by the Secretary of State's office whereby a person importing or acquiring, releasing or marketing GMOs may be subject to certain limitations and conditions (sections 111 and 112).

Similar provisions relating to enforcement, offences and the powers of a court to make orders apply as with other Parts of the EPA.

Part VII: Nature conservation

This Part established Nature Conservancy Council for England, Scotland and Wales and their functions, both generally and specifically.

Part VIII: Miscellaneous

The most significant of the miscellaneous provisions of this Part are:

- power to restrict the importation, use, supply or storage of substances or articles for the purpose of avoiding pollution or harm to human beings, animals or plants
- power to restrict the importation or exportation of waste for the purpose of preventing pollution or harm to human health or for conserving facilities or resources for dealing with waste
- power to make provision for obtaining information about substances that have the potential to cause pollution or harm to human health
- provision of public registers of potentially contaminated land
- amendments of the legislation of control of hazardous substances
- increase in the maximum penalties in respect of water pollution offences
- amendments to legislation as to marine deposits and the creation of public registers as to such deposits and marine incineration
- amendments to the provisions regarding oil pollution offences from ships
- provisions for the control of stray dogs
- provision regarding the burning of straw, stubble and other crop residues.

THE CRIMINAL JUSTICE ACT 1991

The Criminal Justice Act (CJA) brought in provisions relating to *unit fines*. A stated aim of the CJA is to encourage the use of fines, to make their effect fairer on offenders of different means, and to decrease the incidence of fine defaulters becoming imprisoned. Sections 17–24 detail the provisions relating to unit fines and create the situation whereby the actual amount imposed by the courts as a fine will reflect two aspects, namely the seriousness of the offence and the means of the offender.

The seriousness of the offence

This is measured in units and the Act fixes a maximum limit to the number of units attributable to any offence according to the accepted concept of standard levels. These limits are indicated in Table 3.2.

Table 3.2 Units of fines for offences

Level	*Maximum*	*Maximum number of units*
1	£ 200	Up to 2 units
2	£ 500	Up to 5 units
3	£1000	Up to 10 units
4	£2500	Up to 25 units
5	£5000	Up to 50 units

When a court is determining the seriousness of an offence, relevant factors that must be considered are:

- aggravating and mitigating factors relating to the offence itself
- aggravating factors disclosed by previous convictions, such as similarities
- when considering a fine, the facts of all other associated offences.

An *associated offence* may be taken to be one for which an offender is convicted or sentenced, or which is taken into consideration at the same hearing.

Under section 29(1), an offence is not to be regarded as more serious simply because of previous convictions or any failure to respond to previous sentences. Under the CJA, therefore, previous convictions do not, *per se*, aggravate the seriousness of the current offence.

Section 29(2), however, states that where any aggravating factors of an offence are disclosed by the circumstances of other offences committed by the offender, nothing shall prevent the court from taking these factors into account for the purpose of forming an opinion as to the seriousness of the offence. On this basis, where previous offences display similarities to the case before the court, this may be taken to be an aggravating factor with regard to the seriousness of the offence under consideration.

The offender's means

The means of the offender are reflected in a court's calculations of the offender's *disposable weekly income* (DWI). This is essentially one third of what remains of an offender's income after the deduction of general living expenses.

The assessment is made after the offender has submitted a *statement of means*. It is the DWI that will determine the value of the unit used for their fine. Section 18 actually stipulates a minimum and maximum value for a unit, that is, £4 and £100 respectively. On this basis, the maximum fine that could be imposed is £5000, that is, 50 units at £100. Thus, by establishing fines at a level that an offender can afford to pay, it is envisaged that few offenders will be involved in fine default courts, which reduces their risk of being sent to prison for so doing.

Section 20 grants a court the power to require an offender to submit a statement of means. Failure, without reasonable excuse, to provide this information can result in a fine not exceeding level 3 on the standard scale. On the other hand, a person who knowingly or recklessly makes a false statement or fails to disclose any material fact is punishable with up to three months' imprisonment or a level 4 fine.

Table 3.3 Imprisonment related to units

Units	*Maximum days of imprisonment*
1–2	7
3–5	14
6–10	28
11–25	45
26–50	3 months

Table 3.4 Imprisonment related to fines

Amount	*Maximum days of imprisonment*
Up to £200	7
Over £200 and up to £500	14
Over £500 and up to £1000	28
Over £1000 and up to £25000	45
Over £2500 and up to £5000	1–3 months

Default arrangements

Section 22 deals with the maximum periods of imprisonment in the event of an offender defaulting on the payment of a fine (see Table 3.3 and 3.4).

For those cases where a fine has not been set in units, section 23 of the CJA states the maximum period of imprisonment in default for a given amount of fine (see Table 3.4)

Exceptions

Unit fines do not apply in cases where the offender is a company. Certain offences (for instance under the EPA and HSWA) may not be covered by the system as the offence is committed by a corporate body. In other cases, however, identifiable individuals, such as directors, may be responsible for the offence and subject to the unit fine provisions.

Where the maximum fine under a statute or regulations is higher than the normal maximum fine stipulated under the CJA (£5000), the unit fines provisions do not apply. For instance, the maximum fine under the EPA and HSWA is £20 000. However, the unit fine system does apply under, for instance, section 23 of the EPA (obstruction), as this offence carries a maximum of a level 5 penalty.

The unit fine system does not apply to fines imposed by a Crown Court, even when cases are committed to a Crown Court for sentence. On the other hand, even in those instances where unit fines do not apply, section 19 requires that a court, when deciding a figure for a fine, must take into account the means of the offender and this may result in an increase or decrease in the fine imposed.

LEVELS OF STATUTORY DUTY

Statutory duties give rise to *criminal liability*. There are three distinct levels of statutory duty:

1 'absolute' requirements

2 'practicable' requirements

3 'reasonably practicable' requirements.

'Absolute' requirements

Where the risk of injury or disease is inevitable if safety requirements are not followed, a statutory duty may well be absolute.

The classic instance of an absolute duty is in regulation 5(1) of the Provision and Use of Work Equipment Regulations 1992 (PUWER), which states 'Every employer *shall* ensure that work equipment is so constructed or adapted as to be suitable for the purpose for which it is to be used or provided'. Absolute duties are qualified by the terms 'shall' or 'must'.

'Practicable' requirements

A statutory requirement is qualified by the phrase 'so far as is practicable' when it implies that if, *in the light of current knowledge and invention*, it is feasible to comply with this requirement, then, irrespective of the cost or sacrifice involved, such a requirement must be complied with (see *Schwalb* v. *Fass H. & Son* (1946) 175 LT 345).

'Practicable' means more than physically possible and implies a higher duty of care than a duty qualified by the phrase 'so far as is reasonably practicable'.

'Reasonably practicable' requirements

A duty qualified by the phrase 'so far as is reasonably practicable' implies a lower or lesser level of duty than one qualified by 'so far as is practicable'. 'Reasonably practicable' is a narrower term than 'physically possible' (that is, 'practicable'), and implies that a computation must be made in which the *quantum of risk* is placed on one side of the scale and the *sacrifice involved* in carrying out the measures necessary for averting that risk is placed on the other side. If it can be shown that there is a gross disproportion between these two factors, that is, that the risk is insignificant in relation to the sacrifice, then a defendant discharges the onus on themselves (see *Edwards* v. *National Coal Board* (1949) 1 AER 743). All duties under the HSWA are qualified by the term 'so far as is reasonably practicable'.

The 'Reasonable man'

What *is* a reasonable person? What is it about their behaviour that makes them reasonable and how do the courts interpret this term?

The mythical 'reasonable man' was interpreted by one judge in the past as 'the man who travels to work every day on the top deck of the No. 57 Clapham omnibus'. The term is flexible and changes with time according to society and the norms prevalent at the time.

The term 'reasonable' can be found in section 7 of the HSWA, that is, in the duty on employees to take *reasonable* care for the safety of themselves and others, including members of the public, who may foreseeably be affected by their acts or omissions at work.

THE ROLES OF THE ENFORCING AUTHORITIES

The enforcing authorities under the HSWA are:

- the Health and Safety Executive (HSE), which is split into a number of specific inspectorates, for example, Factories, Agricultural, Nuclear Installations
- local authorities, principally through their environmental health departments
- for certain matters, the Fire Authority.

Actual enforcement is undertaken by inspectors appointed under the Act and authorized by a written warrant from the enforcing authority.

The powers of inspectors

Under section 20 of the HSWA, an inspector has the following powers:

- to enter premises at any reasonable time and, where obstruction is anticipated, to enlist the support of a police officer
- on entering premises,
  - to take with them any other person duly authorized by their enforcing authority
  - any equipment or materials required for any purpose for which the power of entry is being exercised
- to make such examinations and investigations as may be necessary
- to direct that premises or any part of such premises, or anything therein, shall remain undisturbed for so long as is reasonably necessary for the purpose of any examination or investigation
- to take such measurements and photographs and make such recordings as they consider necessary for the purpose of any examination or investigation
- to take samples of any articles or substances found in any premises, and of the atmosphere in or in the vicinity of such premises
- where it appears to them that an article or substance has caused or is likely to cause danger to health or safety, to cause it to be dismantled or subjected to any process or test
- to take possession of any article or substance and to detain these for as long as is necessary:
  - to examine these
  - to ensure that they are not tampered with before their examination is completed
  - to ensure that they are available for use as evidence in any proceedings for an offence under the relevant statutory provisions
- to require any person whom they have reasonable cause to believe to be able to give any information relevant to any examination or investigation to answer such questions as the inspector thinks fit to ask and to sign a declaration of the truth of their answers:
- to require the production of, and inspect and take copies of or any entry in:
  - any books or documents that, by virtue of the relevant statutory provisions, are required to be kept
  - any other books or documents that it is necessary for them to see for the purposes of any examination or investigation
- to require any person to afford them such facilities and assistance with respect to any matters or things within that person's control or in relation to which that person has responsibilities that are necessary to enable the

inspector to exercise any of the powers conferred on them by this section

- any other power that is necessary for the purpose of carrying into effect the relevant statutory provisions.

After an inspector has completed an investigation or examination, they have a duty to inform safety representatives of the actual matters they have found (section 28(8)) and must give the employer similar information.

Notices

Enforcing officers may serve two types of notice:

- improvement notices
- prohibition notices.

Improvement notices

If an inspector is of the opinion that a breach has, or is likely to, occur, they may serve an improvement notice on the employer or employee. The notice must state which statutory provision the inspector believes has been contravened and the reason for this belief. It should also state a time limit within which the contravention should be remedied.

Prohibition notices

Where an inspector is of the opinion that a work activity involves or will involve a risk of serious personal injury, they may serve a prohibition notice on the owner and/or occupier of the premises or the person having control of that activity.

Such a notice will direct that the specified activities in the notice shall not be carried out by or under the control of the person on whom the notice is served unless certain specified remedial measures have been complied with.

It should be appreciated that it is not necessary for an inspector to believe that a *legal* provision is being or has been contravened, rather a prohibition notice is served where there is an immediate threat to life and in anticipation of danger. A prohibition notice may have *immediate* effect after its service by the inspector or it may be *deferred*, thereby allowing the person time to remedy the situation, carry out works and so on. The duration of a deferred prohibition notice is stated on the notice.

For a summary of the features of improvement and prohibition notices, see Table 3.5.

Prosecution

Prosecution is frequently the outcome of failure to comply with an improvement or prohibition notice. Conversely, an inspector may simply institute legal proceedings without serving a notice.

Cases are normally heard in a magistrates' court, but there is also provision in the HSWA regarding indictments. Much depends on the gravity of the offence.

HEALTH AND SAFETY EXECUTIVE Serial No. 1

Health and Safety at Work etc. Act 1974, Sections 21, 23 and 24

IMPROVEMENT NOTICE

Name and address (See Section 46)	To ....
	....
(a) Delete as necessary	(a) Trading as ....
(b) Inspector's full name	(b) ....
(c) Inspector's official designation	one of (c) ....
(d) Official address	of (d) ....
	....Tel No ....
	hereby give you notice that I am of the opinion that at..
(e) Location of premises or place and activity	(e) ....
	you, as (a) an employer/a self employed person/a person wholly or partly in control of the premises
(f) Other specified capacity	(f) ....
	(a) are contravening/have contravened in circumstances that make it likely that the contravention will continue to be repeated.
	....
	....
(g) Provisions contravened	(g) ....
	....
	The reasons for my said opinion are: ....
	....
	....
	and I hereby require you to remedy the said contraventions or, as the case may be, the matters occasioning them by
	(h) ....
(h) Date	(a) In the manner stated in the attached schedule which forms part of the notice.
	Signature....................... Date ....
	Being an Inspector appointed by an Instrument in writing made pursuant to Section 19 of the said Act and entitled to issue this notice.
	(a) An Improvement notice is also being served on
	....
	of ....
LP1	related to the matters contained in this notice.

3

• **FIG 3.2 (a) Example of an improvement notice**

HEALTH AND SAFETY EXECUTIVE | Serial No. P

Health and Safety at Work etc. Act 1974, Sections 22–24

PROHIBITION NOTICE

Name and address (See Section 46)	To ....
	....
(a) Delete as necessary	(a) Trading as ....
(b) Inspector's full name	(b) ....
(c) Inspector's official designation	one of (c) ....
(d) Official address	of (d) ....
	....tel no. ....
	hereby give you notice that I am of the opinion that the following activities,
	namely:– ....
	....
	....
	which are (a) being carried on by you/about to be carried on by you/under your control
(e) Location of activity	at (e) ....
	Involve, or will involve (a) a risk/an imminent risk, of serious personal injury. I am further of the opinion that the said matters involve contraventions of the following statutory provisions:– ....
	....
	....
	....
	because ....
	....
	....
	and I hereby direct that the said activities shall not be carried on by you or under your control (a) Immediately /after
(f) Date	(f) ....
	unless the said contraventions and matters included in the schedule, which forms part of this notice, have been remedied.
	Signature ....Date ....
LP2	being an inspector appointed by an instrument in writing made pursuant to Section 19 of the said Act and entitled to issue this notice.

• **FIG 3.2 (b) Example of a prohibition notice**

Table 3.5 A summary of the features of notices

Type of notice	*Circumstances*		*When notice takes effect*	*Effect of appeal (section 24*)*	*Person on whom notice is served*
	Contravention of a 'relevant statutory provision'	*Risk involved*			
Improvement notice (section 21)	Must have been one and it is likely that it will be continued or repeated	No risk specified and covers cases where there is no risk	When specified, but not earlier than 21 days after issue	Suspends the notice until appeal is determined or the apeal is withdrawn	Person contravening provision
Immediate prohibition notice (section 22)	Not necessary	Where there is or will be immediate risk of serious personal injury†	Immediate	No suspension, unless the Industrial Tribunal rules otherwise	Person under whose control the activity is carried out or by whom it is carried out
Deferred prohibition notice (section 22)	Not necessary	Risk of serious personal injury not imminent	At the end of the period specifed in the notice	As in the case of an immediate notice	As in the case of an immediate notice

* Appeals against notices are dealt with in regulations made under section 24 as follows:
– The Industrial Tribunals (Improvement and Prohibition Notices Appeals) Regulations 1974 (SI 1974, No. 1925) – for notices served in England and Wales.
– The Industrial Tribunals (Improvement and Prohibition Notices Appeals) (Scotland) Regulations 1974 (SI 1974, No. 1926).
†'Persons injury' includes any disease and any impairment of a person's physical or mental condition (section 53).

Penalties

The Offshore Safety Act 1992 amended the HSWA and allows magistrates to impose fines of up to £20 000 for a breach of sections 2 to 6 of the Act, and for breach of an improvement notice or prohibition notice. The maximum fine for other offences is £5000.

This Act also widened the range of health and safety offences for which the higher courts can impose prison sentences. The two-year maximum sentence, which existed for offences concerning explosives, licensing regimes and breach of a prohibition notice was extended to cover breach of an improvement notice.

Comment

With the advent of the MHSWR, the role of inspectors may well change to a more management systems-orientated approach. On this basis, instead of examining premises, plant and processes to identify contraventions of current legislation, inspectors appointed under the HSWA will devote more time to reviews of management systems for health and safety. This approach may well be experienced in large multisite organizations where greater attention will be paid to documentation of safety procedures, training systems, the appointment and relative competence of competent persons, emergency procedures and so on from head office level, accompanied by spot checks to ascertain whether or not these procedures and systems are actually implemented at local unit level.

4

The principal regulations

INTRODUCTION

As we saw in the last chapter, statutes enable the Minister or Secretary of State to make regulations. All regulations, such as the Noise at Work Regulations 1989, are made under the HSWA. More recently, regulations have been made in order to implement EC Directives. For instance, the 'Council Directive on the introduction of measures to encourage improvements in the health and safety of workers at work' (the Framework Directive) was implemented in the UK as the Management of Health and Safety at Work Regulations (MHSWR) 1992. Similarly, the 'Council Directive concerning the minimum safety and health requirements for the use by workers of machines, equipment and installations', (the Machinery Safety Directive) was implemented as the Provision and Use of Work Equipment Regulations 1992.

This chapter covers the principal health and safety regulations. The depth of treatment of the various regulations varies from an in-depth treatment, in the case of the more significant regulations, to an overview in other cases, outlining the key provisions.

THE CHEMICALS (HAZARD INFORMATION AND PACKAGING) REGULATIONS 1993

These regulations implement a series of EC Directives on the classification, packaging and labelling of dangerous substances and preparations. They came into force on 1 September 1993 and replace the Classification, Packaging and Labelling of Dangerous Substances (CPL) Regulations 1984. The objective of the Chemicals (Hazard Information and Packaging) (CHIP) Regulations is to help protect people and the environment from the ill-effects of chemicals. It does this by requiring suppliers:

- to identify the hazards (or dangers) of the chemicals they supply
- to give information about the hazards to the people who are supplied

- to package the chemicals safely.

These are known as the *supply requirements* (a *supplier* being someone who supplies chemicals as part of a transaction, including manufacturers, importers and distributors). Similar duties are placed on people who consign chemicals by road, known as the *carriage requirements.*

Supply requirements

The supply requirements implement a series of directives adopted by the member states of the EC on classification, packaging and labelling of dangerous substances and preparations. *Substances* in this case are pure chemicals, like ethanol or water, and *preparations* are mixtures of chemicals, such as paints or gin. The term *chemical* covers substances and preparations.

Carriage requirements

These requirements are based on United Nations (UN) recommendations and are the same as, or very similar to, existing requirements in CPL.

The scope of the CHIP regulations

CHIP is one of the largest packages of regulations derived from international agreements. It is relevant to all chemicals, from the most complicated and esoteric to household commodities such as paint or bleach. It also concerns anyone who supplies or consigns dangerous chemicals in Great Britain or offshore. This includes not only large companies, but also small manufacturers that concentrate on making one or more common chemicals or who retail chemicals to the public. It is intended to enable them to take the right precautions.

CHIP is also the foundation for other health and safety and environmental provisions. For example, substances classified under CHIP as being harmful to health fall within the scope of the Control of Substances Hazardous to Health Regulations (COSHHR). The new safety data sheets required by CHIP will be a major source of information for those who have to prepare COSHH assessments.

Certain substances identified as dangerous by CHIP fall within the scope of the Control of Major Industrial Accidents Hazards Regulations (CIMAHR) 1984. The package of legislation and supporting guidance for CHIP consists of:

- the *regulations*
- the *Approved Supply List: Information Approved for the Classification and Labelling of Substances and Preparations Dangerous for Supply*
- the *Approved Carriage List: Information Approved for the Classification, Packaging and Labelling of Substances Dangerous for Carriage by Road*
- the *Approved Guide to the Classification and Labelling of Substances and Prepa-*

rations Dangerous for Supply
- the *Approved Code of Practice on Safety Data Sheets for Substances and Preparations Dangerous for Supply.*

Classification

Supply requirements

The fundamental requirement is for a supplier to decide if the chemical is dangerous or not. If it *is* dangerous, then it must be classified, and it is an offence to supply a chemical before this classification is done (this is a new requirement under CHIP that did not exist in the CPL).

The first step in classification is to put the chemical into a category of danger. There are three main categories of dangerous chemicals and these are further subdivided:

- substances and preparations dangerous because of their physical or chemical properties:
  - explosive
  - oxidizing
  - exremely flammable
  - highly flammable
  - flammable

4

- substances and preparations dangerous because of their health effects:
  - very toxic
  - toxic
  - harmful
  - corrosive
  - irritant
  - carcinogenic (substances that cause cancer)
  - mutagenic (substances that cause inherited changes)
  - teratagenic (substances that cause harm to the unborn)
- substances dangerous for the environment.

Note that the last four subdivisions of the second category and the third category are new.

Although suppliers are responsible for classification, they do not have to do this themselves. However, the supplier must ensure that the classification has been carried out by someone who is competent to do so.

Some 1400 of the more common dangerous chemicals have already been classified and details are given in the *Approved Supply List.* This new list is more extensive than the previous version and contains more detail on each substance. Each substance is identified by its chemical name or its unique international number and the classification and other information can be read directly from the list.

Where a substance is not on the Approved Supply List, suppliers have to classify the substances themselves on the basis of the properties described in the Regulations. The competent person must find and assemble the available information on the chemical, but it will not be necessary to carry out any new tests. Once the data has been assembled, it can be compared with the criteria in the *Approved Guide to the Classification and Labelling of Substances and Preparations Dangerous for Supply.* The competent person must then decide whether or not the substance is dangerous and what classification (if any) is appropriate.

Preparations must be classified under the same categories, except for the classification for environmental effects, which is not required. One of the objectives of CHIP is to avoid unnecessary animal testing. CHIP therefore sets out a method for calculating which category of danger the preparation should be in. Whereas CPL used several different calculation methods, CHIP sets down one.

Carriage requirements

Chemicals must be classified for carriage by referring to the *Approved Carriage List* or, if the substance is not on the list, then in line with the categories in CHIP. The categories are similar to, but not the same as, those for supply. These provisions, essentially, are the same as in CPL.

If the substance is not dangerous (as specified by CHIP), then no further action is necessary.

Safety data sheets

One of the important new requirements is that safety data sheets must be provided for dangerous chemicals that are supplied for work. A safety data sheet must be provided by the supplier to the recipient and contain information about the chemical that enables the recipient to take the right precautions. The *Approved Code of Practice: Safety Data Sheets for Substances and Preparations Dangerous for Supply* gives advice in this area.

The safety data sheet is invaluable in enabling an employer to carry out a COSHH assessment, but it is not a substitute for an assessment.

Safety data sheets will describe the hazards of the chemicals, but only the user can assess the probability of the danger arising (that is, the risk) in the workplace.

These sheets must be provided whether the chemical is sold in bulk or in packages. They do not have to be provided when chemicals are sold for private use through shops due to the existence of comparable legislation covering such cases.

Labelling

Where a dangerous chemical is supplied in a package, the package must be labelled. The aim is to inform anyone handling the package or using the chemical about its hazards and to give brief advice on any precautions they need to take. For workers, the label is the supplement to information provided by the employer; for others, it is a major way of propagating information.

The label must always contain details about:

- the supplier
- the chemical
- the category of danger
- risk phrases and safety phrases.

Risk phrases and safety phrases are standard phrases set out in CHIP. *Risk phrases* describe the dangers of the chemicals in more detail, such as 'May cause cancer' or 'Toxic by inhalation'. *Safety phrases* tell the user what to do or not to do with the chemical, such as 'Keep away from children' or 'Do not empty into drains'.

A *warning symbol* is also required on most labels, such as a skull and crossbones or a picture of an explosion. Suppliers are responsible for using the correct label for the product.

Labelling follows classification. The first step for substances is to look in the Approved Supply List. Where the substance is not listed, or if the chemical is a preparation then the label is derived from the classification using the advice in the Approved Guide to the Classification and Labelling of Substances and Preparations Dangerous for Supply.

CHIP also requires that labels be provided for packages travelling by road. These labels are similar to the supply labels, but are not as comprehensive, concentrating more on the immediate hazards of transport. The scheme is unchanged from CPL and labels for most of the common substances are to be found on the Approved Carriage List. If necessary, the carriage label can be *combined* with a supply label to avoid the need for repeated labelling as the package goes on and off the road.

Packaging

CHIP requires that chemicals be packaged safely to withstand the conditions of supply and carriage. The requirements are the same as in CPL.

THE CONSTRUCTION REGULATIONS 1961–1966

Employers in the construction industry and related operations must comply with the general provisions of the HSWA and with specific regulations relating to construction made under the FA. What is known as the 'Construction Regulations' is actually comprised of four sets of regulations:

- Construction (General Provisions) Regulations 1961
- Construction (Lifting Operations) Regulations 1961
- Construction (Working Places) Regulations 1966

- Construction (Health and Welfare) Regulations 1966

which were made under the FA. To facilitate understanding of these regulations, their various provisions are covered on a safety topic basis, rather than as individual sets of regulations.

These regulations apply to *building operations* and to *works of engineering construction* undertaken by way of trade or business, or for the purpose of any industrial or commercial undertaking, or by or on behalf of the Crown or any municipal or other public authority and to any line or siding that is part of a railway or tramway used in connection with them.

Section 176 of the FA defines a building operation as the construction, structural alteration, repair or maintenance of a building (including repointing, redecorating, and external cleaning of the structure), the demolition of a building, and the preparation for and laying the foundation of an intended building, but does not include works of engineering construction.

Works of engineering construction are defined as the construction of any railway line or siding otherwise than on an existing railway, and the construction, structural alteration, repair (including repointing and repainting) or demolition of any dock, harbour, inland navigation, tunnel, bridge, viaduct, waterworks reservoir, pipeline, aqueduct, sewer, sewage works or gasholder, except where carried on a railway or tramway.

The term also covers the following operations, except when carried out in a factory, electricity station, railway or tramway, namely the construction, structural alteration, repair, repointing, repainting or demolition of any steel or reinforced concrete structure other than a building, and any road, airfield, sea defence works or river works, and any other civil or constructional engineering works of a similar nature. This part of the definition was added by the Engineering Construction (Extension of Definition) Regulations 1960.

The duties of contractors, employees, safety supervisors and competent persons

Contractors

The duties imposed by the regulations are directed to the contractor or 'employer of workmen'. This is because, in many cases, construction workers are not technically employees but self-employed operators under a contract for service.

Generally, the employer must comply with the regulations in so far as they are relevant to the nature of the work being carried out, whether it be excavations, roof work or whatever. Certain regulations must, however, be complied with *whatever* the work, such as the duty to appoint a safety supervisor.

Employees

Employees are also under a duty to comply with the provisions of the regulations. This means that they must operate in accordance with the regulations and cooperate with the employer in ensuring safety requirements are met. They must report any defect in plant or equipment to their employer or the safety supervisor without delay.

Safety supervisors

Where more than 20 people are employed in building operations or works of engineering construction, at least one safety supervisor must be appointed. The appointment must be made in writing and their name entered on a copy or abstract of the Construction (General Provisions) Regulations (CGPR) 1961).

The safety supervisor should be experienced in construction work and be 'suitably qualified'. Their duties include:

- advising the employer on the observance of safety requirements
- advising in respect of any other safety matters
- general supervision to ensure that safety requirements are being complied with
- promoting the safe conduct of the work generally.

Competent persons

The expression 'competent person' occurs frequently in construction safety legislation. For example, under the CGPR and the Construction (Working Places) Regulations (CWPR) 1966, certain inspections, examinations, operations and supervisory duties must be undertaken by a competent person. 'Competent person', however, is not defined under the regulations and the onus is on the employer to decide whether or not someone is competent to undertake these duties.

It is necessary to look to case law for a definition. Broadly, a competent person should have practical and theoretical knowledge as well as sufficient experience of the particular machinery, plant or procedure involved to enable them to identify defects or weaknesses during plant and machinery examinations, and to assess their importance in relation to the strength and function of that plant and machinery (see *Brazier* v. *Skipton Rock Company Ltd* (1962) 1 AER 955).

Competent persons are needed for the following construction-related activities:

- supervision of demolition work
- supervision of the handling and use of explosives
- inspection of scaffold materials prior to erection of a scaffold
- supervision or erection of, substantial alterations or additions to, and dismantling of scaffolds
- inspections of scaffolds every seven days and after adverse weather conditions that could affect the strength and stability of a scaffold or cause displacement of any part
- inspections of excavations on a daily basis
- supervision of the erection of cranes
- testing of cranes after erection, re-erection and any removal or adjustment

involving changes of anchorage or ballasting
- examination of appliances for anchorage or ballasting prior to crane erection.

A competent person, therefore, must be able to discover defects and be able to understand and act upon the possible outcome of such defects.

General and specific requirements of the Construction Regulations

It should be appreciated that the majority of the duties of employers under the Construction Regulations are of an absolute nature.

Safe working conditions

Places at which people are habitually working must be covered so as to give protection against any falling material. Temporary structures must be of good construction, sound material, adequate strength and stability, free from patent defect and adequately maintained. Suitable and sufficient safe access and egress must be maintained for every working position. All workplaces must be made and kept safe for any person working there. Scaffolds or, if appropriate, ladders or other suitable means of support, must be provided and properly maintained where work cannot be done safely on or from the ground or from part of a building or other permanent structure. Openings, corners, breaks or edges in floors, walls and roofs must be fenced. Safety sheets or nets, or safety belts, must be used when other legal requirements designed to prevent falls cannot be complied with. All practicable steps must be taken to prevent danger from live electric cables or apparatus.

Scaffolding

The erection of scaffolds

A competent person must inspect scaffold materials before each occasion on which they are to be put into use. Any erection, substantial alterations or additions to and dismantling of a scaffold must be under the immediate supervision of a competent person. Competent and experienced workmen must be employed, so far as is possible, for the erection, substantial alterations or additions to and dismantling of scaffolds. Every part of a scaffold must be so fixed, secured or placed as to prevent accidental displacement as far as is practicable. Scaffolds must be constructed of suitable and sound material and of adequate strength. They must be rigidly connected to the building or other structure unless designed and constructed as an independent scaffold. Scaffolds must be securely supported or suspended and strutted or braced where necessary. Parts of buildings or other structures must not be used to support scaffolds unless they are of sound material and sufficiently strong and stable. Gutters must not be used as supports unless they are suitable for the purpose and of adequate strength. Overhanging eaves' gutters must not be so used unless designed as walkways. Loose bricks and other rubble must not be used as supports except for certain low platforms.

The inspection and maintenance of scaffolds

All scaffolds used must have been inspected by a competent person within the preceding seven days unless no part has been erected for over seven days. Scaffolds must be inspected after being exposed to weather conditions likely to affect the strength or stability of the scaffold or to have displaced any part. The results of inspections of scaffolds must be entered in or attached to the prescribed register (except for ladder scaffolds, trestle scaffolds and scaffolds from which persons cannot fall more than 2 metres. Each employer whose employees use a scaffold must satisfy themselves that it complies with the regulations, whether or not their own employees have erected it. All scaffolds must be properly maintained. Platforms, gangways, runs and stairs must be kept clear of unnecessary obstructions, materials or rubbish and from projecting nails. Slippery platforms, gangways, runs and stairs must be sanded, cleaned or otherwise remedied as soon as is practicable. Scaffolds must never be overloaded. Materials must not be kept on scaffolds unless needed within a reasonable time. Movement of materials on or on to scaffolds must be carried out without causing any violent shock. Loads on scaffolds must be evenly distributed as far as is practicable. Partly erected or dismantled scaffolds must either comply with the regulations, even in their incomplete state, or else have prominent warning notices to indicate that they must not be used or have access to them blocked as far as is reasonably practicable.

Ladders

Their construction

Any ladder must be of good construction, suitable and sound material, adequate strength and properly maintained. Ladders with missing or defective rungs must not be used. Wooden stiles and rungs must be used with the grain of the wood running lengthwise. Wooden ladders must not be painted or treated in such a way that defects in the timber may be concealed. Wooden ladders must have reinforcing ties if the tenon joints are not secured by wedges.

Their use

Ladders not standing on a base must be securely, equally and properly suspended by each stile and must be secured, where necessary, to prevent undue swinging or swaying. Ladders standing on a base must be equally and properly supported on each stile. A ladder standing on a base must be securely fixed near its upper resting place (or its upper end, if vertical). If such fixing is impracticable, the ladder must be fixed at or near its lower end. If this is also impracticable, a person must be stationed at the foot of the ladder to prevent it from slipping. Except where there are equal handholds, ladders must rise to a height of at least 1.07 metres above the landing place or above the highest rung reached by the feet of a person using the ladder. The space at each rung of a ladder must be sufficient to provide an adequate foothold. Landing places of adequate size must be provided, if practicable, every 9.14 metres of vertical distance, or more often. Landing places from which people are liable to fall more than 2 metres must have handrails to a height of between 920 millimetres and 1.15 metres and, also, toe boards or other barriers to a height of at least 155 millimetres. The space between the toe board and the nearest guard rail must not be more than 760 millimetres. Openings in landings through which ladders pass must be as small as is practicable. Folding ladders must have a level and firm footing and not stand on loose bricks or other loose packing.

Excavations

Materials and equipment

An adequate supply of timber or other suitable material must be provided. Any machinery in use must have any dangerous parts securely fenced (unless these are safely out of the way because of their position or construction).

Fencing

Barriers must be provided around excavations, shafts, pits and openings into which people can fall a vertical distance of more than 1.98 metres, and such barriers must be as close as is practicable to the edge of the excavation or other opening. Barriers must be kept in position except when necessarily removed for the access of people or materials.

Timbering

Adequate and suitable materials must be used to prevent danger from falls or dislodgement of the sides of any excavation or other opening or materials adjacent to it. Timbering must be undertaken as early as is practicable in the course of the work, and people engaged in timbering must be protected as far as possible from danger. Timbering or other supports must be of good construction, sound materials, free from patent defect, and of adequate strength for the purpose. Struts and braces must be properly and adequately secured to prevent accidental displacement or fall. A competent person must be employed to direct the erection and dismantling of all timbering and other supports, as well as any subsequent alterations or additions to them. Experienced workers must further be employed, as far as possible, for the erection, dismantling and so on of timbering and other supports.

Inspections and examinations

Material for timbering and other supports must be inspected by a competent person before being taken into use. Every part of any excavation, shaft, earthwork or tunnel must be inspected by a competent person at least once during every day that people are employed there. The face of every tunnel and base or crown of every shaft must be inspected by a competent person at the beginning of every shift. The working end of every trench more than 1.98 metres must be inspected by a competent person before the beginning of every shift. No person must work in any excavation or other opening after explosives have been used in or near it, in a manner likely to affect stability, until a thorough examination has been made by a competent person. No person must work in any excavaction or other opening unless it has been thoroughly examined by a competent person within the previous seven days. No person must work in any excavation or other opening after an unexpected fall of rock, earth or other material, or after substantial damage to timber or other supports, unless the part concerned has been thoroughly examined by a competent person. Reports of such examinations must be made on the day of examination, in the form prescribed by the Construction (General Provisions) Reports Order 1962.

Other precautions

Excavations and the approaches to them must be well-lit. Materials must not be placed near the edge of any excavation or other opening so as to endanger those below. If the excavation is likely to affect the security of another structure (permanent or temporary), steps must be taken to safeguard the people employed from the possible collapse of that structure. The means for reaching a place of safety must be provided, as far as practicable, when there may be danger from rising water or irruption of water or material. The means necessary to prevent overrunning must be provided when a vehicle is used to tip material into a pit or excavation or over the edge of any embankment or earthwork. The atmosphere in an excavation must be well-ventilated and free from dust, fumes and so on.

Lifting appliances and lifting gear

Packing or other means must be used to prevent the edges of a load from coming into contact with slings, ropes or chains, if this would cause danger. The angle between the legs of multiple slings must not be so great that the safe working load is exceeded. Every part of a load must be securely suspended, supported and secured to prevent displacement or slipping. Slings must be securely attached to the appliance and in a way not likely to damage the slings of any lifting gear. The hoisting mechanism of a crane must be used only for vertical raising or lowering, unless it can be used otherwise without imposing undue stress or endangering stability and is so used under the supervision of a competent person. The safe working load of the appliance must not be exceeded. The radius of the load must not exceed the maximum working radius of the jib. Where a load is equal to, or nearly equal to the safe working load, lifting must be halted for a moment after the load has been raised for a short distance. All practicable measures must be taken to prevent a load coming into contact with, and displacing, any other object. No load must be left suspended unless a competent person is actually in charge of the lifting appliance. Loads being lowered on to a scaffold must be deposited without causing any violent shock to the scaffold. Where more than one appliance is used for a lift, work must be so arranged that no appliance is overloaded or rendered unstable, and the operation must be supervised by a competent person. Lifting appliances must not be used on soft or uneven surfaces nor on a slope unless precautions are taken to ensure stability. No crane must be used for raising or lowering unless it is either securely anchored or adequately weighted with ballast that is properly placed and secured. (Rails on which cranes are mounted must not be used as anchorages.) Only trained and competent persons must operate a lifting appliance. No person under the age of 18 must operate any lifting appliance driven by mechanical power, or give signals to a driver of a power-operated lifting appliance.

THE CONSTRUCTION (HEAD PROTECTION) REGULATIONS 1989

These regulations impose requirements for the provision of suitable head protection for, and the wearing of suitable head protection by, people at work on building operations or works of engineering construction within the meaning of the FA.

Regulation 3 requires employers to provide suitable head protection (see the definition of this below) for their employees, and for the self-employed to provide it for themselves. It also imposes requirements for the maintenance and replacement of that head protection. Employees are required to report to their employers losses of or defects in their head protection.

Employers, and others having control over workers, must ensure that head protection is worn. The regulations allow rules to be made or directions given as to the wearing of head protection in specified circumstances. There is a specific requirement on people at work to wear head protection.

'Suitable head protection', under the regulations, means head protection that:

- is designed to provide protection, so far as is reasonably practicable, against foreseeable risks of injury to the head to which the wearer may be exposed
- after any necessary adjustment, fits the wearer
- is suitable with regard to the work or activity in which the wearer may be engaged.

THE CONTROL OF ASBESTOS AT WORK REGULATIONS 1987

These regulations came into operation on 1 March 1988 and apply to all workplaces where asbestos products are manufactured, used or handled. They apply to everyone at risk from work with asbestos and give specific statutory protection to all those who may be affected by work activities involving asbestos. They are accompanied by an ACOP, The Control of Asbestos at Work. The following HSE guidance notes provide further information:

EH 10	Asbestos – Control Limits: Measurement of airborne dust concentrations and assessment of control measures
EH 35	Probable asbestos dust concentrations in construction processes
EH 36	Work with asbestos cement
EH 37	Work with asbestos insulating board
EH 41	Respiratory protective equipment for use against asbestos
EH 47	The provision, use and maintenance of hygiene facilities for work with asbestos insulation and coatings.

Regulation 2 incorporates a number of definitions:

- *Action level* refers to one of the following cumulative exposures to asbestos over a continuous 12-week period, namely:
  - where the exposure is to asbestos consisting of or containing any *crocidolite* (blue asbestos) or *amosite* (brown asbestos), 48 fibre-hours per millilitre of air
  - where the exposure is to asbestos consisting of or containing any other types of asbestos (other than crocidolite or amosite), 120 fibre-hours per millilitre of air
  - where both types of exposure are involved, a proportionate number of fibre-hours per millilitre of air
- *control limits* refer to concentrations of asbestos in the atmosphere as follows:
  - 0.2 fibres per millilitre of air averaged over any continuous period of 4 hours (crocidolite or amosite)
  - 0.6 fibres per millilitre of air averaged over any continuous period of 10 minutes (crocidolite or amosite)
  - 0.5 fibres per millilitre of air averaged over any continuous period of 4 hours (asbestos other than crocidolite or amosite)
  - 1.5 fibres per millilitre of air averaged over any continuous period of 10 minutes (asbestos other than crocidolite or amosite).

Prevention or control of exposure (regulation 3)

As with the COSHHR, the emphasis is on the prevention of exposure by employees. Where prevention is not reasonably practicable, employers must *reduce* the exposure of employees, by means other than the use of respiratory protective equipment (RPE), to the lowest level reasonably practicable.

All employers whose employees are, or are liable to be affected, must designate asbestos areas and respiratory protection zones, monitor the exposure of employees to asbestos, ensure that employees undergo periodic medical examinations and keep health surveillance records for a minimum period of 30 years.

Prohibitions on work involving asbestos (regulation 4)

No employer must carry out work that exposes, or is liable to expose, employees to asbestos, unless they have identified the type of asbestos involved in the work activity or they have assumed that the asbestos is either crocidolite or amosite and have treated it accordingly.

Health risk assessment (regulation 5)

No employer must carry out work that exposes, or is liable to expose, their employees to asbestos, unless they have made an assessment of the exposure. Such an assessment must:

- identify the type of asbestos
- determine the nature and degree of exposure
- specify the steps necessary to prevent or reduce exposure to the lowest level reasonably practicable.

This assessment must be reviewed where there is a significant change in working conditions.

Notification to the enforcing authority (regulation 6)

No employer must carry out work that exposes, or is liable to expose, their employees to asbestos unless they have notified the enforcing authority (the HSE) at least 28 days before commencing the work of:

- their name, address and telephone number
- their usual place of business
- the type of asbestos used or handled
- the maximum quantity of asbestos on the premises
- the activities/processes involved on the premises
- the products (if any) manufactured
- the date when the work activity is to start.

Any material change or changes in the work activity must subsequently be notified to the enforcing authority.

Provision of information, instruction and training (regulation 7)

All employers whose employees are, or are liable to be, affected by exposure to asbestos above the action level must provide adequate information, instruction and training for such employees so that they are aware of the risks and can take the necessary precautions.

Prevention and control of exposure to asbestos (regulation 8)

All employers whose employees are, or are liable to be, affected by exposure to asbestos above the action level must:

- prevent exposure of those employees to asbestos, but where prevention of exposure is not reasonably practicable, reduce exposure to the lowest level reasonably practicable by means other than the use of respiratory protective equipment (RPE)
- where reduction to below specified control limits is not reasonably practicable, supply employees in addition with suitable RPE (approved by the HSC) in order to reduce the concentration of airborne asbestos inhaled by employees to a level below the specified control limit.

Use of personal protective equipment (PPE) (regulation 9)

Where PPE is provided, employers must ensure that it is properly used or applied.

Employees must make full and proper use of any control measures, PPE or other facilities provided by the employer and must report any defect in PPE or control measures to the employer.

Maintenance, examination and testing of RPE (regulation 10)

Where RPE is provided to protect employees against the inhalation of asbestos, employers must ensure that such RPE is maintained in a clean, efficient state, that it is in good working order and is regularly tested and examined by a competent person.

A record of such maintenance must be kept for at least five years.

Provision, disposal or cleaning of protective clothing (regulation 11)

Employers must provide adequate and suitable protective clothing and must ensure that such clothing is disposed of as asbestos waste or, alternatively, cleaned at regular intervals.

The clothing must be packed in a suitable container labelled 'Warning – contains asbestos. Breathing asbestos dust is dangerous to health. Follow safety instructions'.

Prevention or reduction of the spread of asbestos (regulation 12)

Employers must prevent the spread of asbestos, but where prevention is not reasonably practicable, reduce its spread to the lowest level that is reasonably practicable.

Cleanliness and design of premises (regulation 13)

Employers must maintain work premises in a clean condition and, in the case of new premises, ensure that they are:

- designed and constructed to facilitate cleaning
- equipped with an adequate and suitable vacuum cleaning system that, ideally, should be a fixed system.

Designated asbestos areas and respirator zones (regulation 14)

All employers must:

- designate as asbestos areas those where exposure to asbestos of an employee exceeds, or is liable to exceed, the action level
- designate respirator zones in any zone where the concentration of asbestos exceeds, or is liable to exceed, the control limit.

Both asbestos areas and respirator zones must be specifically demarcated and identified by notices and, in the case of a respirator zone, the notice must require an employee entering the zone to wear RPE.

An employer must further ensure that:

- employees (other than employees whose work so requires) do not enter or remain in any designated areas or zones respectively
- that employees do not eat, drink or smoke in designated areas or zones.

Employees must not enter or remain in an asbestos area or respirator zone unless their work permits them to do so.

Air monitoring (regulation 15)

All employers must monitor the exposure of employees to asbestos and keep a record of such monitoring for:

- 30 years, if a health record
- otherwise, for five years.

Health records and medical surveillance (regulation 16)

All employers must:

- keep health records of all employees exposed to asbestos above the action level for at least 30 years
- require employees exposed to asbestos above the action level to undergo:
  - a medical examination every two years before the exposure
  - periodic medical examination at least every two years with specific reference to the chest.

Employers must be issued with a certificate of examination and retain this for at least four years, giving a copy to the employees. Such medical examinations are carried out by Employment Medical Advisers (EMAs) during working hours, the cost of these being borne by the employer. The employer must provide adequate facilities for such examinations.

On being given reasonable notice, employers must allow employees access to health records.

Every employee exposed to asbestos above the action level must, when required by their employer, present themselves during working hours for a medical examination or health check.

Provision of washing facilities and so on (regulation 17)

All employers must:

- provide employees exposed to asbestos with adequate and suitable facilities for:
  - washing and for changing clothes
  - storage of protective clothing and personal clothing not worn during working hours
  - the separate storage of respiratory equipment.

Storage and handling of asbestos or asbestos waste (regulation 18)

All employers must ensure that raw asbestos or asbestos waste is not stored, received into or despatched from a place of work, or distributed (unless in a totally enclosed distribution system) within the place of work, unless it is contained in a suitable and sealed container that is clearly labelled and marked.

Labelling/marking of asbestos products (regulation 19)

Raw asbestos must be labelled 'Warning – contains asbestos. Breathing asbestos dust is dangerous to health. Follow safety instructions'. Any waste containing asbestos must:

- be labelled in accordance with the Chemicals (Hazard Information and Packaging) Regulations 1993
- if conveyed by road in a road tanker or tank container, in accordance with the Dangerous Substances (Conveyance by Road in Road Tankers and Tank Containers) Regulations 1981.

Where asbestos is supplied as a product for use at work, it must be labelled as above.

THE CONTROL OF LEAD AT WORK REGULATIONS 1980

These regulations, which are accompanied by an ACOP, are fundamentally concerned with the health protection of people exposed to lead in its various forms while at work. *Lead* is defined in the regulations as meaning lead (including lead alloys and compounds and lead as a constituent of any substance) that is liable to be inhaled, ingested or absorbed by people, whether employees or not.

Where work may expose someone to lead, the employer must assess the risk before the work is commenced to determine the nature and degree of exposure. Adequate information, instruction and training must be provided for those people likely to be affected.

Emphasis is placed on the introduction of measures to control materials, plant and processes so that adequate protection is provided against exposure to lead, thereby eliminating the need for the supply and use of RPE and PPE. Employers have a duty to ensure that any equipment for controlling exposure to lead is properly used and maintained, and employees must use these control measures properly. Employees have a duty further to report defects in the control measures to their employer. Where such control measures do not give adequate protection against airborne lead, approved RPE must be provided and, where the exposure to lead is significant, each employee must be provided with adequate protective clothing.

Adequate washing facilities must be provided and arrangements made for the separate storage of personal clothing not worn during working hours and protective clothing. Workplaces must be kept clean and eating, drinking or smoking is prohibited in places liable to be contaminated by lead.

Where the assessment of risk identifies the need for it, suitable air monitoring procedures must be implemented.

The principal duties of employers that are covered in regulation 16 are those regarding medical surveillance procedures. Thus, every employer must ensure that each of their employees employed in work that exposes them to lead is under medical surveillance by an Employment Medical Adviser (EMA) or appointed doctor if:

- the exposure of that employee to lead is significant
- an EMA or appointed doctor certifies that the employee should be kept under medical surveillance.

In such cases, an employer must not expose that employee to lead, except in circumstances specified in the above certificate.

Every employee who is exposed to lead at work must, when required by the employer, present themselves during normal working hours for either of the following as may be necessary:

- medical examination
- biological tests.

The regulations further require the keeping of records of any air monitoring, medical surveillance and testing, and maintenance of control measures. The ACOP for this area states that exposure to lead is significant if the level of airborne lead is in excess of half the lead-in-air standard or there is a substantial risk of ingesting lead or there is a risk of skin contact with concentrated lead alkyls. For lead-in-air, the standard for an 8-hour time-weighted period is an average concentration of 0.15 milligrams per cubic metre of air, except for tetra-ethyl lead where the level is 0.10 milligrams per cubic metre of air.

THE CONTROL OF INDUSTRIAL MAJOR ACCIDENT HAZARDS REGULATIONS 1984

These regulations are concerned with the prevention of major incidents that can affect not only employees but members of the public living in neighbouring areas to a major industrial installation. The CIMAHR implemented the Seveso Directive.

The regulations apply to certain installations (listed below) and, before commencing activities at any of these, manufacturers must prepare a written report and send a copy to the HSE at least three months before commencing the activity.

Installations, substances used and isolated storage of certain substances

The installations covered by the Regulations and listed in Schedule 4 of the regulations are those for:

- the production, or treatment, or processing of organic or inorganic chemicals, using, among others:
  - alkylation
  - amination by ammonolysis
  - carbonylation
  - condensation
  - dehydrogenation
  - esterification
  - halogenation and manufacture of halogens
  - hydrogenization
  - hydrolysis
  - oxidation
  - polymerization
  - sulphonation
  - desulphurization, manufacture and transformation of sulphur-containing compounds

  - nitration and manufacture of nitrogen-containing compounds
  - manufacture of phosphorus-containing compounds
  - formulation of pesticides and pharmaceutical products
  - distillation
  - extraction
  - solvation
  - mixing

- the purpose of distillation, refining or other processing of petroleum or other products
- the total or partial disposal of solid or liquid substances by incineration or chemical decomposition
- for the production, processing or treatment of energy gases, such as LPG, LNG, SNG
- for the dry distillation of coal or lignite
- for the production of metals or non-metals by a wet process or through electrical energy.

The regulations also apply:

- to substances listed in Schedule 1, which specifies a range of very toxic, other toxic substances and flammable substances that might be used in such installations
- in the case of the isolated storage of certain dangerous substances, such as ammonium nitrate, liquid oxygen and sulphur dioxide, where such a substance is stored and in excess of a quantity specified in Schedule 2.

The duties of manufacturers

Manufacturers in control of industrial activities that have the potential to cause major accidents must:

- identify major accident hazards
- take steps to:
  - prevent major accident hazards and limit their consequences to persons and the environment
  - provide those working on site with information, training and equipment, and, if necessary, produce documentation of this.

The duty to notify of major accidents (regulation 5)

Where a major accident occurs on site, a manufacturer must notify the HSE of the accident. The HSE must then obtain from the manufacturer the following:

- information relating to:
  - the circumstances of the accident

- the dangerous substances involved
- data available for assessing the effects of the accident on human beings and the environment
- emergency measures taken

- the action considered necessary to:

  - alleviate medium- or long-term effects of the accident
  - prevent its recurrence.

The duty to prepare and update reports (regulation 7)

Where industrial activities involve a quantity of *reportable substances* (as listed in Schedule 3) or isolated storage, where the quantity to be stored is equal to or greater than the quantity specified, the manufacturer must, before undertaking the activity or storage, prepare a written report containing the information required under regulation 8 and send such a report to the HSE at least three months before commencing the activity or storage.

Under Schedule 6, the following information relating to every *dangerous substance* involved in an activity in a relevant quantity should be supplied by way of a written report to the HSE:

4

- the name of the dangerous substance or, for a dangerous substance of a general designation, the name corresponding to the chemical formula of the dangerous substance
- a general description of the analytical methods available to the manufacturer for determining the presence of the dangerous substance or reference to such methods in the scientific literature
- a brief description of the hazards that may be created by the dangerous substance
- the degree of purity of the dangerous substance and the names of the main impurities and their percentages.

The following information relating to the *installation* should also be supplied to the HSE:

- a map of the site and its surrounding area to a scale large enough to show any features that may be significant in the assessment of the hazard posed by or the risk associated with the site
- a scale plan of the site, showing the locations and quantities of all significant inventories of the dangerous substance
- a description of the processes or storage involving the dangerous substance and an indication of the conditions under which it is normally held
- the maximum number of people likely to be present on the site
- information about the nature of the land use and the size and distribution of the population in the vicinity of the industrial activity to which the report relates.

Information relating to the *management system* for controlling the industrial activity must also be supplied to the HSE, which should include:

- the staffing arrangements for controlling the industrial activity, with the name of the person responsible for safety on the site and the names of those who are authorized to set emergency procedures in motion and to inform outside authorities
- the arrangements made to ensure that the means provided for the safe operation of the industrial activity are properly designed, constructed, tested, operated, inspected and maintained
- the arrangements for training the people working on the site.

The following information relating to the *potential for major accidents* to occur is also required:

- a description of the potential sources of a major accident and the conditions or events that could be significant in bringing one about
- a diagram of any plant in which the industrial activity is carried out, sufficient to show the features that are significant regarding the potential for a major accident or its prevention or control
- a description of the measures taken to prevent, control or minimize the consequences of any major accident
- information about the emergency procedures laid down for dealing with a major accident occurring at the site
- information about prevailing meteorological conditions in the vicinity of the site
- an estimate of the number of people on site who may be exposed to the hazards considered in the report.

The duty to report modifications made to industrial activities (regulation 8)

Manufacturers must not carry out any modifications to their industrial activities unless a further report to the HSE is made detailing these changes and it is sent to the HSE at least three months before making them.

The duties to prepare safety plans (regulations 10 and 11)

Manufacturers operating on specified major accident sites must prepare and update an adequate:

- on-site emergency plan, detailing how major accidents will be dealt with on site, together with the name of the person responsible for safety and the names of those people authorized to take action
- off-site emergency plan.

THE CONTROL OF PESTICIDES REGULATIONS 1986

The regulations apply to substances used for:

- protecting plants from harmful organisms
- regulating plant growth
- giving protection, for example, against harmful insects, and rendering them harmless
- controlling organisms with harmful effects, such as in buildings
- protecting animals, against parasites, for example.

Prohibitions (regulation 4)

There is a general prohibition on advertising, selling, supplying, storing or using a pesticide without the approval of the Minister of Agriculture, Fisheries and Food and the Secretary of State, as per regulation 5, below.

Approvals (regulation 5)

This regulation authorizes the Minister and Secretary of State to give approval to a pesticide of any description.

Consents (regulation 6)

This regulation authorizes the Minister and Secretary of State to consent to the advertising, sale, supply, storage and use of pesticides under certain conditions.

The seizure or disposal of pesticides (regulation 7)

Under this regulation, the Minister and Secretary of State have the power to seize or dispose of pesticides used in breach of regulation 4.

The release of information to the public (regulation 8)

Evaluations of pesticides may be revealed to any member of the public who requests them, for a fee.

Schedules 1–3

These Schedules detail the conditions operating with regard to giving consent to advertise, sell, store or use pesticides.

Schedule 4

This Schedule details the conditions that apply to regulate crop spraying by air.

THE CONTROL OF SUBSTANCES HAZARDOUS TO HEALTH REGULATIONS 1988

The COSHHR came into force on 1 October 1989 and apply to *all* forms of workplace and *every* form of work activity involving the use of hazardous substances. The regulations are supported by a number of ACOPS, such as Control of substances hazardous to health, Control of substances hazardous to health in fumigation operations and Control of carcinogenic substances. As such, they set out a strategy for safety regarding hazardous substances that covers more than 40 000 chemicals and materials, together with hazardous substances generated by industrial processes.

The strategy established in the COSHHR divides into four main areas:

- the acquisition and dissemination of information and knowledge about hazardous substances
- the assessment of risks to health associated with the use, handling, storage and so on of such substances at work
- the elimination or control of health risks by the use of appropriate engineering applications, operating procedures and personal protection
- monitoring the effectiveness of the measures taken.

The regulations have seven principal objectives:

1 to maintain and improve existing standards of health and safety in relation to work involving substances hazardous to health

2 to simplify greatly the existing law and, consequently, the task of employers and employees in complying with it and of inspectors in enforcing it

3 to provide one set of regulations covering substances hazardous to health, including those not specifically covered by any existing provision, or covered only where they occur in factories

4 to set out clear objectives that will be cost-effective by matching precautions to the risks involved

5 to provide a suitable framework for implementing existing and future EC Directives on worker protection

6 to enable the Government to ratify ILO Convention No. 139 on carcinogenic substances

7 to repeal or revoke, wholly or partially, legislation that is no longer relevant to present-day conditions.

The principal requirements of the regulations – that is regulations 6–12 – apply to all substances hazardous to health that may be encountered at work and result from the purpose of the work activities, with the exception of:

- lead, so far as the Control of Lead at Work Regulations 1980 apply (see pages 84–85)

- asbestos, so far as the Control of Asbestos at Work Regulations 1987 apply
- substances that are only hazardous because of any one or any combination of the following:
  - radioactivity
  - explosive properties
  - flammable properties
  - high pressure
  - high temperature
  - low temperature
- substances administered as part of a medical treatment or in the course of research
- substances found below ground in any mine within the meaning of section 180 of the Mines and Quarries Act 1954
- micro-organisms that do not arise out of or in connection with work that is under the employer's control, such as chest infections caught incidentally from other workers
- asphyxiants – these must be purely asphyxiants and non-toxic (the COSHHR do not prejudice any requirements imposed by existing public health and environmental health law, such as the Public Health Acts 1936–61 and food hygiene legislation.

Definitions (regulation 2)

The following definitions given in regulation 2 are of significance:

- the *maximum exposure limit* for a substance hazardous to health means the maximum exposure limit for that substance set out in Schedule 1 in relation to the reference period specified there when calculated by a method approved by the HSC
- the term *micro-organism* includes any microscopic biological entity that is capable of replication
- the *occupational exposure standard* for a substance hazardous to health means the standard approved by the HSC for that substance in relation to the specified reference period when calculated by a method approved by the HSC
- the term *substance* means any natural or artificial substance, whether in solid or liquid form or in the form of a gas or vapour (including micro-organisms).
- a *substance hazardous to health* means any substance (including any preparation) that is:
  - a substance that is listed as dangerous for supply because of its health effects within the meaning of the Chemicals (Hazard Information and Packaging) Regulations 1993 (Approved Supply List) and for which the

general indication of the nature of the risk is specified as very toxic, toxic, harmful, corrosive or irritant
- a substance for which a maximum exposure limit is specified in Schedule 1 of the regulations or for which the HSC has approved an occupational exposure standard (see the current HSE guidance note, EH 40 Occupational exposure limits)
- a micro-organism that creates a hazard to the health of any person
- dust of any kind when present at a substantial concentration in air
- a substance, other than one mentioned in the first four points directly above, that creates a hazard to the health of any person comparable with the hazards created by the substances mentioned in these points.

The assessment of health risks created by work involving substances hazardous to health (regulation 6)

This regulation requires that an employer shall not carry out any work that is liable to expose any employees to any substance hazardous to health unless they have made a *suitable and sufficient assessment* (see below for what is meant by this) of the risks created by this work to the health of these employees and of the steps that need to be taken to meet the requirements of the regulations. Moreover, this assessment must be reviewed straight away if there is reason to suspect that the assessment is no longer valid or there has been a significant change in the work to which the assessment relates and when as a result of the review, changes in the assessment are required, these changes shall be made.

The employer must keep a written record of the assessment in all but the simplest cases, and must inform their employees of the results of the assessment.

What is 'suitable and sufficient' assessment?

The general ACOP indicates that a suitable and sufficient assessment should include:

- an assessment of the risks to health
- the steps that need to be taken to achieve adequate control of exposure in accordance with regulation 7 (see below)
- identification of other actions necessary to comply with regulations 8–12.

An assessment of the risks created by any work should involve:

- a consideration of:
  - the substances or types of substances (including micro-organisms) employees are liable to be exposed to (taking into account the consequences of possible failure of any control measures provided to meet the requirements of regulation 7 – see below)
  - what effects these substances can have on the body

  - where the substances are likely to be present and in what form
  - the ways and the extent to which, any groups of employees or others could potentially be exposed, taking into account the nature of the work and process and any reasonably foreseeable deterioriation in, or failure of, any control measure provided for the purpose of regulation 7 (see below)

- an estimate of the exposure, taking into account engineering measures and systems of work currently employed for controlling potential exposure
- where valid standards exist that represent adequate control, comparison of the estimate with these standards.

Detailed guidance on COSHHR assessment is provided in the HSE publication *A step-by-step Guide to COSHH Assessment* (HMSO).

The prevention or control of exposure to substances hazardous to health (regulation 7)

The emphasis here is on the *prevention* of exposure to hazardous substances but, where this is not reasonably practicable, there must be adequate *control* of such exposure. This applies whether the route of entry into the body is through inhalation, ingestion or through the skin, or if the substance is dangerous when in contact with the skin.

4

In the case of substances that are hazardous when inhaled and have been assigned maximum exposure limits (MELs), exposure must never exceed these limits and should be reduced to below these limits as much as is reasonably practicable (a list of substances assigned MELs is given in Schedule 1 of the regulations).

Where there is exposure to a substance for which an occupational exposure standard (OES) has been approved, the control of this exposure shall, so far as the inhalation of the substance is concerned, only be treated as adequate if, first, the OES is *not* exceeded or, second, where the OES *is* exceeded, the employer identifies the reasons for the standard being exceeded and takes appropriate action, as soon as is reasonably practicable, to remedy the situation.

In particular, where reasonably practicable, the prevention or adequate control of exposure to a substance hazardous to health shall be secured by means other than the provision of PPE, such as respiratory protection. Where control cannot be achieved by these means, it must be achieved by the use of suitable PPE that also conforms to specific standards, where any exist. If the PPE includes RPE, this must be suitable, of an approved type or comply with a standard approved by the HSE.

The use of control measures and so on (regulation 8)

Under this regulation, specific duties are placed on both employers and employees (see Figure 4.1 for a summary of these). Every employer who provides any control measure, PPE or other thing or facility pursuant to these regulations shall take all reasonable steps to ensure that it is properly used or applied, as the case may be. Equally, every employee shall make full and proper use of any control measure, or other thing provided to this end and, if they discover any defect in these shall report it straight away to their employer.

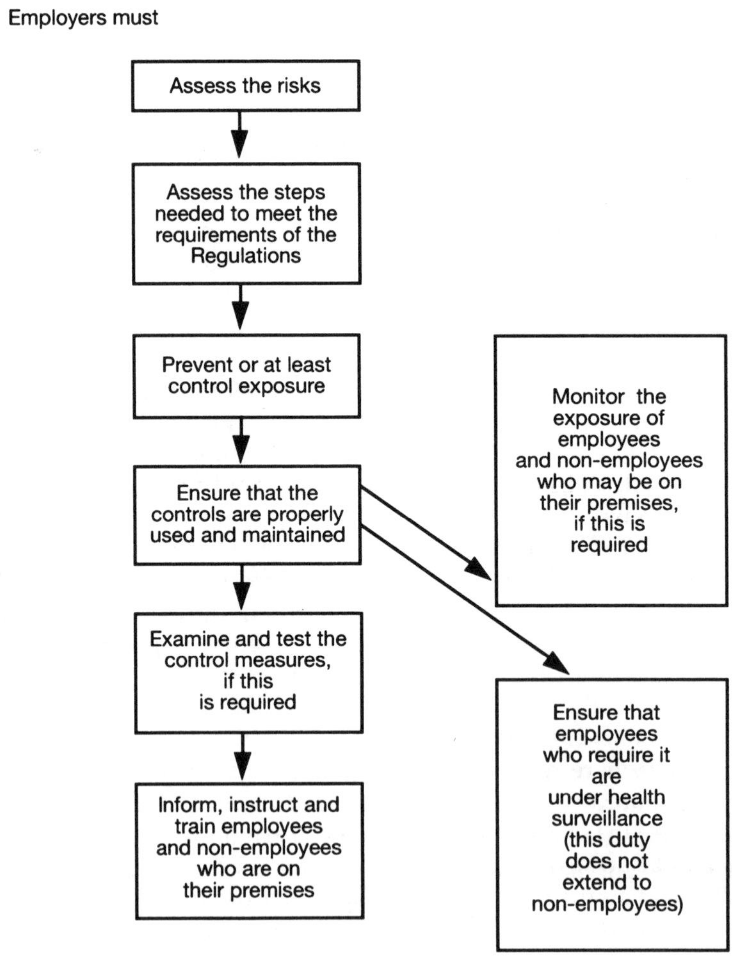

• **FIG 4.1 The main duties imposed on employers by the COSHHR**

The maintenance, examination and test of control measure and so on (regulation 9)

This regulation places an absolute duty on any employer who provides any control measure, such as local exhaust ventilation (LEV), to meet the requirements of regulation 7, to ensure that it is maintained *in an efficient state, in efficient working order and in good repair*. A clearly documented, planned preventative maintenance programme for all engineering controls is called for in this case. Where engineering controls are provided, the employer shall ensure that thorough examinations and tests of these engineering controls are carried out:

- in the case of LEV plant, at least once every 14 months
- in any other case, at suitable intervals.

Where RPE (other than disposable RPE) is provided, the employer shall ensure that, at suitable intervals, thorough examinations and, where appropriate, tests of this equipment are carried out. A suitable record of examinations and tests carried out in accordance with the above requirements (that is, for engineering controls and RPE) shall be kept by the employer and such a record shall be kept available for at least five years from the date on which it was made.

Monitoring exposure at the workplace (regulation 10)

Monitoring of exposure implies the taking of samples of airborne contamination, either by using personal dosemeters or static sampling equipment, or both. The need for monitoring exposure would normally be identified in the health risk assessment made under regulation 6 (see above).

Regulation 10 requires that, in any case in which

- it is a requisite for ensuring the maintenance of adequate control of the exposure of employees to substances hazardous to health
- it is otherwise requisite for protecting the health of employees,

the employer shall ensure that the exposure of employees to substances hazardous to health is monitored in accordance with a suitable procedure.

Where a substance or process is specified in column 1 of Schedule 4, monitoring shall be carried out at the frequency specified in the corresponding entry in column 2 of that Schedule.

The employer shall keep a record of any monitoring carried out for the purpose of the regulation and that record or a suitable summary of it shall be kept available:

- where the record is representative of the personal exposure of identifiable employees, for at least 30 years
- in any other case, for at least five years.

Health surveillance (regulation 11)

'Health surveillance' is simply defined as 'including biological monitoring'. As such, health surveillance can take many forms, including respiratory and lung function tests, blood tests and routine health examinations by an occupational health nurse. Where a health risk assessment made under regulation 6 identifies the need for some form of health surveillance of exposed employees, or those liable to be exposed to a dangerous substance, the employer must ensure that such employees are kept under suitable health surveillance.

Health surveillance shall be considered appropriate where:

- the employee is exposed to one of the substances and engaged in a process specified in Schedule 5 (such as vinyl chloride monomer (VCM) manufacture) unless that exposure is not significant
- the exposure of the employee to a substance hazardous to health is such that an identifiable disease or adverse health effect may be related to the exposure, there is a reasonable likelihood that the disease or effect may occur under the particular conditions of their work and there are valid techniques for detecting indications of the disease or the effect.

The employer shall ensure that a health record, containing particulars approved by the HSE, in respect of each of his employees who may be exposed to substances hazardous to health is made and maintained and that the record is kept in a suitable form for at least 30 years from the date of the last entry made in it. Where an employer ceases to trade, such records must be offered to the HSE.

Information, instruction and training for those who may be exposed to substances hazardous to health (regulation 12)

This regulation places an absolute duty on employers to provide information, instruction and training for employees who may be exposed to substances hazardous to health. Such information, instruction and training shall be suitable and sufficient if they know:

- the risks to health created by such exposure
- the precautions that should be taken.

The information that must be provided includes:

- information on the results of any monitoring of exposure at the workplace and, in the case of a substance with a listed MEL, the employee or their representatives shall be informed straight away if the results of such monitoring show that the MEL has been exceeded
- information on the collective results of any health surveillance undertaken

in a form calculated to prevent it being identified as relating to a particular person.

Every employer shall ensure that any person (whether or not their employee) who carries out work in connection with the employer's duties under these regulations has the necessary information, instruction and training. On this basis, the employees of, for instance, a contractor, who are exposed or might be exposed to substances hazardous to health, must receive appropriate information, instruction and training.

Prohibited substances

Regulation 4 ensures that prohibitions contained in the legislation repealed by the COSHHR are carried forward. The full list of the prohibited substances and the circumstances under which they are prohibited is contained in Schedule 2.

The use or importation of the following substances is prohibited:

- 2-Naphthylamine
- Benzidine
- 4-Aminodiphenol
- 4-Nitrodiphenol.

Defences under the regulations

Regulation 16 states:

> In any proceedings for an offence consisting of a contravention of these Regulations it shall be a defence for any person to prove that he took *all reasonable precautions* and exercised *all due diligence* to avoid the commission of that offence.

To rely on this defence, the employer must establish that, on the balance of probabilities, they have taken *all* precautions that were reasonable and exercised *all* due diligence to ensure that these precautions were implemented in order to avoid such a contravention.

It is unlikely that an employer could rely on a regulation 16 defence if:

- precautions were available that had not been taken
- that they had not provided sufficient information, instruction and training, together with adequate supervision, to ensure that the precautions were effective.

Thus, a stated policy on the use of substances hazardous to health, company code of practice or other form of instructions to staff are insufficient without evidence that such staff are being provided with the appropriate information, instruction, training and supervision.

THE ELECTRICITY AT WORK REGULATIONS 1989

These regulations are made under the HSWA and apply to all work associated with electricity. The purpose of the regulations is to require that precautions be taken against the risk of death or personal injury from electricity when it is involved in work activities.

The regulations impose duties on duty holders (see regulation 3) in respect of systems, electrical equipment and conductors, and work activities on or near electrical equipment. They replace the 1908 and 1944 regulations and extend to all premises.

The regulations also establish general principles for electrical safety rather than state detailed requirements. Further detailed advice is given in the supporting Memorandum of Guidance and other authoritative documents, such as the IEE Wiring Regulations, British and European standards and HSE publications.

As the regulations state principles of electrical safety in a form that may be applied to any work activity having a bearing on electrical safety, they apply to *all* electrical equipment and systems, wherever manufactured, purchased, installed or taken into use, even if this predates them. If, however, electrical equipment *does* predate the regulations, it does not, of itself, mean that the continued use of such equipment is prohibited. The equipment may continue to be used, provided the requirements of the regulations can continue to be satisfied. In other words, the equipment need only be replaced if it becomes unsafe or there is a risk of injury when it is used.

The duties in some of the regulations are subject to the qualifying term 'reasonably practicable'. Where qualifying terms are absent, the requirement is said to be *absolute*, which means that it must be met, regardless of cost or any other consideration.

Regulation 29 provides a defence for a duty holder who can establish that they took *all reasonable steps and exercised all due diligence* to avoid committing an offence under certain Regulations.

Part I: Introduction

Interpretation (regulation 2)

This regulation incorporates a number of important definitions, including:

- *circuit conductor*, meaning any conductor in a sysem that is intended to carry electric current in normal conditions, or to be energized in normal conditions, and includes a combined neutral and earth conductor, but does not include a conductor provided solely to perform a protective function by connection to earth or other reference point
- *conductor* means a conductor of electrical energy
- *danger* means risk of injury
- *electrical equipment* includes anything used, intended to be used or installed for use, to generate, provide, transmit, transform, rectify, con-

vert, conduct, distribute, control, store, measure or use electrical energy
- *injury* means death or personal injury from electric shock, electric burns, electrical explosion or arcing, or from fire or explosion initiated by electrical energy, where any such death or injury is associated with the generation, provision, transmission, rectification, conversion, conduction, distribution, control, storage, measurement or use of electrical energy.
- *system* means any electrical system in which all the electrical equipment is, or may be, electrically connected to a common source of electrical energy, and includes such source and such equipment.

Those on whom duties are imposed (regulation 3)

It shall be the duty of every:

- employer and self-employed person to comply with the provisions of these Regulations, in so far as they relate to matters that are within their control
- manager of a mine or quarry to ensure that all requirements or prohibitions imposed by or under these regulations are complied with in so far as they related to the mine or quarry or part of a quarry of which they are the manager and to matters that are within their control

It shall be the duty of every employee while at work to:

- to cooperate with their employer so far as is necessary to enable any duty placed on that employer by the provisions of these regulations to be complied with
- to comply with the provisions of these regulations in so far as they relate to matters that are within their control.

Part II: General

Systems, work activities and protective equipment (regulation 4)

All systems shall, at all times, be of such construction as to prevent danger, so far as is reasonably practicable.

As may be necessary to prevent danger, all systems shall be maintained so as to prevent, so far as is reasonably practicable such danger.

Every work activity, including operation, use and maintenance of a system and work near a system, shall be carried out in such a manner as not to give rise, so far as is reasonably practicable, to danger.

Any equipment provided under these regulations for the purpose of protecting those at work on or near electrical equipment shall be suitable for this purpose, be maintained in a condition suitable for this use and be properly used.

The strength and capability of electrical equipment (regulation 5)

No electrical equipment shall be put into use where its strength and capability may be exceeded in such a way as to give rise to danger.

Adverse or hazardous environments (regulation 6)

Electrical equipment that may, reasonably foreseeably, be exposed to:

- mechanical danger
- the effects of the weather, natural hazards, temperature or pressure
- the effects of wet, dirty, dusty or corrosive conditions
- any flammable or explosive substance including dusts, vapours or gases, shall be of such construction or, as necessary, protected so as to prevent, so far as is reasonably practicable, danger arising from such exposure.

Insulation, protection and placing of conductors (regulation 7)

All conductors in a system that may give rise to danger shall either:

- be suitably convered with insulating material and, as necessary, protected so as to prevent danger, so far as is reasonably practicable
- have such precautions taken in respect of them (including, where appropriate, their being suitably placed) as will prevent danger, so far as is reasonably practicable.

Earthing or other suitable precautions (regulation 8)

Precautions shall be taken, either by earthing or other suitable means, to prevent danger arising when any conductor (other than a circuit conductor) that may, reasonably foreseeably, become charged as a result of either the use of the system or a fault in a system becomes so charged. Also, for the purposes of complying with this regulation, a conductor shall be regarded as earthed when it is connected to the general mass of earth by conductors of sufficient strength and current-carrying capability to discharge electrical energy to earth.

Integrity of referenced conductors (regulation 9)

If a circuit conductor is connected to earth or to any other reference point, nothing that might reasonably be expected to give rise to danger by breaking the electrical continuity or introducing high impedance shall be placed in that conductor unless suitable precautions are taken to prevent danger.

Connections (regulation 10)

Where necessary to prevent danger, every joint and connection in a system shall be mechanically and electrically suitable for use.

The means for protecting from excess current (regulation 11)

Efficient means, suitably located, shall be provided for protecting every part of a system from excess current as may be necessary to prevent danger.

The means for cutting off the supply and for isolation (regulation 12)

Where necessary, to prevent danger, suitable means (including, where appropriate, methods of identifying circuits) shall be available for:

- cutting off the supply of electrical energy to any electrical equipment
- the isolation of any electrical equipment.

Isolation here means the disconnection and separation of the electrical equipment from every source of electrical energy in such a way that this disconnection and separation is secure.

These means shall not apply to electrical equipment that is itself a source of electrical energy, but, in such a case, as is necessary, precautions shall be taken to prevent danger, so far as is reasonably practicable.

Precautions for work on equipment made dead (regulation 13)

Adequate precautions shall be taken to prevent electrical equipment that has been made dead in order to prevent danger while work is carried out on or near that equipment from becoming electrically charged during that work if danger may arise as a result.

Work on or near live conductors (regulation 14)

No one shall be engaged in any work activity on or so near any live conductor (other than one suitably covered with insulating material so as to prevent danger) such that danger may arise unless:

- it is unreasonable in all circumstances for it to be dead
- it is reasonable in all circumstances for the person concerned to be at work on or near it while it is live
- suitable precautions (including, where necessary, the provision of suitable protective equipment) are taken to prevent injury.

Working space, access and lighting (regulation 15)

For the purposes of enabling injury to be prevented, adequate working space, adequate means of access and adequate lighting shall be provided at all electrical equipment on which, or near which, work is being done in circumstances that may give rise to danger.

People to be competent to prevent danger and injury (regulation 16)

No one shall be engaged in any work activity where technical knowledge or experience is necessary to prevent danger or, where appropriate, injury, unless they possess such knowledge or experience, or are under such degree of supervision as may be appropriate, having regard to the nature of the work.

Part III: Regulations applying only to mines

Part III of the regulations makes specific provision for electrical safety in mines.

Part IV: Miscellaneous and general

Regulation 29 defence

In any proceedings for an offence consisting of a contravention of regulations 4(4), 5, 8, 9, 10, 11, 12, 13, 14, 15, 16 or 25, it shall be a defence for any person to prove that they *took all reasonable precautions and exercised all due diligence* to avoid the commission of that offence.

THE HEALTH AND SAFETY (DISPLAY SCREEN EQUIPMENT) REGULATIONS 1992

These regulations implement the EC VDU Directive and came into force on 1 January 1993. Workstations put into service on or after that date must meet the requirements laid down in the Schedule to the Regulations. Workstations in operation prior to 31 December 1992 must comply with the Schedule no later than 31 December 1996.

Compliance with the Regulations is based on an analysis of workstations by an employer, taking into account the criteria outlined in the Schedule. The Regulations should be read in conjunction with the MHSWR as far as the general duties of employers are concerned.

Interpretation (regulation 1)

A number of important definitions are incorporated in regulation 1, including:

- *display screen equipment* means any alphanumeric or graphic display screen, regardless of the display process involved
- *operator* means a self-employed person who habitually uses display screen equipment as a significant part of their normal work
- *use* means use for or in connection with work
- *user* means an employee who habitually uses display screen equipment as a significant part of their normal work
- *workstation* means an assembly comprised of:
  - display screen equipment (whether provided with software determining the interface between the equipment and its operator or user, a keyboard or any other input device
  - any optional accessories to the display screen equipment
  - any disk drive, telephone, modem, printer, document holder, work chair, work desk, worksurface or other item peripheral to the display screen equipment
  - the immediate work environment around the display screen equipment.

Exemptions from the regulations

The regulations do *not* apply to:

- drivers' cabs or control cabs for vehicles or machinery
- display screen equipment on board a means of transport
- display screen equipment mainly intended for public operation
- portable systems not in prolonged use
- calculators, cash registers or any equipment having a small data or measurement display required for direct use of the equipment
- window typewriters.

The analysis of workstations to assess and reduce risks (regulation 2)

Every employer shall perform a suitable and sufficient analysis of those workstations that:

- regardless of who has provided them, are used for the purposes of their undertaking by users
- have been provided by them and are used for the purposes of their undertaking by operators,

for the purpose of assessing the health and safety risks to which these people are exposed in consequence of such use.

Any assessment made by an employer shall be reviewed by them if:

- there is reason to suspect that it is no longer valid
- there has been a significant change in the matters to whcih it relates

and where, as a result of any such review, changes in an assessment are required, the employer concerned shall make them.

The employer shall reduce the risks identified in consequence of the above assessment to the lowest extent reasonably practicable.

Requirements for workstations (regulation 3)

Every employer shall ensure that any workstation first put into service on or after 1 January 1993 meets the requirements laid down in the Schedule to these regulations.

Every employer shall ensure that any workstation first put into service on or before 31 December 1992 meets the requirements laid down in the Schedule not later than 31 December 1996.

The daily work routine (regulation 4)

Every employer shall so plan the activities of users at work in their undertaking that their daily work on display screen equipment is periodically interrupted by breaks or changes of activity as will reduce their workload at that equipment.

Eyes and eyesight (regulation 5)

Where a person:

- is already a user on the date of coming into force of these regulations
- is an employee who does not habitually use display screen equipment as a significant part of their normal work, but is to become a user in the undertaking in which they are already employed,

their employer shall ensure that they are provided with an appropriate eye and eyesight test, requested by their employer, and that any such test is carried out by a competent person.

Any eye and eyesight test carried out shall:

- in any case where the person is already a user, be carried out as soon as practicable after being requested by the user concerned
- in any case where the person will become a user, be carried out before the employee concerned becomes a user.

At regular intervals after an employee has been provided with an eye and eyesight test, their employer shall ensure that they are provided with a further eye and eyesight test of an appropriate nature – any such test being carried out by a competent person.

Where a user experiences visual difficulties that may reasonably be considered to be caused by work on display screen equipment, their employer shall ensure that they are provided, at the employer's request, with an appropriate eye and eyesight test – any such test being carried out by a competent person as soon as is practicable after it has been requested.

Every employer shall ensure that each user employed by them is provided with special corrective appliances appropriate for the work being done by the user concerned where:

- normal corrective appliances cannot be used
- the result of any eye and eyesight test that the user has been given in accordance with this regulation shows such provision to be necessary.

Nothing in the regulations regarding follow-up eye tests shall require an employer to provide any employee with an eye and eyesight test against that employee's will.

The provision of training (regulation 6)

Where a person:

- is already a user on the date of coming into force of these regulations
- is an employee who does not habitually use display screen equipment as

a significant part of their normal work, but is to become a user in the undertaking in which they are already employed,

their employer shall ensure that they are provided with adequate health and safety training in the use of any workstation on which they may be required to work.

Every employer shall ensure that each user at work in their undertaking is provided with adequate health and safety training whenever the organization of any workstation there which they may be required to work is substantially modified.

The provision of information (regulation 6)

Every employer shall ensure that operators and users at work in their undertaking are provided with adequate information about:

- all aspects of health and safety relating to their workstations
- the measures taken by the employer in order to comply with their duties under regulations 2 and 3 that relate to the operators and users and their work.

Every employer shall also ensure that users working in their undertaking are provided with adequate information about the measures taken by the employer in order to comply with their duties under regulations 4, 5, 6(1) and 6(2) that relate to them and their work.

The schedule

This sets out the minimum requirements for workstations contained in the annex to the Council Directive 90/270/EEC on the minimum safety and health requirements for work with display screen equipment.

The extent to which employers must ensure that workstations meet the requirements laid down in this Schedule

An employer shall ensure that a workstation meets the requirements laid down in this Schedule to the extent that:

- the requirements relate to a component that is present in the workstation concerned
- the requirements have an effect in terms of securing the health, safety and welfare of people at work
- the inherent characteristics of a given task do not make compliance with the requirements inappropriate for the workstation concerned.

The equipment

General comment

Using the equipment must not be a source of risk for operators or users.

The display screen

The characters on the screen shall be well-defined and clearly formed, of adequate size and with adequate spacing between the characters and lines.

The image on the screen should be stable, with no flickering or other form of instability.

The brightness and the contrast between the characters and the background shall be easily adjustable by the user, and also easily adjustable in response to ambient conditions.

The screen must swivel and tilt easily and freely to suit the needs of the operator or user.

It shall be possible to use a separate base for the screen or an adjustable table.

The screen shall be free of reflective glare and reflections liable to cause discomfort to the user.

The keyboard

The keyboard shall be tiltable and separate from the screen so as to allow the operator or user to find a comfortable working position, avoiding fatigue in the arms or hands.

The space in front of the keyboard shall be sufficient to provide support for the hands and arms of the operator or user.

The keyboard shall have a matt surface to avoid reflective glare.

The arrangement of the keyboard and the characteristics of the keys shall be such as to facilitate the use of the keyboard.

The symbols on the keys shall be adequately contrasted and legible from the working position.

The work desk or worksurface

The work desk or worksurface shall have a sufficiently large, low-reflective surface and allow a flexible arrangement of the screen, keyboard, documents and related equipment.

The document holder shall be stable and adjustable and shall be positioned so as to minimize the need for uncomfortable head and eye movement.

There shall be adequate space for operators or users to find a comfortable position.

The work chair

The work chair shall be stable and allow the user easy freedom of movement and a comfortable position.

The seat shall be adjustable in height.

The seat back shall be adjustable in both height and tilt and a footrest shall be made available to any user who wishes to have one.

The work environment

Space requirements

The workstation shall be dimensioned and designed so as to provide sufficient space for the user to change position and vary movements.

Lighting

Any room lighting or task lighting provided shall ensure satisfactory lighting conditions and an appropriate contrast between the screen and the background environment, taking into account the type of work and the vision requirements of the operator or user.

Possible disturbing glare and reflections on the screen or other equipment shall be prevented by coordinating workplace and workstation layout with the positioning and technical characteristics of the artificial light sources.

Reflections and glare

Workstations shall be so designed that sources of light, such as windows and other openings, transparent or translucid walls and brightly coloured fixtures or walls cause no direct glare and no distracting reflections on the screen.

Windows shall be fitted with a suitable system of adjustable covering to attenuate the daylight that falls on the workstation.

Noise

Noise emitted by equipment belonging to any workstation shall be taken into account when a workstation is being equipped, with a view, in particular, to ensuring that attention is not distracted and speech is not disturbed.

Heat

Equipment belonging to any workstation shall not produce excess heat that could cause discomfort to operators or users.

Radiation

All radiation, with the exception of the visible part of the electromagnetic spectrum, shall be reduced to negligible levels from the point of view of the protection of operators or users' health and safety.

Humidity

An adequate level of humidity shall be established and maintained.

The interface between computer and operator/user

In designing, selecting, commissioning and modifying software, and in designing tasks using display screen equipment, the employer shall take into account the following principles:

- software must be suitable for the task
- software must be easy to use and, where appropriate, adaptable to the

user's level of knowledge or experience; no quantitative or qualitative checking facility may be used without the knowledge of the operators or users
- systems must provide feedback to operators or users on the performance of these systems
- systems must display information in a format and at a pace that are adapted to the operators or users
- the principles of software ergonomics must be applied, in particular to human data processing.

The regulations are accompanied by a comprehensive guide issued by the HSE.

THE HEALTH AND SAFETY (ENFORCING AUTHORITY) REGULATIONS 1989

These regulations re-enact the main provisions of the 1977 regulations, which provided that where the *main activity* carried out in any premises was specified in Schedule 1 to these regulations then, subject to specified exceptions, the local authority (LA) was the enforcing authority in respect of all activities carried out on these premises (regulation 3).

Schedule 1 of the 1989 regulations includes activities not specified in the former Schedule 1. The new activities are:

- the display or demonstration of goods at exhibitions
- cosmetic or therapeutic treatments
- sports, cultural or recreational activities
- hiring out of pleasure craft for use on inland waters
- care, treatment, accommodation or exhibition of animals
- activities of an undertaker
- church worship of religious meetings.

The 1989 regulations also introduced a new provision for multioccupied premises. Subject to specified exceptions, each part separately occupied is to be regarded as being separate premises for the purposes of enforcement allocation (regulation 3).

Regulation 4 made the HSE the enforcing authority for any part of a premises occupied by a body specified in the regulations, and for enforcement against such a body or its officers or servants. The HSE was also made the enforcing authority for any part of the premises occupied by another person for the purpose of providing services at the premises for a specified body. Parish councils, community councils, visiting forces, international headquarters and defence organizations were added to the list of bodies that were specified in the 1977 regulations (regulation 4).

These regulations also made the HSE the enforcing authority for premises where the main activity is indoor sports, if specified conditions are met (regulation 4). They also made the HSE the enforcing authority for the enforcement of section 6 of the HSWA (general duties of manufacturers and so on regarding articles and substances used at work), even though the main activity is listed in Schedule 1.

The activities set out in Schedule 2 are allocated for enforcement by the HSE, even though the main activity carried out is listed in Schedule 1). Further, these regulations provide that, regardless of the main activity, the licensing or registration authority for an explosives factory, magazine, store or premises for keeping explosives shall be the enforcing authority for such provisions of the Explosives Act 1875 and legislation made under it as a relevant statutory provision (regulation 4).

The regulations enable the responsibility for enforcement to be assigned by the HSE and LA jointly (to either of them) where they agree there is uncertainty in the particular case as to which one is the enforcing authority (regulation 6).

Schedule 1: The main activities that determine whether or not the local authorities will be the enforcing authorities

The following activities determine that the local authorities will be the enforcing authorities:

- the sale or storage of goods for retail or wholesale distribution except:
  - where it is part of the business of a transport undertaking
  - at container depots where the main activity is the storage of goods in the course of transit to or from dock premises, an airport or railway
  - where the main activity is the sale or storage for wholesale distribution of any dangerous substance
  - where the main activity is the sale or storage of water or sewage or their by-products or natural or town gas

and, for the purposes of this point, where the main activity carried out on premises is the sale and fitting of motor car tyres, exhausts, windscreens or sunroofs, the main activity shall be deemed to be sale of goods

- the display or demonstration of goods at an exhibition for the purposes of offer or advertisement for sale
- office activities
- catering services
- the provision of permanent or temporary residential accommodation, including the provision of a site for caravans or campers
- consumer services provided in a shop, except dry cleaning or radio and television repairs (and, here, *consumer services* means services of a type ordinarily supplied to people who receive them otherwise than in the course of a trade, business or other undertaking carried out by them, whether for profit or not)
- cleaning (wet or dry) in coin-operated units in launderettes and similar premises

- the use of a bath, sauna or solarium, massaging, hair transplanting, skin-piercing, manicuring or other cosmetic services and therapeutic treatments, except where they are carried out under the supervision or control of a registered medical practitioner, or dentist registered under the Dentists Act 1984, a physiotherapist, an osteopath or chiropractor
- the practise or presentation of the arts, sports, games, entertainment or other cultural or recreational activities except where carried out in a museum, art gallery or theatre or where the main activity is the exhibition of a cave to the public
- the hiring out of pleasure craft for use in inland waters
- the care, treatment, accommodation or exhibition of animals, birds or other creatures, except where the main activity is horse breeding or horse training at a stable, or is an agricultural activity or veterinary surgery
- the activities of an undertaker, except where the main activity is the making of coffins
- church worship or religious meetings.

Schedule 2: Activities in respect of which the HSE is the enforcing authority

These activities include:

- any activity in a mine or quarry, other than a mine or quarry in which notice of abandonment has been given under section 139(2) of the Mines and Quarries Act 1954
- any activity in a fairground
- any activity in premises occupied by a radio, television or film undertaking in which the activity of broadcasting, recording or filming is carried out, and the activity of broadcasting, recording or filming wherever they are carried out (for this purpose, *film* includes video)
- the following activities carried out at premises by those who do not normally work on the premises:

  - construction work if:

    (i) section 127(6) of the FA (which requires certain work to be notified to an inspector) applies to such work

    (ii) the whole or part of the work contracted to be undertaken by the contractor at the premises is to the external fabric or other external part of a building or structure

    (iii) it is carried out in a physically segregated area of the premises, the activities normally carried out in this area have been suspended for the purpose of enabling the construction work to be carried out, the contractor has authority to exclude from this area persons who are not attending it in connection with the carrying out of the work and the work is not the maintenance of insulation on pipes, boilers or other parts of heating or water systems or its removal from them

- the installation, maintenance or repair of any gas system, or any work in relation to a gas fitting
- the installation, maintenance or repair of electricity systems
- work with ionizing radiations, except work in one or more of the categories set out in Schedule 3 to the Ionising Radiations Regulations 1985

- the use of ionizing radiations for medical exposure (within the meaning of regulation 2(1) of the Ionising Radiations Regulations 1985)
- any activity in premises occupied by a radiography undertaking in which work is carried out with ionizing radiation
- agricultural activities, and any activity at an agricultural show that involves the handling of livestock or the working of agricultural equipment
- any activity on board a sea-going ship
- any activity in relation to a ski slope, ski lift, ski tow or cable car
- fish, maggot and game breeding, except in a zoo.

THE HEALTH AND SAFETY (FIRST AID) REGULATIONS 1981

These regulations apply to nearly all workplaces in the UK. Within the Regulations, *first aid* means:

- in cases where a person will need help from a medical practitioner or nurse, treatment for the purpose of preserving life and minimizing the consequences of injury or illness until such help is obtained
- treatment of minor injuries that would otherwise receive no treatment or do not need treatment by a medical practitioner or nurse.

The duties of employers

Under section 3(1), an employer shall provide, or ensure that there are provided, such equipment and facilities as are *adequate and appropriate* in the circumstances for enabling first aid to be rendered to their employees if they are injured or become ill at work.

Two main duties are imposed on employers by the regulations:

- to provide first aid
- to inform employees of the first aid arrangements.

Self-employed people must provide first aid equipment for their own use.

The Approved Code of Practice regarding first aid

This Code emphasizes the duty of employers to consider a number of factors and determine for themselves what is adequate and appropriate in all the circumstances. Furthermore, where there are particular risks associated with the operation of an enterprise, the employer must ensure that first aiders receive training to deal with these specific risks.

Factors to be considered in assessing first aid provision include:

- the number of employees
- the nature of the undertaking
- the size of the establishment and the distribution of employees
- the location of the establishment and the locations employees go to in the course of their employment
- use of shift working (each shift would have the same level of first aid cover/protection)
- the distance from external medical services, such as the local casualty department.

The general guidance suggests that even in a simple office, there ought to be a first aider for every 50 people there.

First aid boxes

There should be at least one first aid box, the contents of which are listed in the ACOP.

THE HEALTH AND SAFETY (INFORMATION TO EMPLOYEES) REGULATIONS 1989

These regulations require information relating to health, safety and welfare to be furnished to employees by means of posters or leaflets in the form approved and published for the purposes of the regulations by the HSE (copies of the form of poster or leaflets may be obtained from the HSE and the actual posters from HMSO).

The regulations also require that the name and address of the enforcing authority and the address of the Employment Medical Advisory Service be written in the appropriate space on the poster. Where the leaflet is given to employees, the same information must be specified in a written notice accompanying it.

The regulations provide for the issuing of certificates of exemption by the HSE, provide for a defence for a contravention of the regulations and repeal, revoke and modify various enactments relating to the provision of information to employees.

The regulations do not apply to the master and crew of a seagoing ship.

THE HIGHLY FLAMMABLE LIQUIDS AND LIQUEFIED PETROLEUM GASES REGULATIONS 1972

These regulations lay down requirements for the following matters in relation to highly flammable liquids and so on used in a factory:

- manner of storage
- marking of storage accommodation and vessels
- precautions to be observed for the prevention of fire and explosion
- provision of fire fighting apparatus
- securing means of escape in the event of fire.

By *highly flammable liquids* is meant both liquefied flammable gas, although not aqueous ammonia, and liquefied petroleum gases and so this term includes any liquid, liquid solution, emulsion or suspension that:

- gives off a flammable vapour at a temperature less than 32°C when tested in the manner set out in Schedule 1 of the regulations (closed cup flashpoint determination method)
- supports combustion when tested in a manner set out in Schedule 2 (combustibility test).

4

Liquefied flammable gas is any substance that would be a flammable gas at a temperature of 20°C and a pressure of 760 millimetres of mercury, but is in a liquid form as a result of the application of pressure or refrigeration or both.

The term *liquefied petroleum gas* covers both commercial butane and commercial propane, and any mixture of them.

The application of the regulations

The regulations apply to factories and impose duties on the occupier of the premises or, in some cases, the owner of the substances.

General storage requirements for highly flammable liquids

When not in use or being conveyed, all highly flammable liquids (HFLs) should be stored in a safe manner. All HFLs should be stored in one of the following ways:

- in suitable fixed storage tanks in a safe position
- in suitable closed vessels kept in a safe position in the open air and, where necessary, protected against direct sunlight
- in suitable closed vessels kept in a store room that either is in a safe position or is of fire-resisting structure
- in the case of a workroom where the aggregate quantity of HFL stored does not exceed 50 litres, in suitable closed vessels kept in a suitably placed cupboard or bin that is a fire-resisting structure.

Other storage precautions

Bund walls

Storage tanks should be provided with a bund wall enclosure that is capable of containing 110 per cent of the capacity of the largest tank within the bund.

Ground beneath vessels

The ground beneath storage vessels should be impervious to liquid and be so sloped that any minor spillage will not remain beneath the vessels, but will run away to the sides of the enclosure.

Bulk storage

Bulk storage tanks should not be located inside buildings or on the roof of a building. Underground tanks should not be sited under the floors of process buildings.

Drum storage

The area to be utilized for drum storage should be surrounded with a sill capable of containing the maximum spillage from the largest drum in store.

The marking of store rooms and containers

Every store room, cupboard, bin, tank and vessel used for storing HFLs should be clearly and boldly marked 'Highly flammable' or 'Flashpoint below 32°C' or 'Flashpoint in the range of 22°C to 32°C'.

Specific provisions for the storage of liquefied petroleum gas

All liquefied petroleum gas (LPG) must be stored in one of the following ways:

- in suitable underground reservoirs or in suitable fixed storage tanks located in a safe position, either underground or in the open air
- in suitable movable storage tanks/vessels kept in a safe position in the open air
- in pipelines or pumps forming part of an enclosed system
- in suitable cylinders kept in safe positions in the open air or, where this is not reasonably practicable, in a store room constructed of non-combustible material, having adequate ventilation, being in a safe position, of fire-resisting structure, and being used solely for the storage of LPG and/or acetylene cylinders.

LPG cylinders must be kept in a store until they are required for use, and any expended cylinder must be returned to the store as soon as is reasonably practicable. This should ensure that only the minimum amount of LPG is kept in any workplace.

The marking of store rooms and containers

Every tank, cylinder, store room and so on used for the storage of LPG should be clearly and boldly marked 'Highly flammable – LPG'.

Precautions against spills and leaks (all HFLs)

Where HFLs are to be conveyed within a factory, a totally enclosed piped system should be used, where reasonably practicable. Where not reasonably practicable, a system using closed, non-spill containers will be acceptable.

Portable vessels, when emptied, should be removed to a safe place without delay.

Where, in any process or operation, any HFL is liable to leak or be split, all reasonably practicable steps should be taken to ensure that any such HFL should be contained or immediately drained off to a suitable container, or to a safe place, or rendered harmless.

Precautions against escaping vapours

No means likely to ignite vapour from any HFL should be present where there may be a dangerous concentration of vapours from HFL.

Where any HFL is being utilized in the workplace, reasonably practicable steps should be taken so as to minimize the risk of escape of HFL vapours into the general workplace atmosphere. Where such escape cannot be avoided, then the safe dispersal of HFL vapours should be effected, so far as is reasonably practicable.

The relaxation of fire resistance specifications in certain circumstances

In cases where either explosion pressure relief or adequate natural ventilation are required in a fire-resistant structure, a relaxation of the specification of a fire-resistant structure is allowable.

Fire escapes and fire certificates

There must be adequate and safe means of escape in case of fire from every room in which any HFL is manufactured, used or manipulated. This regulation does not apply where there is storage only.

Fire certificates are generally necessary where:

- HFLs are manufactured
- LPG is stored
- liquefied flammable gas is stored.

The prevention of a build-up of deposits

Whenever, as a result of any process or, operation involving any HFL, a deposit of any solid waste residue liable to give rise to a risk of fire may occur on any surface:

- steps must be taken to prevent the occurrence of all such deposits, so far as is reasonably practicable
- where any such deposits occur, effective steps must be taken to remove all such residues, as often as necessary, to prevent danger.

Smoking controls

No person may smoke in any place in which any HFL is present and where the circumstances are such that smoking will give rise to the risk of fire.

The provision of fire-fighting equipment

Appropriate fire-fighting equipment should be made readily available for use in all factories where HFLs are manufactured, used or manipulated.

The duties of employees

It is the duty of every employee to comply with them and cooperate in carrying them out.

If an employee discovers any defect in plant, equipment or appliance, it is their duty to report the defect without delay to the occupier, manager or other responsible person.

THE IONISING RADIATIONS REGULATIONS 1985

These comprehensive regulations impose duties on employers to protect employees and other persons against ionizing radiation arising from work with radioactive substances and other sources of ionizing radiation. They also impose certain duties on employees.

The regulations provide an excellent framework for safe working practices involving the use of radioactive substances and sources of ionizing radiation and the controls necessary for these. The principal requirements of the regulations are outlined below, together with many of the definitions that are important in the interpretation of the regulations.

Interpretation (regulation 2)

The meanings of the following terms are significant:

- *appointed doctor* means a registered medical practitioner who is, for the time being, appointed in writing by the HSE for the purposes of these regulations
- *approved* means approved for the time being by the HSE or the HSC, as the case may be
- *approved dosimetry service* means a dosimetry service approved in accordance with regulation 9(1)
- *classified person* means a person who has been so designated in accordance with regulation (1)
- *contamination* means contamination by a radioactive substance of any surface (including any surface of the body or clothing) or any part of absorbent objects or materials or the contamination of liquids or gases by any radioactive substance
- *controlled area* means an area that has been so designated by the employer in accordance with regulation 8(1) or (3)
- *dose* means, in relation to ionizing radiation, any dose quantity or sum of dose quantities mentioned in Schedule 1
- *dose limit* means, in relation to persons of a specified class, the dose limit specified in Schedule 1 in relation to a person of that class and is with respect to:
    - the whole body, the relevant dose limit specified in Part I
    - any individual organ or tissue except the lens of the eye, the relevant dose limit specified in Part II
    - the lens of the eye, the relevant dose limit specified in Part III
    - the abdomen of a woman of reproductive capacity, the dose limit specified in Part IV
    - the abdomen of a pregnant woman, the dose limit specified in Part V.

- *dose rate* means, in relation to a place, the rate at which a person or part of a person would receive a dose of ionizing radiation from external radiation if they were at that place; *instantaneous dose rate* means a dose rate at that place averaged over one minute; *time average dose rate* means a dose rate at that place averaged over any 8-hour working period
- *dose record* means, in relation to a person, the record of the doses received by that person as a result of their exposure to ionizing radiation, being the record made and maintained on behalf of the employer by the approved dosimetry service in accordance with regulation 13(3)(a)
- *external radiation* means, in relation to a person, ionizing radiation coming from outside the body of that person
- *health record* means, in relation to an employee, the record of medical surveillance of that employee maintained by the employer in accordance with regulation 16(c)
- *internal radiation* means, in relation to a person, ionizing radiation coming from inside the body of that person
- *ionizing radiation* means gamma rays, X-rays or corpuscular radiations that are capable of producing ions either directly or indirectly

- *maintained*, where the reference is to maintaining plant, apparatus or facilities, means maintained in an efficient state, in efficient working order and in good repair
- *medical exposure* means exposure of a person to ionizing radiation for the purpose of their medical or dental examination or treatment that is conducted under the direction of a suitably qualified person and includes any such examination or treatment conducted for the purposes of research
- *overexposure* means any exposure of a person to ionizing radiation to the extent that the dose received by that person causes a dose limit relevant to that person to be exceeded
- *qualified person* means a person who has been so appointed for the purposes of regulation 24(3) in accordance with regulation 10(7)
- *radiation generator* means any apparatus in which charged particles are accelerated in a vacuum vessel through a potential difference of more than 5 kilovolts (whether or not in one or more steps), except an apparatus in which the only such generator is a cathode ray tube or visual display unit that does not cause, under normal operating conditions, an instantaneous dose rate of more than 5 μSvh^{-1} (micro-Sievert per hour, a unit of dose rate) at a distance of 50 millimetres from any accessible surface
- *radioactive substance* means any substance having an activity concentration of more than 100 Bqg^{-1} (Becquerel, a unit of quantity or activity of a radionuclide) and any other substance that contains one or more radionuclides whose activity cannot be disregarded for the purposes of radiation protection, and the term includes a radioactive substance in the form of a sealed source
- *radiation protection adviser* means a person appointed in accordance with regulation 10(1)
- *sealed source* means a radioactive substance bonded wholly within a solid, inactive material or encapsulated within an inactive receptacle of, in either case, sufficient strength to prevent any dispersion of the substance under reasonably foreseeable conditions of use and shall include the bonding or encapsulation, except that:

  - where such bonding or encapsulation is solely for the purpose of storage, transport or disposal, the radioactive substance, together with its bonding or encapsulation, shall not be treated as a sealed source
  - the term 'sealed source' shall not include any radioactive substance inside a nuclear reactor or any nuclear fuel element.

- *short-lived daughters of radon* 222 means polonium 218, lead 214, bismuth 214 and polonium 214
- *supervised area* means any area that has been so designated by the employer in accordance with regulation 8(2) or (3)
- *trainee* means a person aged 16 years or over (including a student) who is undergoing instruction or training that involves operations which would,

in the case of an employee, be work with ionizing radiation

- *woman of reproductive capacity* means a woman who is made subject to the additional dose limit for a woman of reproductive capacity specified in Part IV of Schedule I by an entry in her health record made by an employment medical adviser or appointed doctor
- *work with ionizing radiation* means any work:
  - involving the production, processing, handling, use, holding, storage, moving, transport or disposal of any radioactive substance
  - involving the operation or use of any radioactive generator
  - in which there is any exposure of a person to an atmosphere containing the short-lived daughters of radon 222 at a concentration in air, averaged over any 8-hour working period, of greater than 6.24×10^{-7} Jm^{-3} a unit of alpha radiation energy concentration per cubic metre of air) (0.03 working levels).
- *working level* means the special unit of potential alpha energy concentration in air and is any combination of short-lived daughters of radon 222 in unit volume of air such that the total potential alpha energy concentration for complete decay to lead 210 is 2.08×10^{-5} Jm^{-3}.

4

The principal provisions of the regulations

Part II: Dose limitation

Restriction of exposure (regulation 6)

This regulation places a general duty on employers to restrict, so far as is reasonably practicable, the exposure of employees, and other people who could foreseeably be affected, to ionizing radiation.

In addition, every employer shall, so far as is reasonably practicable, achieve this restriction of exposure to ionizing radiation by means of engineering controls and design features that include shielding, ventilation, containment of radioactive substances and minimization of contamination and, in addition, by the provision and use of safety features and warning devices.

Furthermore, in addition to taking the steps required above, every employer shall provide such systems of work as will, so far as is reasonably practicable, restrict the exposure of employees and other people to ionizing radiation. Also, in the case of employees or others who enter or remain in controlled or supervised areas, employers must provide them with adequate and suitable PPE (including RPE) unless:

- it is not reasonably practicable to further restrict exposure to ionizing radiation by such means
- the use of PPE of a particular kind is not appropriate to the nature of the work or the circumstances of the particular case.

An employee who is engaged in work with ionizing radiation:

- shall not knowingly expose themselves or any other person to ionizing

radiation to any extent greater than is reasonably necessary for the purposes of their work, and shall exercise reasonable care while carrying out such work
- shall make full and proper use of any PPE provided
- shall report to their employer straight away if they find any defect in any PPE.

The employer shall ensure that:

- no radioactive substance in the form of a sealed source is held in the hand or manipulated directly by hand unless the instantaneous dose rate to the skin of the hand does not exceed 75 μSvh^{-1}
- so far as is reasonably practicable, no unsealed radioactive substance nor any article containing a radioactive substance is held in the hand or directly manipulated by hand.

No employee shall eat, drink, smoke, take snuff or apply cosmetics in any area that the employer has designated as a controlled area, but they can drink from a drinking fountain so constructed that there is no contamination of the water.

Dose limits (regulation 7)

Under this regulation, employers must ensure that employees and other people are not exposed to ionizing radiation to an extent that any dose limit specified in Schedule 1 for each such employee or other person, as the case may be, is exceeded.

Schedule 1: Dose limits

Part 1: Dose limits for the whole body

The dose limit for the whole body resulting from exposure to the whole or part of the body, being the sum of the following dose quantities resulting from exposure to ionizing radiation, namely the effective dose equivalent from external radiation and the committed effective dose equivalent from that year's intake of radionuclides, shall, in any calendar year, be:

- for employees aged 18 years or over — 50 micro-sievert
- for trainees aged under 18 — 15 micro-sievert
- for any other person — 5 micro-sievert

Part II: Dose limits for individual organs and tissues

Without prejudice to Part I above, the dose limit for individual organs or tissues, being the sum of the following dose quantities resulting from exposure to ionizing radiation, namely the dose equivalent from external radiation, the dose equivalent from contamination and the committed dose equivalent from that year's intake of radionuclides averaged throughout any individual organ or tissue (other than the lens of the eye) or any body extremity or over any area of skin, shall, in any calendar year, be:

• for employees aged 18 or over	500 micro-sievert
• for trainees aged under 18	150 micro-sievert
• for any other person	50 micro-sievert

In assessing the dose quantity to the skin, whether it is from contamination or external radiation, the area of skin over which the dose quantity is averaged shall be appropriate to the circumstances, but, in any event, shall not exceed 100 square centimetres.

Part III: Dose limits for the lens of the eye

The dose limit for the lens of the eye resulting from exposure to ionizing radiation, being the average dose equivalent from external and internal radiation delivered between 2.5 and 3.5 millimetres behind the surface of the eye, shall, in any calendar year, be:

• for employees aged 18 or over	150 micro-sievert
• for trainees aged under 18	45 micro-sievert
• for any other person	15 micro-sievert

Part IV: Dose limit for the abdomen of a woman of reproductive capacity

The dose limit for the abdomen of a woman of reproductive capacity who is at work, being the dose equivalent from external radiation resulting from exposure to ionizing radiation averaged throughout the abdomen, shall be 13 micro-sievert in any consecutive three-month interval. 4

Part V: Dose limit for the abdomen of a pregnant woman

The dose limit for the abdomen of a pregnant woman who is at work, being the dose equivalent from external radiation resulting from exposure to ionizing radiation averaged throughout the abdomen, shall be 10 micro-sievert during the declared term of pregnancy.

Note that the sievert is the SI unit of dose equivalent, an index of the risk of harm from exposure of a particular body tissue to various radiations. The micro-sievert is one thousandth of a sievert.

Part III: Regulation of work with ionizing radiation

Part III lays down general procedures for ensuring safe working practices and the designation and appointment of certain people.

Designation of controlled and supervised areas (regulation 8)

Employers must designate as *controlled areas* any area where doses are likely to exceed three tenths of any dose limit for employees of 18 or over.

Employers must designate as a *supervised area* any area, not being a controlled area, where any person is likely to be exposed to an extent that exceeds one third of the extent they would be exposed to in a controlled area.

The employer shall not permit any employee or other person to enter or remain in a controlled area unless that employee or other person:

- is a classified person
- enters or remains in the area under a written system of work (that is, a permit to work system), such that:
  - in the case of an employee aged 18 or over, they do not receive, in any calendar year, a dose of ionizing radiation exceeding three tenths of any relevant dose limit
  - in the case of any other person, they do not receive, in any calendar year, a dose of ionizing radiation exceeding any relevant dose limit.

An employer shall not permit an employee or other person to enter or remain in a controlled area in accordance with a written system of work unless they can demonstrate, by personal dose assessment or other measurements, that the doses are restricted in accordance with the above paragraph.

The designation of classified persons (regulation 9)

The employer shall designate as *classified persons* those of their employees who are likely to receive a dose of ionizing radiation that exceeds three tenths of any relevant dose limit and shall inform those employees that they have been so designated straight away.

An employer shall not designate an employee as a classified person unless:

- that employee is aged 18 or over
- an employment medical adviser (EMA) or appointed doctor has certified in the health record that, in their professional opinion, that employee is fit to be designated as a classified person.

The appointment of radiation protection advisers and classified persons (regulation 10)

In any case where:

- any employee is exposed to an instantaneous dose rate that exceeds 7.5 μSvh^{-1}
- the employer has designated a controlled area that people enter,

the employer carrying out work with ionizing radiation shall appoint one or more *radiation protection advisers* (RPAs) for the purpose of advising them as to the observance of these regulations and as to other health and safety matters in connection with ionizing radiation.

No employer shall appoint a person as an RPA unless:

- that person is suitably qualified and experienced
- they have notified the HSE in writing of the intended appointment at least 28 days in advance
- they have received an acknowledgement in writing of the notification from the HSE.

The employer shall provide any RPA with adequate information and facilities for the performance of their functions and shall, whenever appropriate, consult that RPA.

The above provisions relating to qualifications, notification of the HSE and the provision of information and facilities apply similarly in the case of a 'qualified person' for the purpose of regulation 24 (monitoring of levels of radiation and contamination).

Local rules, supervision and radiation protection supervisors (regulation 11)

Every employer who undertakes work with ionizing radiation shall make and set down in writing local rules for the purpose of enabling the work with ionizing radiation to be carried out in compliance with the requirements of these regulations and shall ensure that the rules that are relevant are brought to the attention of those employees and others who may be affected by them.

The employer shall ensure that the work with ionizing radiation is supervised to the extent necessary to enable the work to be carried out in accordance with the requirements of these regulations and shall take all reasonable steps to ensure that any local rules relevant to this work are observed.

Where the work with ionizing radiation is any other than that specified in Schedule 3 (work not required to be notified under regulation 5(2)), the employer shall appoint one or more employees as *radiation protection supervisors* for the purpose of securing compliance with the above, and any such appointment shall be in writing and the names of the people appointed shall be included in the local rules.

Information, instruction and training (regulation 12)

In addition to the general duty on employers under the HSWA to inform, instruct and train employees and others, this regulation specifies groups of people who must receive information, instruction and training.

Every employer shall ensure that:

- those *employees* who are engaged in work with ionizing radiation receive such information, instruction and training as will enable them to conduct the work in accordance with the requirements of these regulations
- adequate information is given to *others* who are directly concerned with the work with ionizing radiation carried out by the employer to ensure their health and safety, so far as is reasonably practicable
- *classified persons and trainees* are informed of the health hazard, if any, associated with their work, the precautions to be taken, the importance of complying with the medical and technical requirements and given appropriate training in the field of radiation protection
- those employees who are engaged in work with ionizing radiation who are *women* are informed of the possible hazard arising from ionizing radiation to the foetus in early pregnancy and of the importance of informing the employer as soon as they discover that they have become pregnant.

Part IV: Dosimetry and medical surveillance

This Part deals with:

- the procedures for dose assessment (regulation 13)
- dosimetry in the event of an accident, occurrence or incident that is likely to result in a person being exposed to ionizing radiation to an extent greater than three tenths of any relevant dose limit (regulation 14)
- medical surveillance of certain groups (regulation 16)
- approved arrangements for the protection of certain employees (regulation 17).

Part V: Arrangements for the control of radioactive substances

Sealed sources and articles containing or embodying radioactive substances (regulation 18)

Regulation 18 imposes duties on employers with regard to the control of radioactive substances.

Where a radioactive substance is used as a source of ionizing radiation in work with ionizing radiation, the employer shall ensure that, whenever reasonably practicable, the substance is in the form of a sealed source.

The employer shall ensure that the design, construction and maintenance of any article containing or embodying a radioactive substance, including its bonding, immediate container or other mechanical protection is such as to prevent the leakage of any radioactive substance:

- in the case of a sealed source, so far as is practicable
- in the case of any other article, so far as is reasonably practicable.

Where appropriate, the employer shall ensure that suitable tests are carried out at suitable intervals, which shall, in no case, exceed 26 months, to detect leakage of radioactive substances from any article, and the employer shall keep a suitable record of these tests for at least 3 years from the date of the tests to which it refers.

Accounting for radioactive substances (regulation 19)

This regulation requires an employer to take such steps as are appropriate to account for and keep records of the quantities and locations of radioactive substances, and to keep records for at least two years from that date and at least two years from the date of disposal of a radioactive substance.

Keeping of radioactive substances (regulation 20)

Every employer shall ensure, so far as is reasonably practicable, that any radioactive substance under their control that is not, for the time being, in use or being moved, transported or disposed of:

- is kept in a suitable receptacle
- is kept in a suitable store.

Transporting and moving radioactive substances (regulation 21)

Every employer who causes or permits a radioactive substance to be transported shall ensure that, so far as is reasonably practicable, the substance is kept in a suitable receptacle, suitably labelled, while it is being transported. So far as is reasonably practicable, any written information accompanying the radioactive substance shall enable a person receiving it:

- to know the nature and quantity of the radioactive substance
- to comply with the requirements of regulations 6, 7, 8 and 18(2) and the points mentioned above in so far as such compliance depends on this information.

Washing and changing facilities (regulation 22)

Where an employer is required to designate an area as a controlled area or a supervised area, they shall ensure that adequate washing and changing facilities are provided for those who enter or leave that area and that these facilities are properly maintained.

Personal protective equipment (regulation 23)

Every employer shall ensure that, where PPE is provided, it includes RPE and that the RPE is of a type, or conforms to a standard, approved in either case by the HSE.

Every employer shall ensure that all PPE (including RPE) is thoroughly examined at suitable intervals, is properly maintained and that, in the case of RPE, a suitable record of such examinations are made and kept for at least two years from the date on which the examination was made and that the record includes a statement of the condition of the equipment at the time of the examination.

Part IV: Monitoring ionizing radiation

Monitoring levels of radiation and contamination (regulation 24)

Regulation 24 places the following duties on the employer:

- to take such steps, otherwise than by the use of the assessed doses of individuals, to ensure that levels of radiation are adequately monitored for each controlled area or supervised area
- to provide equipment for such monitoring that:
  - is properly maintained
  - is thoroughly examined and tested at least once every 14 months
  - has had its performance established by tests before being taken into use for the first time
- to ensure that the above examinations and tests are carried out by, or under the immediate supervision of, a *qualified person*
- to make suitable records of the results of the monitoring and the tests carried out and to keep such records for at least two years from the respective dates on which they were made.

Part VII: Assessments and notifications

The assessment of hazards (regulation 25)

Before work with ionizing radiation is carried out, an employer must make an assessment that adequately identifies the nature and magnitude of the radiation hazard to employees that is likely to arise from this work in the event of any reasonably foreseeable accident, occurrence or incident.

Where such an assessment shows that a radiation hazard to employees or others exists, the employer shall take all reasonably practicable steps to:

- prevent any such accident, occurrence or incident
- limit the consequences of any such accident, occurrence or incident that does occur
- provide employees with the information, instruction, training and equipment necessary to restrict their exposure to ionizing radiation.

Special hazard assessments and reports (regulation 26)

An employer shall not undertake any work with ionizing radiation that involves:

- having on any site
- providing facilities for there to be on any site
- transporting

more than the quantity of any radioactive substance specified in column 6 of Schedule 2 or, in the case of fossil material, the mass of this material specified below, unless they have made an assessment of the radiation hazard that could arise from the work and have sent a report of the assessment to the HSE at least 28 days before commencing the work or within such shorter time in advance as the HSE may agree.

The specified mass of fossil material shall be:

- plutonium, as Pu 239 or as a mixture of plutonium isotopes containing Pu 239 or Pu 241, 150 grams
- uranium, as U 233, 150 grams
- uranium enriched in U 235 to more than 1 per cent but not more than 5 per cent, 500 grams
- uranium enriched in U 235 to more than 5 per cent, 250 grams.

Contingency plans (regulation 27)

Where the assessment made in accordance with regulation 25 shows that, as a result of any reasonably foreseeable accident, occurrence or incident:

- employees or others are likely to receive a dose of ionizing radiation that exceeds any relevant dose limit
- any area other than a controlled area would be required to be so designated,

the employer shall prepare a contingency plan designed to secure, so far as is reasonably practicable, the restriction of exposure to ionizing radiation and the health and safety of those who may be affected by the accident, occurrence or incident to which the plan relates.

The investigation of exposure (regulation 28)

The employer shall ensure that an investigation is carried out straight away when any of their employees are exposed to ionizing radiation to an extent that three tenths of the annual dose limit for employees aged 18 or over specified in Part I of Schedule I (whole body dose limit; is exceeded for the first time in any calendar year, to determine whether or not the requirements of regulation 6 are being met. A report of any such investigation shall be kept for at least two years.

The investigation and notification of exposure (regulation 29)

This regulation lays down procedures for notifying the HSE and making a detailed investigation where an employer suspects or has been informed that an employee is likely to have received an overexposure to ionizing radiation.

The notification of certain occurrences (regulation 31)

Every employer shall notify the HSE without delay when a quantity of radioactive substance that was under their control and that exceeds the quantity specified for that substance in column 7 of Schedule 2:

- has been released, or is likely to have been released, into the atmosphere as a gas, aerosol or dust
- has been spilled or otherwise released in such a manner as to give rise to significant contamination.

The employer shall make an immediate investigation and, unless nothing has occurred, notify the HSE. A report of this investigation shall be kept for at least 50 years from the date on which it was made.

Part VIII: Safety of articles and equipment

The duties of manufacturers and so on regarding articles for use in work with ionizing radiation (regulation 32)

This regulation modifies the duties of manufacturers and so on under section 6 of the HSWA to include the duty to ensure that any such article is so designed and constructed as to restrict, so far as is reasonably practicable, the extent to which employees and others are, or are likely, to be exposed to ionizing radiation.

Specific duties are also placed on those who erect or install an article for use at work. Such people shall:

- where appropriate, together with an RPA, undertake a critical examination of the way in which the article was erected or installed for the purpose of ensuring, in particular, that:

- the safety features and warning devices operate correctly
- there is sufficient protection for people from exposure to ionizing radiation

- provide the employer with adequate information about proper use, testing and maintenance of the article.

The equipment used for medical exposure (regulation 33)

Every employer shall ensure that any equipment or apparatus under their control that is used in connection with medical exposure is of such a design or construction and is so installed and maintained as to be capable of restricting, so far as is reasonably practicable, the exposure to ionizing radiation of anyone who is undergoing a medical exposure to the extent that this is compatible with the clinical purpose or research objective in view.

The employer must investigate any incident where a person has been overexposed as a result of malfunction of, or a defect in, such radiation equipment and, unless such an investigation shows, beyond reasonable doubt, that no such incident has occurred, shall notify the HSE straight away. They shall then make a detailed investigation of the circumstances of the exposure and an assessment of the dose received. Such a report shall be kept for at least 50 years from the date on which it was made.

The misuse of or interference with the sources of ionizing radiation (regulation 34)

No one shall intentionally or recklessly misuse or, without reasonable excuse, interfere with any radioactive substance or radiation generator.

Part IX: Miscellaneous and general

The defence for the contravention of certain regulations (regulation 35)

It shall be a defence in proceedings against any person for an offence consisting of a contravention of regulations 5(4), 17(1) and 26(4) for the person to prove that, at the time proceedings were commenced:

- an improvement notice under section 21 of the HSWA relating to the contravention had not been served on them
- if such a notice had been served on them, that:
  - the period for compliance had not expired
  - they had appealed against the notice and that appeal had not been dismissed or withdrawn.

The Schedules to the regulations

The ten Schedules cover the following matters:

1 dose limits
2 quantities of radionuclides:

- Part I: Table of radionuclides
- Part II: Quantity ratios for more than one radionuclide

3 work not required to be notified under regulation 5(2)
4 particulars to be supplied in a notification under regulation 5(2)
5 additional particulars that the HSE may require
6 designation of controlled areas:

- Part I: Designation in relation to external radiation
- Part II: Designation in relation to internal radiation
- Part III: Designation in relation to external radiation and internal radiation together
- Part IV: Designation in relation to short-lived daughters of Radon 222

7 particulars to be included in an assessment report
8 further particulars that the HSE may require
9 sealed sources to which regulation 26 does not apply
10 revocations and modifications.

THE LIFTING PLANT AND EQUIPMENT (RECORDS OF TEST AND EXAMINATION, ETC.) REGULATIONS 1992

These regulations remove the legal requirement to report the results of the testing and examination of lifting plant and equipment by a competent person on prescribed forms. They also remove the requirement to provide a written report, except when required by an inspector, thus allowing for the storage of records of tests and so on by electronic means.

On this basis, the competent person may provide the record in a way that suits them and the owner or user of the plant and equipment. Effectively, this means that a competent person is able to use the same form on which to provide the written record for the majority of lifting plant and equipment likely to be tested and so on, or, if they wish can record the results of the test and so on by electronic means. The only proviso is that the record *must* contain the particulars prescribed by these Regulations, which are outlined in its Schedule and Appendix 1.

The prescribed particulars

The prescribed particulars cover the:

- record of the test, test and examination or test and thorough examination of lifting plant and equipment
- record of thorough examination of lifting plant and equipment.

THE MANAGEMENT OF HEALTH AND SAFETY AT WORK REGULATIONS 1992

These regulations came into operation on 1 January 1993 and are accompanied by an ACOP issued by the HSC. The duties, because of their wide-ranging general nature, overlap with many existing regulations, such as the Control of Substances Hazardous to Health Regulations (COSHHR) 1988. Where duties overlap, compliance with the duty in the more *specific* regulation will normally be sufficient to comply with the corresponding duty in the MHSWR. However, where the duties in these regulations go *beyond* those in the more specific regulations, additional measures will be needed to comply fully with the MHSWR.

Because of their importance in the areas of health and safety management, the principal requirements of the regulations are dealt with below.

Interpretation (regulation 1)

The important definitions included here are as follows:

- *the assessment* – means, in the case of an employer, the assessment made by them in accordance with regulation 3(1) and changed by them when necessary in accordance with regulation 3(3); and, in the case of a self-employed person, the assessment made by them in accordance with regulation 3(2) and changed by them in accordance with regulation 3(3)
- *employment business* – means a business (whether or not carried out with a view to profit and whether or not carried out in conjunction with any other business) that supplies people (other than seafarers) who are employed in it to work for and under the control of others in any capacity
- *fixed-term contract of employment* – means a contract of employment for a specific term that is fixed in advance or can be ascertained in advance by reference to some relevant circumstance
- *the preventive and protective measures* – means the measures that have been identified by the employer or by the self-employed person in consequence of the assessment as the measures they need to take to comply with the requirements and prohibitions imposed on them by or under the relevant statutory provisions.

The disapplication of these Regulations (regulation 2)

These regulations shall not apply to or in relation to the master or crew of a sea-going ship or to the employer of these people in respect of the normal shipboard activities of a ship's crew under the direction of the master.

Risk assessment (regulation 3)

Every employer shall make a suitable and sufficient assessment of:

- the risks to the health and safety of their employees to which they are exposed while at work
- the risks to the health and safety of those not in their employ arising out of or in connection with the conduct by them of their undertaking, for the purpose of identifying the measures they need to take to comply with the requirements and prohibitions imposed on them by or under the relevant statutory provisions.

Similar provisions to these apply in the case of self-employed people.

Any assessment shall be reviewed by the employer or self-employed person who made it if:

- there is reason to suspect that it is no longer valid
- there has been a significant change in the matters to which it relates,

and where, as a result of any such review, changes to an assessment are required, the employer or self-employed person shall make them.

Where the employer employs five or more employees, they shall record:

- the significant findings of the assessment
- any group of their employees identified by it as being especially at risk.

Comment

Risk assessment is the principal feature of these regulations. Guidance on risk assessment is provided in the ACOP.

Health and safety arrangements (regulation 4)

Every employer shall make and give effect to such arrangements as are appropriate, having regard to the nature of their activities and the size of his undertaking, for the effective planning, organization, control, monitoring and review of the preventive and protective measures.

Where the employer employs five or more employees, they shall record these arrangements.

Comment

There is a need here to consider the systems necessary to ensure the effective management of health and safety requirements. Such systems should be integrated with other management systems, such as those for the financial, personnel, production, engineering, purchasing and other areas of management activity. The principal elements of management practice, that is planning, organizing, controlling, monitoring and reviewing, should be taken into account.

Health surveillance (regulation 5)

Every employer shall ensure that their employees are provided with such health surveillance as is appropriate, having regard to the risks to their health and safety that are identified by the assessment.

Comment

Health surveillance may already be required in order to comply with existing legislation, such as the Control of Substances Hazardous to Health Regulations (COSHHR) 1988. However, health surveillance may also be necessary where the risk assessment under these MHSWR indicates that:

- there is an identifiable disease or adverse health condition related to the work concerned
- valid techniques are available to detect indications of the disease or condition, such as certain forms of biological monitoring
- there is a reasonable likelihood that the disease or condition may occur under the particular conditions of work
- surveillance is likely to further the protection of the health of the employees to be covered.

The principal objective of any health surveillance activity is to detect adverse health effects at an early stage, thereby enabling further harm to be prevented.

Health and safety assistance (regulation 6)

Every employer (except a qualified self-employed person or a partnership that includes a qualified person; see below) shall appoint one or more competent persons to assist them in undertaking the measures they need to take to comply with the requirements and prohibitions imposed on them by or under the relevant statutory provisions.

Where an employer appoints competent persons in accordance with the above, they shall make arrangements for ensuring adequate cooperation between them.

The employer shall ensure that the number of persons appointed under the first paragraph, the time available for them to fulfil their functions and the means at their disposal are adequate for the size of their undertaking, the risks to which their employees are exposed and the distribution of those risks throughout the undertaking.

The employer shall ensure that:

- any person appointed by them in accordance with the first paragraph who is not in their employ:
  - is informed of the factors known by them to affect, or suspected by them of affecting, the health and safety of any other person who may be affected by the conduct of their undertaking
  - has access to the information referred to in regulation 8

- any person appointed by them in accordance with the first paragraph is given such information about any person working in their undertaking who is:
  - employed by them under a fixed-term contract of employment
  - employed in an employment business, as is necessary to enable that person to carry out the function specified in the paragraph properly.

A person shall be regarded as competent for the purposes of the first paragraph where they have sufficient training and experience or knowledge and other qualities to undertake the measures referred to in that paragraph properly.

The first paragraph shall *not* apply to a self-employed employer who is not in partnership with any other person where they have sufficient training and experience or knowledge and other qualities to undertake the measures referred to in that paragraph properly.

The first paragraph shall not apply to individuals who are employers and who are together carrying on business in partnership where at least one of the individuals concerned has sufficient training and experience or knowledge and other qualities to:

- properly undertake the measures they need to take to comply with the requirements and prohibitions imposed on them by or under the relevant statutory provisions
- properly assist their fellow partners in undertaking the measures they need to take to comply with the requirements and prohibitions imposed on them or under the relevant statutory provisions.

Comment

The concept of 'competent persons' is not new to health and safety legislation, the appointment of such people being required under the Construction Regulations, Noise at Work Regulations, Pressure Systems and Transportable Gas Containers Regulations and so on.

The degree of competence of the competent person for the purposes of these Regulations will depend on the risks identified in the risk assessment. While there is no specific emphasis on the qualifications of such people, broadly, a competent person should have such skill, knowledge and experience as to enable them to identify defects and understand the implications of these defects. The depth of training, accountabilities and responsibilities, authority and level of reportability within the management system of the competent person is, therefore, important. The competent person should not be placed so far down the management system that their recommendations carry no weight.

The procedures for serious and imminent danger and for danger areas (regulation 7)

Every employer shall:

- establish and, where necessary, give effect to appropriate procedures to be followed in the event of serious and imminent danger to people at work in their undertaking
- nominate a sufficient number of competent people to implement these procedures in so far as they relate to the evacuation from the premises of employees and others at work
- ensure that none of their employees have access to any area occupied by them to which it is necessary to restrict access on grounds of health and safety unless the employee concerned has received adequate health and safety instruction.

Without prejudice to the generality of the first point above, the procedures referred to in it shall:

- so far as is practicable, require any one at work who is exposed to serious and imminent danger to be informed of the nature of the hazard and of the steps to be taken to protect them from it
- enable those concerned (if necessary by taking appropriate steps in the absence of guidance or instruction and in the light of their knowledge and the technical means at their disposal) to stop work and immediately proceed to a place of safety in the event of their being exposed to serious, imminent or unavoidable danger
- save in exceptional cases for reasons duly substantiated (which cases and reasons shall be specified in those procedures), require the people concerned to be prevented from resuming work in any situation where there is still a serious imminent danger.

A person shall be regarded as competent for the purposes of the second point given in the first paragraph where they have sufficient training and experience or knowledge and other qualities to enable them to implement the evacuation procedures referred to there properly.

Comment

The aim here is that employers establish procedures to be followed by workers if situations present serious and imminent danger, and under what circumstances they should stop work and move to a place of safety. Fundamentally, the requirement is for organizations' emergency plans/procedures to cover foreseeable high-risk situations, such as fire, explosion and so on and ensure that staff are trained in these procedures.

Information for employees (regulation 8)

Every employer shall provide their employees with comprehensible and relevant information on:

- the risks to their health and safety identified by the assessment
- the preventative and protective measures
- the procedures referred to in regulation 7(1)(a)
- the identity of those people nominated by them in accordance with regulation 7(1)(b)
- the risks notified to them in accordance with regulation 9(1)(c).

Comment

The significant feature of this regulation is that the information provided to workers must be 'comprehensible', that is written in such a way as to be easily understood by the people to which it is addressed. On this basis, the mode of presentation of such information should take account of their level of training, knowledge and experience. It may also need to consider people with language difficulties or with disabilities that may impede their receipt of information. Information can be provided in whatever form is most suitable in the circumstances, so long as it is comprehensible, such as a staff handbook, posters or other media.

Cooperation and coordination (regulation 9)

Where two or more employers share a workplace (whether on a temporary or permanent basis), each such employer shall:

- cooperate with the other employers concerned so far as is necessary to enable them to comply with the requirements and prohibitions imposed on them by or under the relevant statutory provisions
- taking into account the nature of their activities, take all reasonable steps to coordinate the measures they take to comply with the requirements and prohibitions imposed on him by or under the relevant statutory provisions with the measures the other employers concerned are taking to comply with those that apply to them
- take all reasonable steps to inform the other employers concerned of the risks to their employees' health and safety arising from or in connection with how they conduct their undertaking.

The first paragraph shall apply to employers sharing a workplace with self-employed people and to self-employed people sharing a workplace with other self-employed people in the same way that it applies to employers sharing a workplace with other employers, the words 'employers' and 'employees' being construed accordingly.

Comment

This regulation makes provision for employers jointly occupying a work site, such as in cases of construction sites, trading estates or office blocks, to cooperate and coordinate their health and safety activities, particularly where there are risks that are common to everyone, irrespective of their work activity. Fields of cooperation and coordination include health and safety training, safety monitoring procedures, emergency arrangements and welfare amenity provisions. In some cases, the appointment of a health and safety coordinator should be considered.

People working in host employers' or self-employed people's undertakings (regulation 10)

Every employer and every self-employed person shall ensure that the employer of any employees from an outside undertaking who are working in their undertaking are provided with comprehensible information on:

- the risks to those employees' health and safety arising out of or in connection with the conduct by the host employer's or self-employed person's undertaking
- the measures taken by the host employer or self-employed person in compliance with the requirements and prohibitions imposed on them by or under the relevant statutory provisions in so far as the requirements and prohibitions relate to those employees coming to work in their undertaking

The first paragraph shall apply to a self-empoyed person who is working in the undertaking of an employer or a self-employed person as it applies to employees from an outside undertaking who are working there, and the words 'employer', 'employees' and 'self-employed person' shall be construed accordingly.

Every employer shall ensure that every person working in their undertaking who is not their employee and every self-employed person (who is not themselves an employer) shall ensure that any person working in their undertaking is provided with appropriate instructions and comprehensible information regarding any risks to that person's health and safety that arise from the way they conduct their undertaking.

Every host employer shall:

- ensure that the employer of any employees from an outside undertaking working in their undertaking is provided with sufficient information to enable the employees' employer to identify any person nominated by the host employer in accordance with regulation 7(1)(b) to implement evacuation procedures as far as these employees are concerned
- take all reasonable steps to ensure that the employees from an outside undertaking receive sufficient information to enable them to identify any person nominated by the host employer in accordance with regulation 7(1)(b) to implement evacuation procedures as far as they are concerned.

This last paragraph above shall also apply to a self-employed person who is working in an employer's undertaking and the words 'employer' and 'employees' shall be construed accordingly.

Comment

This regulation applies to a wide range of work activities where employees undertake work in other people's premises, such as contract cleaners, maintenance staff and so on. These people must be provided with adequate information and instructions regarding relevant risks to their health and safety.

Capabilities and training (regulation 11)

Every employer shall, in entrusting tasks to their employees, take into account their capabilities as regards health and safety.

Every employer shall ensure that their employees are provided with adequate health and safety training:

- on their being recruited into the employer's undertaking
- on their being exposed to new or increased risks because of:
  - their being transferred or given a change of responsibilities within the employer's undertaking
  - the introduction of new work equipment into or a change respecting work equipment already in use within the employer's undertaking
  - the introduction of new technology into the employer's undertaking
  - the introduction of a new system of work into or a change respecting a system of work already in use within the employer's undertaking.

The training referred to the points above shall:

- be repeated periodically where appropriate
- be adapted to take account of new or changed risks to the health and safety of the employees concerned
- take place during working hours.

Comment

This regulation introduces, for the first time in health and safety legislation, a human factors approach to ensuring appropriate levels of health and safety provision. When allocating work to employees, employers should ensure that the demands of the job do not exceed the employees' ability to carry out the work without risk to themselves and others. There is a need, therefore, for employers to consider both the physical and mental abilities of employees before allocating tasks, together with their level of knowledge, training and experience. Training, in particular, should reflect this aspect of human capability.

Employees' duties (regulation 12)

Every employee shall use any machinery, equipment, dangerous substance, transport equipment, means of production or safety device provided for them by their employer in accordance both with any training in the use of this equipment and the instructions for using it that have been provided by the employer in compliance with the requirements and prohibitions imposed on them by or under the relevant statutory provisions.

Every employee shall inform their employer or any other employee of that employer with specific responsibility for the health and safety of fellow employees:

- of any work situation that a person with the first-mentioned employee's training and instruction would reasonably consider represented a serious and immediate danger to health and safety
- of any matter that would reasonably be considered to represent a shortcoming in the employer's protection arrangements for health and safety,

in so far as that situation or matter either affects the health and safety of the employee or arises out of or in connection with their own activities at work, and has not previously been reported to their employer or to any other employee of that employer in accordance with this paragraph.

Comment

This regulation reinforces and expands the duties of employers towards employees under section 7 of the HSWA. In the light of these requirements, employers should install some form of hazard reporting system, whereby employees can report hazards to their employer or appointed competent person. Such a system should ensure a prompt response where hazards are identified, with the competent person signing off the hazard report when the hazard has been eliminated or controlled.

Temporary workers (regulation 13)

Every employer shall provide any person they have employed under a fixed-term contract with comprehensible information on:

- any special occupational qualifications or skills required to be held by that employee if they are to carry out their work safely
- any health surveillance required to be provided to that employee by or under any of the relevant statutory provisions

and shall provide such information before the employee concerned commences their duties.

Every employer and every self-employed person shall provide any person employed in an employment business who is to carry out work in their undertaking with similar comprehensible information to that mentioned in the first paragraph above.

Every employer and every self-employed person shall ensure that every person running an employment business, the employees of which are to carry out work in their undertaking, is provided with comprehensible information on:

- any special occupational qualifications or skills that these employees are required to hold if they are to carry out their work safely
- the specific features of the jobs to be filled by these employees (in so far as those features are likely to affect their health and safely)

and the person running the employment business concerned shall ensure that the information so provided is given to the said employees.

Comment

This regulation supplements previous regulations as it requires the provision of information but with additional requirements for temporary workers, that is, those employed on fixed duration contracts and those employed in employment businesses, but working under the control of a user company. The use of temporary workers will also have to be notified to the competent person.

Exemption certificates (regulation 14)

These regulations may, by certification from the Secretary of State for Defence, exempt members of the forces generally from having to comply with them.

The exclusion of civil liability (regulation 15)

Breach of a duty imposed by these regulations shall not confer a right of action in any civil proceedings. (Similar provisions apply in the case of the HSWA.)

The Schedule

The following regulation shall be inserted after regulation 4 of the Safety Representatives and Safety Committees Regulations 1977:

Employer's duty to consult and provide facilities and assistance

4A 1 Without prejudice to the generality of section 2(6) of the Health and Safety at Work Act 1974, every employer shall consult safety representatives in good time with regard to:

(a) the introduction of any measure at the workplace which may substantially affect the health and safety of the employees the safety representatives concerned represent;
(b) his arrangements for appointing or, as the case may be, nominating persons in accordance with regulations 6(1) and 7(1)(b) of the MHSWR 1992;
(c) any health and safety information he is required to provide to the employees the safety representatives concerned represent by or under the relevant statutory provisions;
(d) the planning and organisation of any health and safety training he is

required to provide to the employees' safety representatives concerned represent by or under the relevant statutory provisions; and

(e) the health and safety consequences for the employees the safety representatives concerned represent of the introduction (including planning thereof) of new technologies into the workplace.

2 Without prejudice to regulations 5 and 6 of these Regulations, every employer shall provide such facilities and assistance as safety representatives may reasonably require for the purpose of carrying out their functions under section 2 of the 1974 Act and under these Regulations.

Comment

This Schedule specifies the situations where there is a legal duty on the part of employers to consult with safety representatives, reinforcing existing provisions of the Safety Representatives and Safety Committees Regulations 1977.

The ACOP

These regulations are supported by a comprehensive ACOP issued by the HSC.

Footnote to the MHSWR

It must be appreciated that the vast majority of the duties specified in these regulations are of an *absolute* nature, qualified as they are by the word 'shall', compared with the HSWA, where the duties are qualified by the phrase 'so far as is reasonably practicable', a lower level of duty.

THE MANUAL HANDLING OPERATIONS REGULATIONS 1992

These regulations came into force on 1 January 1993 and implement the European 'Heavy Loads' Directive. They supplement the general duties placed on employers and others by the HSWA and the broad requirements of the MHSWR 1992. They are supported by guidance notes issued by the HSE.

A number of terms are defined as follows:

- The term *injury* does not include injury caused by any toxic or corrosive substance that:
  - has leaked or spilled from a load
  - is present on the surface of a load but has not leaked or spilled from it
  - is a constituent part of a load.
- The term *load* includes any person and any animal.

- The term *manual handling operations* means any transporting or supporting of a load (including the lifting, putting down, pushing, pulling, carrying or moving thereof) by hand or by bodily force.

The duties of employers (regulation 4)

Each employer shall:

- so far as is reasonably practicable, avoid the need for their employees to undertake any manual handling operations at work that involve a risk of their being injured
- where it is *not* reasonably practicable to avoid such a need the employer shall:
  - make a suitable and sufficient assessment of all such manual handling operations to be undertaken by them, having regard to the factors that are specified in the Schedule
  - take appropriate steps to reduce the risk of injury to these employees to the lowest level reasonably practicable
  - take appropriate steps to provide any of these employees with general indications and, where it is reasonably practicable to do so, precise information on:

    (i) the weight of each load

    (ii) the heaviest side of any load the centre of gravity of which is not positioned centrally.

  Any such assessment shall be reviewed by the employer if:

- there is reason to suspect that it is no longer valid
- there has been a significant change in the manual handling operations to which it relates

and where, as a result of any such review, changes to an assessment are required, the relevant employer shall make them.

The regulations further require that each employee while at work shall make full and proper use of any system of work provided for their use by their employer to reduce the risk of injury as mentioned above in compliance with these regulations.

Schedule 1

Factors the employer must bear in mind and questions they must consider when making an assessment of manual handling operations are as follows.

The tasks

Do they involve:

- holding or manipulating loads at distance from the trunk?
- unsatisfactory bodily movement or posture, especially:

- twisting the trunk
- stooping
- reaching upwards?

- excessive movement of loads, especially:
  - excessive lifting or lowering distances
  - excessive carrying distances?
- excessive pushing or pulling of loads?
- risk of sudden movement of loads?
- frequent or prolonged physical effort?
- insufficient rest or recovery periods?
- a rate of work imposed by a process?

The loads

Are they:

- heavy?
- bulky or unwieldy?
- difficult to grasp?
- unstable or with contents likely to shift?
- sharp, hot or otherwise potentially damaging?

The working environment

Are there:

- space constraints preventing good posture?
- uneven, slippery or unstable floors?
- variations in level of floors or work surfaces?
- extremes of temperature or humidity?
- conditions causing ventilation problems or gusts of wind?
- poor lighting conditions?

Individual capability

Does the job:

- require unusual strength, height or other feature?
- create a hazard to those who might reasonably be considered to be pregnant or have a health problem?
- require special information or training for its safe performance?

Other factors

Is movement or posture hindered by personal protective equipment or clothing?

For an example of an assessment check-list, see Figure 4.2.

Manual handling of loads

EXAMPLE OF AN ASSESSMENT CHECKLIST

Note: This checklist may be copied freely. It will remind you of the main points to think about while you:

- consider the risk of injury from manual handling operations
- identify steps that can remove or reduce the risk
- decide your priorities for action.

SUMMARY OF ASSESSMENT	Overall priority for remedial action: Nil/Low/Med /High*
Operations covered by this assessment	Remedial action to be taken: ....
....	....
....	....
Locations:	Date by which action is to be taken ....
Personnel involved:	Date for reassessment: ....
Date of assessment:	Accessor's name: ....Signature ....

*circle as appropiate

Section A – Preliminary:

Q1 Do the operations involve a significant risk of injury? Yes/No*

If '**Yes**' go to Q2. If '**No**' the assessment need go no further.
If in doubt answer '**Yes**'. You may find the guidelines in Appendix 1 helpful.

Q2 Can the operations be avoided/mechanised/automated at reasonable cost? Yes/No*

If '**No**' go to Q3. If '**Yes**' proceed and then check that the result is satisfactory.

Q3 Are the operations clearly within the guidelines in Appendix 1? Yes/No*

If '**No**' go to Section B. If '**Yes**' you may go straight to Section C if you wish.

Section C – Overall assessment of risk:

Q What is your overall assessment of the risk of injury? Insignificant/Low/Med/High*

If not '**Insignificant**' go to Section D. If '**Insignificant**' the assessment need go no further.

Section D – Remedial action:

Q What remedial steps should be taken, in order of priority?

i ....

ii ....

iii ....

iv ....

v ....

And finally:

- complete the SUMMARYabove
- compare it with your other manual handling assessments
- decide your priorities for action

– TAKE ACTION ....AND CHECK THAT IT HAS THE DESIRED EFFECT

• FIG 4.2 Example of an assessment check-list

4

Section B – More detailed assessment, where necessary:

Questions to consider: (If the answer to a question is 'Yes' place a tick against it and then consider the level of risk)	Yes	**Level of risk:** (Tick as appropriate) Low	Med	High	**Possible remedial action** (Make rough notes in this column in preparation for completing Section D)
The tasks – do they involve:					
• holding loads away from trunk?					
• twisting?					
• stooping?					
• reaching upwards?					
• large vertical movement?					
• long carrying distances?					
• strenuous pushing or pulling?					
• unpredictable movement of loads?					
• repetitive handling?					
• insufficient rest or recovery?					
• a workrate imposed by a process?					
The loads – are they:					
• heavy?					
• bulky/unwieldy?					
• difficult to grasp?					
• unstable/unpredictable?					
• intrinsically harmful (eg sharp/hot?)					
The working environment – are there:					
• constraints on posture?					
• poor floors?					
• variations in levels?					
• hot/cold/humid conditions?					
• strong air movements?					
• poor lighting conditions?					
Individual capability – does the job:					
• require unusual capability?					
• hazard those with a health problem?					
• hazard those who are pregnant?					
• call for special information/training?					
Other factors–					
is movement or posture hindered by clothing or personal protective equipment?					

Deciding the level of risk will inevitably call for judgement. The guidelines in Appendix 1 may provide a useful yardstick.

When you have completed Section B go to Section C.

• **FIG 4.2 continued**

THE NOTIFICATION OF COOLING TOWERS AND EVAPORATIVE CONDENSERS REGULATIONS 1992

These regulations require the notification to local authorities of wet cooling towers and evaporative condensers, which are components of many of the air-conditioning systems found in large buildings, and of industrial cooling towers.

Knowledge of the whereabouts of such equipment is of particular help to local authorities in the investigation of outbreaks of legionnaires' disease.

Notification is done by completing a standard form available from the local authority (LA). Any changes to the information contained in the form must be notified within one month of their occurring. The LA must also be informed, as soon as reasonably practicable, when equipment ceases to be operational.

The regulations came into operation on 2 November 1992.

The information required

The information required on a notification form includes:

- the name and address of the premises where the cooling towers and evaporative condensers are situated
- the number of such devices there are on site
- the name, address and telephone number of the person in control of the premises
- brief information on the whereabouts in the premises of the equipment.

THE NOISE AT WORK REGULATIONS 1989

These regulations came into operation on 1 January 1990 and are accompanied by a number of Noise Guides issued by the HSE. They give effect in Great Britain to provisions of the Council Directive 86/188/EEC on the protection of workers from the risks related to exposure to noise.

The regulations bring in the concepts of 'daily personal noise exposure' and 'action levels' (see Figure 4.3).

The relevant definitions regarding these concepts are:

- *daily personal noise exposure*, which means the level of daily personal noise exposure of an employee ascertained in accordance with Part 1 of the Schedule to the regulations, but taking no account of the effect of any personal ear protector used
- *exposed* means exposed to while at work, and *exposure* shall be construed accordingly
- the *first action level* means a daily personal noise exposure of 85 decibels (A)

- the *peak action level* means a daily personal noise exposure of 90 decibels (A).

The assessment of exposure (regulation 4)

Under regulation 4, every employer shall, when any of their employees is likely to be exposed to the first action level or above or to the peak action level or above, ensure that a competent person makes a noise assessment that is adequate for the purposes of:

- identifying which employees are so exposed
- providing them with information about the noise to which these employees may be exposed that will facilitate compliance with the employer's duties under regulations 7, 8, 9 and 11.

This noise assessment shall be reviewed when:

- there is reason to suspect that the assessment is no longer valid
- there has been a significant change in the work to which the assessment relates,

and where, as a result of the review, changes in the assessment are required, these changes shall be made.

Assessment records (regulation 5)

Following any noise assessment, the employer shall ensure that an adequate record (see Figure 4.4) of the assessment and of any review of it that is carried out, is kept until a further noise assessment is made.

Reducing the risk of damage to hearing (regulation 6)

This regulation places a general duty on every employer to reduce the risk of damage to the hearing of their employees due to exposure to noise to the lowest level reasonably practicable.

Reducing exposure to noise (regulation 7)

Every employer shall, when any of their employees are likely to be exposed to the second action level or above or to the peak action level or above, reduce, so far as is reasonably practicable (other than by the provision of ear protectors), the exposure to noise of that employee.

ACTION REQUIRED WHERE Lep.d IS LIKELY TO BE: (see note 1 below)	below 85dB(A)	85dB(A) 1st AL	90dB(A) 2nd AL (2)
EMPLOYER'S DUTIES			
General Duty to Reduce Risk			
Risk of hearing damage to be reduced to the lowest level	●	●	●
Assessment of Noise Exposure			
Noise assessments to be made by a Competent Person (Reg. 4)		●	●
Record of assessments to be kept until a new one is made (Reg. 5)		●	●
Noise Reduction			
Reduce exposure to noise as far as is reasonably practicable by means other than ear protectors (Reg. 7)			●
Provision of Information To Workers			
Provide adequate information, instruction and training about risks to hearing, what employees should do to minimise risk, how they can obtain ear protectors if they are exposed between 85 and 90 dB(A), and their obligations under the Regulations. (Reg. 11)		●	●
Mark ear protection zones and notices, so far as reasonably practicable (Reg. 9)			●
Ear Protectors			
Ensure so far as is practicable that protectors are:–			
– provided to employees who ask for them (Reg.8(1))		●	●
– provided to all exposed (Reg.8(2))			●
– maintained and repaired (Reg.10(1)(b))		●	●
– used by all exposed (Reg.10(1)(a))			●
Ensure so far as is reasonably practicable that all who go into a marked area protection zone use ear protectors. (Reg.9)(1)(b))			(3)
Maintenance and Use of Equipment			
Ensure so far as is practicable that:–			
– all equipment provided under the Regulations is used except for the ear protectors provided between 85 and 90 dB(A). (Reg.10(1)(a))		●	●
ensure all equipment is maintained. (Reg.10(1)(b))		●	●
EMPLOYEES DUTIES			
Use of Equipment			
So far as practicable:–			
use ear protectors (Reg.10(2))		●	●
use any other protective equipment (Reg.10(2))			●
report any defects discovered to his/her employer (Reg. 10(2))		●	●
MACHINE MAKER'S AND SUPPLIERS DUTIES			
Provision of Information			
Provide information on the noise likely to be generated (Reg.12)		●	●

NOTES: *(1) The dB(A) action levels are values of daily personal exposure to noise LEP.d)*
(2) All the actions indicated at 90dB(A) are also required where the peak sound pressure above 200 Pa (140dB re 20 uPa).
(3) Lep.d is the daily personal noise exposure of an employee derived from a formula incorporated in the Schedule to the Regulations.

• **FIG 4.3 The action levels specified in the Noise at Work Regulations 1989**

NOISE EXPOSURE RECORD

Name and address of premises, department etc. ____________________

____

____

____

____

Date of survey ____________ Survey made by ____________

Workplace Number of persons	Noise level (Leq(s) or sound level)	Daily exposure period	LEP.d dB(A)	Peak pressure (where appropriate)	Comments remarks

General comments ______________________________

Instruments used ______________________________

Date of last calibration ____________ Signature ____________

Date ____________

• **FIG 4.4 Example of a noise exposure record**

Ear protection (regulation 8)

While the emphasis under the regulations is on noise control, the regulations do recognize the need for ear protection. Under regulation 8, every employer shall ensure, so far as is practicable, that when any of their employees are likely to be exposed to the first action level or above in circumstances where the daily personal noise exposure of that employee is likely to be less than 90 decibels (A), that employee is provided, at their own request, with suitable and sufficient personal ear protectors.

Furthermore, when any of their employees is likely to be exposed to the second action level or above or to the peak action level or above, every employer shall ensure, so far as is practicable, that this employee is provided with suitable ear protectors which, when properly worn, can reasonably be expected to keep the risk of damage to the employee's hearing to below that arising from exposure to the second action level or, as the cause may be, to the peak action level.

Ear protection zones (regulation 8)

Regulation 8 is concerned with the demarcation and identification of ear protection zones, that is, areas where employees must wear ear protection.

4

Thus, every employer shall, in respect of any premises under their control, ensure, so far as is reasonably practicable, that:

- each ear protection zone is demarcated and identified by means of a sign (specified in paragraph A.3.3 of Appendix A to Part 1 of BS 5878) that includes text indicating:
  - that is an ear protection zone
  - the need for their employees to wear personal ear protectors while in any such zone
- none of their employees enters any such zone unless that employee is wearing personal ear protectors.

In this regulation, *ear protection zone* means any part of the premises referred to above where any employee is likely to be exposed to the second action level or above or to the peak action level or above, and *Part 1 of BS 5378* has the same meaning as in regulation 2(1) of the Safety Signs Regulations 1980.

The maintenance and use of equipment (regulation 10)

Every employer shall ensure, so far as is practicable, that anything provided by them:

- to or for the benefit of an employee complies with their duties under these regulations (other than personal ear protectors provided pursuant to regulation 8) and is fully and properly used
- complies with their duties under these regulations and is maintained in an

efficient state, in efficient working order and in good repair.

Every employee shall, so far as is practicable, use personal ear protectors fully and properly when they are provided by their employer pursuant to regulation 7 and any other protective measures provided by their employer in compliance with the employer's duties under these regulations. If the employee discovers any defect in the protective equipment or other measures, they shall report it to their employer straight away.

The provision of information to employees (regulation II)

Every employer shall, in respect of any premises under their control, provide each of their employees who is likely to be exposed to the first action level or above or to the peak action level or above with adequate information, instruction and training on:

- the risk of damage to that employee's hearing that such exposure may cause
- what steps that employee can take to minimize the risk
- the steps that the employee *must* take in order to obtain the personal ear protectors referred to in regulation 8
- that employee's obligations under these regulations.

The modification of the duties of manufacturers and so on regarding articles for use at work and articles of fairground equipment (regulation 12)

The duties under section 6 of the HSWA on the part of manufacturers, designers and so on were modified to include a duty to ensure that, where any such article is likely to cause any employee to be exposed to the first action level or above or to the peak action level or above, adequate information is provided concerning the noise likely to be generated by this article.

THE PERSONAL PROTECTIVE EQUIPMENT AT WORK REGULATIONS 1992

People at work use a wide range of personal protective equipment (PPE), including safety boots, aprons, wellingtons, eye protectors and ear protectors, among others. Up to 1993, there was very little guidance or, indeed, legislation covering this matter, other than the duty to *provide* such equipment under, for instance, the Protection of Eyes Regulations 1974.

The PPER came into operation on 1 January 1993. As such, they revoke much of the older, more specific pieces of legislation, replacing them with one, complete set of regulations covering all forms of PPE.

The regulations:

- amend certain regulations made under the HASWA that deal with PPE, so that they fully implement the EC Directive in circumstances where they apply
- cover all aspects of the *provision, maintenance and use* of PPE at work and in other circumstances
- revoke and replace almost all pre-HASWA and some post-HASWA legislation that deals with PPE.

It should be appreciated that specific requirements of current regulations dealing with PPE, namely the Control of Lead at Work Regulations 1980, the Ionising Radiations Regulations 1985, the Control of Asbestos at Work Regulations 1987, the Control of Substances Hazardous to Health Regulations (COSHHR) 1988, the Noise at Work Regulations 1989 and the Construction (Head Protection) Regulations 1989, take precedence over the more general requirements of the PPER.

Under the regulations *personal protective equipment* means 'all equipment (including clothing affording protection against the weather) which is intended to be worn or held by a person at work and which protects him against one or more risks to his health and safety, and any addition or accessory designed to meet this objective'; – a very broad definition indeed.

Regulations 4 to 12 do not apply in respect of PPE, which include:

- ordinary working clothes and uniforms that do not specifically protect the health and safety of the wearer
- an offensive weapon (within the meaning of section 1(4) of the Prevention of Crime Act 1953) used as self-defence or deterrent equipment
- portable devices for detecting and signalling risks and nuisances
- PPE used for protection while travelling on a road
- equipment used during the playing of competitive sports.

The provision of PPE (regulation 4)

Under regulation 4, every employer *shall* ensure that *suitable* PPE is provided to their employees who may be exposed to a risk to their health and safety while at work, except where and to the extent that such risk has been adequately controlled by other means that are equally or more effective. Similar provisions to these apply in the case of self-employed people.

PPE shall not be considered suitable unless it:

- is appropriate for the risk or risks involved and the conditions at the place where exposure to the risk may occur
- takes account of ergonomic requirements and the state of health of the person or people who may wear it
- is capable of fitting the wearer correctly, if necessary after adjustments have been made within the range for which it is designed
- *so far as is practicable*, is effective in preventing or adequately controlling the risk or risks involved without increasing the overall risk.

The compatibility of PPE (regulation 5)

Every employer shall ensure that, where the presence of more than one risk to health or safety makes it necessary for their employees to wear or use more than one item of PPE, such equipment is compatible and continues to be effective against the risk or risks in question. Similar provisions as above apply in the case of self-employed people.

Assessing PPE requirements (regulation 6)

As with the other regulations that came into operation at the same time, considerable emphasis is placed on assessment. regulation 6 is quite clear on this matter, as follows:

- before choosing any PPE that they are required to provide, an employer or self-employed person shall ensure that an assessment is made to determine whether the PPE they intend to provide is suitable
- the assessment shall include:
  - an assessment of any risk or risks that have not been avoided by other means
  - the definition of the characteristics that the PPE must have in order to be effective against the risks identified in the assessment above, taking into account any risks that the equipment itself may create
  - a comparison of the characteristics of the PPE available with the characteristics referred to defined above.
- The assessment shall be reviewed if:
  - there is reason to suspect that it is no longer valid
  - there has been a significant change in the matters to which it relates

and where, as a result of any such review, changes in the assessment are required, the relevant employer or self-employed person shall ensure that they are made.

The maintenance and replacement of PPE (regulation 7)

Regulation 7 places a duty on the employer to maintain PPE. The word 'maintenance' here includes the replacement or cleaning of PPE, as appropriate, and keeping it *in an efficient state, in efficient working order and in good repair*. Again, similar provisions to these apply in the case of self-employed people. From a management viewpoint, 'maintenance in an efficient state, in efficient working order and in good repair' implies the need for a formal system for checking all forms of PPE issued to staff on a regular basis and the recording of such checks.

Accommodation for PPE (regulation 8)

Employers and the self-employed must ensure that 'appropriate accommodation', such as a locker, is provided for PPE when it is not being used.

Information, instruction and training (regulation 9)

Employers must provide adequate and appropriate information to enable the employee to know:

- the risk or risks that the PPE will avoid or limit
- the purpose for which and the manner in which the PPE is to be used
- any action to be taken by the employee to ensure that the PPE remains in an efficient state, in efficient working order and in good repair.

The information and instruction provided shall not be considered adequate and appropriate unless it is comprehensible to the people to whom it is given.

The use of PPE (regulation 10)

Under regulation 10, there are the following duties on both employers and employees:

- every employer shall take *all reasonable steps* to ensure that any PPE provided to their employees is properly used
- every employee shall use any PPE in accordance with both any training in the use of the PPE concerned that has been received by them and the instructions regarding the use of it that have been given to them
- every self-employed person shall make full and proper use of any PPE
- every employee and self-employed person shall take all reasonable steps to ensure that the PPE is returned to the accommodation provided for it after use.

Reporting loss or defect (regulation 11)

Employees who have been provided with PPE are required to report to their employer any loss of or obvious defect in it straight away.

HSE guidance notes

These regulations are accompanied by extensive guidance on the selection, use and maintenance of PPE, including a specimen risk survey table for the use of PPE.

THE PRESSURE SYSTEMS AND TRANSPORTABLE GAS CONTAINERS REGULATIONS 1989

These Regulations impose safety requirements with respect to pressure systems and transportable gas containers that are used or intended to be used at work. They further impose safety requirements with a view to preventing certain pressure vessels from becoming pressurized. The Regulations replace the earlier relevant sections of the FA 1961 and are accompanied by an ACOP. The majority of duties are of an absolute nature.

Part I Interpretation (regulation 3)

The regulations incorporate a number of definitions, including the following:

- *pressure system* means:
  - a system comprising one or more pressure vessels of rigid construction, and associated pipework and protective devices
  - the pipework with its protective devices to which a transportable gas container is, or is intended to be connected
  - a pipeline and its devices
- *transportable gas container* (TGC) means a container, including any permanent fitting of such a container, that is used, or is intended to be used, to contain a relevant fluid and is:
  - designed to be transportable for the purpose of refilling and has an internal volume of at least 0.5 litres and not greater than 3000 litres
  - a non-refillable container having an internal volume of at least 1.4 litres and not greater than 5 litres
  - for the purposes of regulation 17(3) only, a non-refillable container
- *competent person* means a competent individual (other than an employee) or a competent body, corporate or unincorporate, and, accordingly, any reference in the regulations to a competent person performing a function includes a reference to their performing it through their employees
- *danger* in relation to a pressure system means reasonably foreseeable danger to people from a system failure, but (except in the case of steam) it does not mean danger from the hazardous characteristics of the relevant fluid other than from its pressure.
- *design specification* means a specification for the design of one type of TGC
- *design standard* means a standard for the design of more than one type of TGC
- *examination* means a careful and critical scrutiny of a pressure system, part of a pressure system or TGC, in or out of service as appropriate, to assess:
  - its actual condition

  - whether, for the period up to the next examination, it will not cause danger when properly used if normal maintenance is carried out, and for this purpose *normal maintenance* means such maintenance as is reasonable to expect the user (in the case of an installed system) or owner (in the case of a mobile system or TGC) to ensure is carried out independently of any advice from the competent person making the examination
- *framework directive* means the Council Directive 76/767/EEC concerning the approximation of the laws of the member states relating to common provisions for pressure vessels and methods of inspecting them
- *installed system* means a pressure system other than a mobile system
- *mobile system* means a pressure system that can be readily moved between and used in different locations, but it does not include a steam locomotive
- *owner* in relation to a pressure system or TGC means the employer or self-employed person who owns the pressure system or TGC or, if they do not have a place of business in Great Britain, their agent in Great Britain or, if there is no such agent, the user
- *pipeline* means a pipe or system of pipes used for the conveyance of relevant fluid across the boundaries of premises, together with any apparatus for inducing or facilitating the flow of relevant fluid through, or through a part of, the pipe or system, and any valves, valve chambers, pumps, compressors or similar works that are annexed to, or incorporated in the course of, the pipe or system

- *pipework* means a pipe or system of pipes together with associated valves, pumps, compressors and other pressure-containing components and includes a hose or bellows, but does not include a pipeline or any protective device
- *relevant fluid* means:
  - steam
  - any fluid or mixture of fluids that is at a pressure greater than 0.5 bar above atmospheric pressure, and that is:
    (i) a gas
    (ii) a liquid that would have a vapour pressure greater than 0.5 bar above atmospheric pressure when in equilibrium with its vapour at either the actual temperature of the liquid or 17.5°C
  - a gas dissolves under pressure in a solvent contained in a porous substance at ambient temperature and that could be released from the solvent without the application of heat
- *safe operating limits* means the operating limits (incorporating a suitable margin of safety) beyond which failure is liable to occur
- *scheme of examination* means the written scheme referred to in regulation 8
- *system failure* means the unintentional release of stored energy (other than from a pressure relief system) from a pressure system or TGC.

PART II OF THE REGULATIONS APPLIES GENERALLY, AS FOLLOWS:

Design, construction, repair and modification (regulation 4)

This regulation imposes safety requirements on any person who designs, manufactures, imports or supplies any pressure system or TGC. In particular, they must ensure that:

- they are properly designed and properly constructed from suitable material
- they are so designed and constructed that all necessary examinations for preventing danger can be carried out
- where means of access to the interior of the system is incorporated, such access can be gained without danger
- they are provided with such protection devices as may be necessary for preventing danger, and any such device designed to release contents shall do so safely, so far as is practicable.

The employer of a person who modifies or repairs a pressure system or TGC at work shall ensure that nothing about the way this work is done gives rise to danger or otherwise impairs the operation of any protective device or inspection facility.

Part III of the Regulations deals specifically with pressure systems, as follows:

The provision of information and marking (regulation 5)

Regulation 5 requires designers and suppliers of pressure systems to provide sufficient information concerning the design, construction, examination, operation and maintenance of them as may reasonably foreseeably be needed to enable the provisions of the regulations to be complied with. Similar requirements apply in the case of employers of those who modify or repair such systems.

Manufacturers must mark pressure systems with specified information (see Schedule 4 of the regulations), and no person shall remove such a mark from or falsify any mark on a pressure system, or on a plate attached to it, relating to its design, construction, test or operation.

Installation (regulation 6)

The employer of someone who installs a pressure system at work shall ensure that nothing about the way in which it is installed gives rise to danger or otherwise impairs the operation of any protective device or inspection facility.

Safe operating limits (regulation 7)

This regulation places specific duties on the users of installed systems and owners of mobile systems. They must not operate the system or allow it to be operated unless they have established the safe operating limits of the system.

Furthermore, the owner of a mobile system shall, if they are not also the user of it:

- supply the user with a written statement specifying the safe operating limits of the system
- ensure that the system is legibly and durably marked with the safe operating limits and that the mark is clearly visible.

Written scheme of examination (regulation 8)

The user of an installed system and owner of a mobile system shall not operate the system or allow it to be operated unless they have a *written scheme for the periodic examination*, by a competent person, of the following parts of the system, namely:

- all protective devices
- every pressure vessel and every pipeline in which (in either case) a defect may give rise to danger
- those parts of the pipework in which a defect may give rise to danger

and these parts of the system shall be identified in the scheme.

The user or owner shall ensure that:

- the scheme has been drawn up, or certified as being suitable, by a competent person
- the content of the scheme is reviewed at appropriate intervals by a competent person so that it can be determined whether or not it is suitable in the current conditions of use of the system
- the content of the scheme is modified in accordance with any recommendations made by the competent person arising from the review.

No person shall certify or draw up a scheme of examination as above unless the scheme is suitable and:

- specifies the nature and frequency of examination
- specifies any measures necessary to prepare the pressure system for safe examination other than those it would be reasonable to expect the user or owner respectively to take without specialist advice
- where appropriate, provides for an examination to be carried out *before* the pressure system is used for the first time.

The references made above to the suitability of the scheme are references to its suitability for the purpose of preventing danger from those parts of the pressure system included in the scheme.

Comment

Regulation 8 is the most important requirements of these regulations, and careful consideration must be given to the information provided in the ACOP regarding this area.

Making examinations in accordance with the written scheme (regulation 9)

This regulation goes into considerable depth regarding the procedures to be followed in the examination of pressure systems. Here are the main points:

- the user of an installed system and owner of a mobile system shall:
  - ensure that those parts of the system included in the scheme are examined by a competent person within the intervals specified and, where appropriate, before the system is used for the first time
  - before each examination, take all appropriate safety measures to prepare the system for examination, including any such measures as are specified in the scheme of examination
- where a competent person undertakes an examination for the purposes of the first point above, they shall carry out this examination properly and in accordance with the scheme of examination
- where a competent person undertakes an examination for the purposes of the first point above, they shall (subject to the next point and regulation 13(4)) make a *written report of examination*, sign or otherwise authenticate it, date it and send it to the user or owner respectively; and this report shall be sent as soon as is practicable after completing the examination, but, in any event, to arrive:
  - within 28 days of the completion of the examination
  - before the date specified in the report for any repairs or modifications to be made by,

  whichever is the sooner
- where the competent person is the user or owner respectively, the requirement to send the report to the user or owner shall not apply, but they shall make the report by the time it would have been required to have been sent to them if they had not been the competent person
- the written report of examination specified above shall:
  - state which parts of the pressure system have been examined, the condition of these parts and the results of the examination
  - specify any repairs or modifications to, or changes in the established safe operating limits of, the parts examined that, in the opinion of the competent person, are necessary to prevent danger or to ensure the continued effective working of the protective devices, and specify the date by which any such repairs or modifications must be completed or any such changes to the safe operating limits must be made
  - specify the date within the limits set by the scheme of examination after

which the pressure system may not be operated without a further examination under the scheme of examination
- state whether, in the opinion of the competent person, the scheme of examination is suitable (for the purposes of preventing danger from those parts of the pressure system included in it) or should be modified, and if the latter, state the reason for this view
- the user or owner, respectively, of a system that has been examined under this regulation shall ensure that the system is not operated, and no person shall supply such a mobile system for operation, after (in each case):
- the date specified for repairs or modifications to made by in the report, unless the repairs or modifications specified have been completed, and the changes in the safe operating limits so specified have been made
- the date specified in the report after which it cannot be operated without a further examination (or if that date has been postponed as given in the next point, the postponed date) unless a further examination has been carried out under the scheme of examination

- the date specified in the report after which it cannot be operated without a further examination may be postponed to a later date by agreement in writing between the competent person who made the report and the user or owner respectively if:
  - any such postponement does not give rise to danger
  - only one such postponement is made for any one examination
  - such postponement is notified by the user or owner in writing to the enforcing authority for the premises in which the pressure system is situated, before the date specified in the report
- where the competent person is the user or owner, respectively, the reference to an agreement in writing shall not apply, but there shall be included in the notification just mentioned above a declaration that the postponement will not give rise to danger
- The owner of a mobile system shall ensure that the date specified in the report after which the pressure system may not be operated without a further examination is legibly and durably marked on the mobile system and that the mark is clearly visible.

4

The action to take in case of imminent danger (regulation 10)

Where a competent person is of the opinion that the pressure system or part of the pressure system will give rise to imminent danger unless certain repairs or modifications have been carried out or unless suitable changes to the operating conditions have been made, then, without prejudice to the requirements of regulation 9, they shall make a written report to that effect straight away, identifying the system and specifying the repairs, modifications or changes concerned and give it:

- in the case of an installed system, to the user
- in the case of a mobile system, to the owner and to the user, if any,

and the competent person shall, within 14 days of the completion of the examination, send a written report containing the same particulars to the enforcing authority for the premises at which the pressure system is situated.

Where a report is given in accordance with the above, the user or owner, respectively, shall ensure that the system is not operated until the repairs, modifications or changes have been carried out or made.

Operation (regulation 11)

The user or owner, respectively, shall provide for anyone operating the system adequate and suitable instructions for:

- the safe operation of the system
- the action to be taken in the event of an emergency.

The user of a pressure system shall ensure that it is not operated except in accordance with the instructions provided in respect of that system.

Maintenance (regulation 12)

This regulation places a duty on users and owners, respectively, to ensure that systems are properly maintained and in good repair, so as to prevent danger.

The keeping of records and so on (regulation 13)

This regulation details the record-keeping requirements for installed and mobile systems. Such records must include:

- the last report by the competent person
- previous reports, if they contain information that will materially assist in assessing whether or not:
  - the system is safe to operate
  - any repairs or modifications to the system can be carried out safely
- any documents provided pursuant to regulation 5 that relate to those parts of the pressure system included in the written scheme of examination
- any agreement made pursuant to regulation 9(7) and, in a case to which regulation 9(8) applies, a copy of the notification referred to in regulation 9(7)(c), until a further examination has been carried out since that agreement or notification under the scheme of examination.

Part IV of the regulations covers the precautions to be taken to prevent the pressurization of certain vessels. Regulation 14 specifies such vessels as being those that:

- are constructed with a permanent outlet to the atmosphere or to a space where the pressure does not exceed atmospheric pressure
- could become a pressure vessel if that outlet were obstructed.

The precautions to be taken to prevent pressurization (regulation 15)

Under regulation 15, the user of a vessel to which Part IV applies shall ensure that the outlet referred to in regulation 14(a) is kept open and free from obstruction at all times when the vessel is in use.

Part V of the regulations covers general and specific provisions for TGCs, as follows:

Design standards, approval and certification (regulation 16)

No one shall:

- supply for the first time
- import
- manufacture and use

a TGC unless the conditions specified below have been met.

The conditions are as follows:

- that the container has been verified (either by certificate in writing or by means of stamping the container) as conforming to a design standard or design specification approved by the HSE:
  - by a person or body, corporate or unincorporate, approved by the HSE for this purpose
  - in accordance with a quality assurance scheme approved by the HSE
- the container is an EC-type cylinder, that is:
  - there is an EC Verification Certificate in force for it issued by an inspection body that, under the law of any member state, is authorized to grant such a certificate for the purposes of the framework Directive and the separate Directive relating to that type of cylinder, or, in the case of a cylinder not subject to EC verification under any of the separate Directives, it conforms to the requirements of the framework Directive and the separate Directive relating to that type of cylinder
  - it bears all the marks and inscriptions required by the framework Directive and the separate Directive relating to that type of cylinder.

Any approval under this regulation shall be by a certificate in writing, may be made subject to conditions and may be revoked by a certificate in writing at any time

The filling of containers (regulation 17)

The employer of a person who is to fill a TGC with a relevant fluid at work shall ensure that, before it is filled, this person:

- checks from the marks on the cylinder that:
  - it appears to have undergone proper examination at appropriate intervals by a competent person (unless the manufacturer's mark reveals that such an examination is not yet due)
  - it is suitable for containing that fluid
- makes all other appropriate safety checks.

The employer of a person who fills a TGC with a relevant fluid at work shall ensure that this person:

- checks that, after filling, it is within its safe operating limits
- checks that it is not overfilled
- removes any excess fluid in a safe manner in the event of overfilling.

An employer shall ensure that no person employed by them refills at work a non-refillable container with a relevant fluid.

The examination of containers (regulation 18)

The owner of a TGC shall, for the purpose of determining whether or not it is safe, ensure that the container is examined at appropriate intervals by a competent person.

Where a competent person undertakes such an examination, they shall carry out that examination properly and if, on completing the examination, they are satisfied that the container is safe, they shall ensure that there is fixed to the container a mark showing the date of the examination.

No person other than the competent person, or person authorized by them, shall fix to a TGC the above mark or a mark liable to be confused with it.

The modification of containers (regulation 19)

Subject to the next paragraph:

- an employer shall ensure that no one employed by them modifies at work the body of a TGC:
  - of seamless construction
  - that has contained acetylene

- an employer shall ensure that no one person employed by them modifies at work the body of another type of TGC if this modification would put the TGC outside the scope of the design standard or design specification to which it was originally constructed
- a person shall not supply any modified TGC for use unless, following such work, a person or body approved by the HSE has marked or certified it as being fit for use or, in the case of an EC-type cylinder, an inspection body has so marked or certified it.

The information above shall not apply to the remaking of a thread if this is done in accordance with a standard approved by the HSE.

Repair work (regulation 20)

An employer shall ensure that no one employed by them carries out at work any major repair on the body of a TGC:

- of seamless construction
- that has contained acetylene.

An employer shall ensure that no one employed by them carries out at work any major repair on the body of any other type of TGC unless they are competent to do so.

No one shall supply a TGC that has undergone a major repair unless, following such work, a person or body approved by the HSE has marked or certified it as being fit for use or, in the case of an EC-type cylinder, an inspection body has so marked or certified it.

In this regulation, *major repair* means any repair involving hot work or welding on the body of the TGC but, except in the case of a TGC that has contained acetylene, it does not mean heat treatment applied for the purpose of restoring the metallurgical properties of the container.

Rerating (regulation 21)

This regulation applies to the rerating of a TGC, that is, the reassessment of its capability to contain compressed gas safely with a view to improving its capacity by means of an increase in the charging pressure (or, in the case of liquefied gas, the filling ratio) to that which was originally assessed and marked on the container at the time of manufacture.

An employer shall ensure that no one employed by them rerates a TGC at work unless they are competent to do so and does it in accordance with suitable written procedures drawn up by the owner of the container.

No one shall supply a TGC that has been rerated unless, following the rerating, a person or body approved by the HSE has certified it as being safe for use.

In this regulation *filling ratio* means the ratio of the volume of liquefied gas in the container to the total volume of the container.

Records (regulation 22)

The manufacturer or their agent or the importer of a TGC:

- made to an approved design specification, shall keep a copy of this specification, together with any certificate of conformity issued in accordance with regulation 16(2)(a)
- made to an approved design standard, shall keep a copy of any certificate of conformity issued in accordance with regulation 16(2)(a)
- that is an EC-type cylinder, shall keep the EC Verification Certificate referred to in regulation 16(2)(b)(i) where one has been issued.

The owner of a hired-out TGC:

- made to an approved design specification, shall keep a copy of this specification, together with a copy of any certificate of conformity issued in accordance with regulation 16(2)(a)
- made to an approved design standard, shall keep a copy of any certificate of conformity issued in accordance with regulations 16(2)(a)
- that is an EC-type cylinder, shall keep a copy of the EC Verification Certificate referred to in regulation 16(2)(b)(i) where one has been issued
- that:
  - is a refillable container
  - is used solely for containing liquefied petroleum gas
  - has a water capacity up to and including 6.5 litres,

shall keep a copy of the design specification for the container.

The owner of a TGC for acetylene shall keep records of the tare weight of the container, including the porous substance and acetone or other solvent, the nature of the solvent and the maximum pressure allowed in the container.

Miscellaneous provisions of the Regulations are covered in Part VI, as follows:

Defence (regulation 23)

In any proceedings for an offence for a contravention of the provisions of these regulations, it shall, subject to the next two paragraphs, be a defence for the person charged to prove:

- that the offence committed was due to *the act or default of another person* who was not one of their employees (now called 'the other person')
- that they took *all reasonable precautions* and exercised *all due diligence* to avoid committing the offence.

The person charged shall not, without leave of the court, be entitled to rely on the above defence unless, within a period ending seven clear days before the hearing, they have served on the prosecutor a notice in writing giving such information about the other person as was then in their possession.

For the purpose of enabling the other person to be charged with and convicted of the offence by virtue of section 36 of the HSWA, a person who establishes a defence under this regulation shall, nevertheless, be treated, for the purposes of this section, as having committed the offence.

Schedule 4: The marking of pressure vessels

The information referred to in regulation 5(4) is as follows:

- the manufacturer's name
- the serial number that identifies the vessel
- the date of manufacture of the vessel
- the standard to which the vessel was built
- the maximum design pressure of the vessel
- the maximum design pressure of the vessel where it is other than atmospheric
- the design temperature.

THE PROVISION AND USE OF WORK EQUIPMENT REGULATIONS 1992

These regulations implement the Council Directive of 30 November 1989 'concerning the minimum safety and health requirements for the use of work equipment by workers at work', generally known as the 'Machinery Safety' Directive 89/655/EEC. Regulations 1 to 10 came into force on 1 January 1993, but regulations 11 to 24, 27 and Schedule 2 do not come into force until 1 January 1997 for work equipment first provided before 1 January 1993 ('existing equipment').

They revoke much of the old legislation, including 17 codes of regulations, 7 sections of the Factories Act 1961, a section of the Offices, Shops and Railway Premises Act 1963 and 2 sections of the Mines and Quarries Act 1954.

These comprehensive regulations are intended:

- to implement the Machinery Safety Directive
- to simplify and clarify existing laws on the provision and use of work equipment by reforming older legislation
- to form a coherent, single set of key health and safety requirements concerning the provision and use of work equipment.

The regulations are supported by Guidance Notes prepared by the HSE and HSC that contain practical advice on implementing the regulations.

Generally, the regulations are framed in a simple and straightforward way. They cover the more general requirements relating to the selection, suitability and maintenance of work equipment, together with procedures for dealing with specific risks and the giving of information, instruction and training. The more specific risks associated with dangerous parts, machinery failure, temperature and operating conditions, and the procedures and precautions necessary to avert these risks are also dealt with.

The majority of these requirements are of an absolute nature, implying that no form of defence is available to an employer, self-employed person or manufacturer, designer, supplier, importer or installer of work equipment when charged with an offence under the regulations.

Interpretation (regulation 2)

The following two terms are important:

- the term *work equipment* includes any machinery, appliance, apparatus or tool and any assembly of components that, in order to achieve a common end, are arranged and controlled so that they function as a whole
- the term *use* in relation to work equipment means any activity involving work equipment, including starting, stopping, programming, setting, transporting, repairing, modifying, maintaining, servicing and cleaning, and related expressions shall be construed accordingly.

The application of the requirements specified under these regulations (regulation 4)

The requirements imposed by these regulations on an employer shall apply in respect of work equipment provided for or used by any of their employees at work.

The requirements imposed by these regulations on an employer shall also apply to:

- a self-employed person regarding work equipment they use at work
- any one who has control, to any extent, of non-domestic premises made available to people as a place of work, regarding work equipment used in these premises by these people and to the extent of their control
- any one to whom the provisions of the Factories Act 1961 apply by virtue of section 17(5) of that Act as if they were the occupier of a factory, regarding work equipment used in the premises deemed to be a factory by that section.

Any reference in the second point above to a person having control of any premises or matter is a reference to the person having this control in connection with their carrying out the trade, business or other undertaking (whether for profit or not).

The suitability of work equipment (regulation 5)

Every employer shall ensure that work equipment is so constructed or adapted as to be suitable for the purpose for which it is used or provided.

In selecting work equipment, every employer shall bear in mind the working conditions and risks to the health and safety of workers that exist in the premises or undertaking in which the work equipment is to be used, as well as any additional risk posed using the equipment is to be used, as well as any additional risk posed using the equipment.

Every employer shall ensure that work equipment is used only for those operations and under those conditions for which it is suitable.

In this regulation 'suitable' means suitable in any respect which it is reasonably foreseeable will affect the health or safety of any person.

Maintenance (regulation 6)

Every employer shall ensure that work equipment is *maintained in an efficient state, in efficient working order and in good repair.*

Every employer shall ensure that where any machinery has a maintenance log, the log is kept up to date.

Specific risks (regulation 7)

Where the use of work equipment is likely to involve a specific risk to health or safety, every employer shall ensure that:

- the use of this equipment is restricted to those given the task of using it
- repairs, modifications, maintenance or servicing of the work equipment is restricted to those who have been specifically designated to do this (whether or not they are also authorized to perform other operations).

The employer shall ensure that those designated to do the repairs and so on mentioned above have received adequate training in the operations they will need to carry out to fulfil this role

Information and instructions (regulation 8)

Every employer shall ensure that all those who use work equipment have available to them adequate health and safety information and, where appropriate, written instructions pertaining to the use of the equipment.

Every employer shall ensure that any of their employees who supervise or manage the use of work equipment have available to them similar adequate information.

Without prejudice to the generality of first two paragraphs above, the information and instructions required by either of these paragraphs shall include information and, where appropriate, written instructions on:

- the conditions in which and the methods by which the work equipment may be used

- foreseeable abnormal situations and the action to be taken if such a situation were to occur
- any conclusions to be drawn from experience in using the work equipment.

Information and instruction required by this regulation shall be readily comprehensible to those concerned.

Training (regulation 9)

Every employer shall ensure that all those who use work equipment have received adequate training for the purposes of health and safety, including training in the methods that may be adopted when using the work equipment, any risks that such use may entail and the precautions to be taken.

Every employer shall ensure that any of their employees who supervise or manage the use of work equipment have received similar adequate training.

Conformity with community requirements (regulation 10)

Every employer shall ensure that any item of work equipment provided for use in the premises or undertaking of the employer complies with any enactment (whether in an Act or instrument) that implements in Great Britain any of the relevant EC Directives listed in Schedule 1 that is applicable to that item of work equipment.

Where it is shown that an item of work equipment complies with an enactment (whether an Act or instrument) to which it is subject by virtue of the paragraph above, the requirements of regulations 11–24 shall apply regarding this item of work equipment, but only to the extent that the relevant Directive implemented by the enactment is not applicable to the item of work equipment.

Dangerous parts of machinery (regulation 11)

Every employer shall ensure that the measures listed below are taken in order to:

- prevent access to any dangerous part of machinery to any rotating stock-bar
- stop the movement of any dangerous part of machinery or rotating stock-bar before any part of a person enters a danger zone.

These measures shall consist of the provision of:

- fixed guards enclosing every dangerous part or rotating stock-bar where and to the extent that it is practicable to do so, but where or to the extent that it is not, then
- other guards or protection devices where and to the extent that it is prac-

ticable to do so, but where or to the extent that it is not, then

- jigs, holders, push-sticks or similar protection appliances used in conjunction with the machinery where and to the extent that it is practicable to do so, but where or to the extent that it is not, then
- information, instruction, training and supervision.

All guards and protection devices provided in relation to the first two points in the list above shall:

- be suitable for the purpose for which they are provided
- be of good construction, sound material and adequate strength
- be maintained in an efficient state, in efficient working order and in good repair
- not give rise to any increased risk to health or safety
- not be easily bypassed or disabled
- be situated at sufficient distance from the danger zone
- not unduly restrict the view of the operating cycle of the machinery, where such a view is necessary
- be so constructed or adapted that they allow operations necessary to fit or replace parts and for maintenance work, but restrict this access so that it is allowed only to the area where the work is to be carried out and, if possible, without having to dismantle the guard or protection device.

All jigs, holders, push-sticks or similar protection appliances provided shall comply with the requirements as to suitability, construction and so on listed above.

In this regulation:

- *danger zone* – means any zone in or around machinery in which a person is exposed to a risk to health or safety from contact with a dangerous part of machinery or a rotating stock-bar
- *stock bar* – means any part of a stock bar that projects beyond the headstock of a lathe.

Protection against specified hazards (regulation 12)

Every employer shall take measures to ensure that the exposure of a person using work equipment to any risk to their health or safety from any of the hazards listed below is either prevented or, where this is not reasonably practicable, adequately controlled.

The measures required by the above paragraph shall:

- be measures other than the provision of the PPE or of information, instruction, training and supervision, so far as is reasonably practicable
- include, where appropriate, measures to minimize the effects of the hazard as well as to reduce the likelihood of the hazard occurring.

The hazards referred to above are:

- any article or substance falling or being ejected from work equipment
- rupture or disintegration of parts of work equipment

- working equipment catching fire or overheating
- the unintended or premature discharge of any article or of any gas, dust liquid, vapour or other substance that, in each case, is produced, used or stored in the work equipment
- the unintended or premature explosion of the work equipment or any article or substance produced, used or stored in it.

For the purposes of this regulation, *adequate* means adequate only in relation to the nature of the hazard and the nature and degree of exposure to the risk, and *adequately* shall be construed accordingly.

High or very low temperatures (regulation 13)

Every employer shall ensure that work equipment, parts of work equipment and any article or substance produced, used or stored in work equipment that, in each case, is at a high or very low temperature shall have protection, where appropriate, so as to prevent burns, scalds or searing.

Control systems and controls (regulations 14–17)

These regulations deal with general and specific safety requirements covering thus:

- regulation 14: Controls for starting or making a significant change in operating conditions
- regulation 15: Stop controls
- regulation 16: Emergency stop controls
- regulation 17: Controls.

Control systems (regulation 18)

Every employer shall ensure, so far as is reasonably practicable, that all the control systems of work equipment are safe.

Without prejudice to the generality of this statement, a control system shall not be safe unless:

- its operation does not create an increased risk to health or safety
- it ensures, so far as is reasonably practicable, that any fault in or damage to any part of the control system or the loss of supply of any source of energy used by the work equipment cannot result in additional or increased risk to health or safety
- it does not impede the operation of any control required by regulations 15 or 16

Isolation from sources of energy (regulation 19)

Every employer shall ensure that, where appropriate, work equipment is provided with suitable means to isolate it from all its sources of energy.

Without prejudice to the generality of the first paragraph, the means mentioned in it shall not be suitable unless they are clearly identifiable and readily accessible.

Every employer shall take appropriate measures to ensure that the reconnection of any energy source to work equipment does not expose any person using the work equipment to any risk to their health or safety.

Stability (regulation 20)

Every employer shall ensure that work equipment, or any part of work equipment, is stabilized by clamping or otherwise, where necessary, for the purposes of health or safety.

Lighting (regulation 21)

Every employer shall ensure that suitable and sufficient lighting, which takes account of the operations to be carried out, is provided at any place where a person uses work equipment.

Maintenance operations (regulation 22)

Every employer shall take appropriate measures to ensure that work equipment is so constructed or adapted that, so far as is reasonably practicable, maintenance operations that involve a risk to health or safety can be carried out while the work equipment is shut down or, in other cases:

- without exposing the person carrying them out to a risk to their health or safety
- appropriate measures can be taken for the protection of any person carrying out maintenance operations that involve a risk to their health or safety.

Markings (regulation 23)

Every employer shall ensure that work equipment is marked in a clearly visible manner with any marketing appropriate for reasons of health and safety.

Warnings (regulation 24)

Every employer shall ensure that work equipment incorporates any warnings or warning devices that are appropriate for reasons of health and safety.

Without prejudice to the generality of this statement, warnings given by means of warning devices on work equipment shall not be appropriate unless they are unambiguous, easily perceived and easily understood.

Comments

These regulations incorporate important new provisions of both a general and specific nature. It must be appreciated that the term 'work equipment' covers just about every form of machine, appliance and hand tool used by people at work. The implications for employers are:

- the assessment of risks at the selection stage of new work equipment
- ongoing safety assessments of existing work equipment
- the implementation of formally documented, planned maintenance systems
- the designation of certain trained people for high-risk activities
- the provision of information, instruction and training for staff using any form of work equipment
- the development and implementation of management procedures aimed at ensuring the safe use of work equipment in all work situations.

Second-hand, hired and leased work equipment

Second-hand equipment

In situations where existing work equipment is sold by one company to another and brought into use by the second company, it becomes 'new equipment' and must meet the requirements for such equipment, *even though* it is second-hand. This means that the purchasing company will need to ascertain that the equipment meets the specific hardware provisions of regulations 11–24 before putting it into use.

Hired and leased equipment

Such equipment is treated in the same way as scond-hand equipment, namely that it is classed as 'new equipment' at the hire/lease stage. On this basis, organizations hiring or leasing an item of work equipment will need to check that it meets the requirements of regulations 11–24 before putting it into use.

THE REPORTING OF INJURIES, DISEASES AND DANGEROUS OCCURRENCES REGULATIONS 1985

Interpretation

In these regulations, the following definitions are significant:

- *specified major injury or condition* means:
  - fracture of the skull, spine or pelvis
  - fracture of any bones:
    (i) in the arm or wrist, but not a bone in the hand
    (ii) in the leg or ankle, but not a bone in the foot
  - amputation of:
    (i) a hand or foot

(ii) a finger, thumb or toe, or any part thereof, if the joint or bone is completely severed
- the loss of sight of an eye, a penetrating injury to the eye or a chemical or hot metal burn to the eye
- either injury (including burns) requiring immediate medical treatment or involving loss of consciousness, resulting, in either case, from an electric shock from any electrical circuit or equipment, whether or not due to direct contact
- loss of consciousness resulting from lack of oxygen
- decompression sickness (unless suffered during an operation to which the Diving Operations at Work Regulations 1981 apply) requiring immediate medical treatment
- either acute illness requiring medical treatment or involving loss of consciousness, resulting, in either case, from absorption of any substance by inhalation, ingestion or through the skin
- acute illness requiring medical treatment where there is reason to believe this resulted from exposure to a pathogen or infected material
- any other injury that results in the person injured being admitted immediately into hospital for more than 24 hours.

- *a reportable disease* is one specified in column 1 of Schedule 2 of the Regulations and involving one of the activities specified in the corresponding entry in column 2 of the Schedule, for example:

Column 1 **Disease**	*Column 2* **Work activity**
2 Chrome ulceration of: • the nose or throat • the skin of the hands or forearm	Work involving exposure to chromic acid or to any other chromium compound
10 Byssinosis	Work in any room where any process up to and including the weaving process is performed in a factory in which the spinning or manipulation of raw or waste cotton or of flax, or the weaving of cotton or flax, is carried out
16 Hepatitis	Work involving exposure to human blood products or body secretions or excretions

and the responsible person must send a report to the enforcing authority on the approved form (Form 2508A) straight away wherever a person suffers from one of these diseases

- a *dangerous occurrence* is one that arises out of or in connection with work and is of a class specified in Part 1 of Schedule 1 of the regulations, for example:
  - explosion, collapse or bursting of any pressure vessel, including a boiler or boiler tube, in which the internal pressure was above or below atmospheric pressure, that might have caused the death of, or any of the injuries or conditions covered by regulation 3(2) to, anyone or that resulted in stoppage of the plant involved for more than 24 hours
  - a collapse or partial collapse of any scaffold that is more than 5 metres high resulting in a substantial part of the scaffold falling or overturning, and, where the scaffold is slung or suspended, a collapse or partial collapse of the suspension arrangements (including any outrigger) that causes a working platform or cradle to fall more than 5 metres
  - any ignition or explosion of explosives, where the ignition or explosion was not intentional
- *responsible person*, in the case of a reportable accident or disease, means:
  - involving an employee at work, the employer
  - involving someone undergoing training for employment, the person who is the immediate provider of this training

  or any other case, the person who, for the time being, has control of the premises in connection with the running of their trade, business or other undertaking (whether for profit or not) at which, or in connection with the work at which, the accident, disease or dangerous occurrence happened.
- *work* means work as an employee, as a self-employed person or as someone undergoing training for employment (whether or not under any scheme administered by the Manpower Services Commission).

The duty to notify and report fatal and major injuries and dangerous occurrences (regulation 3)

Where any person, as a result of an accident arising from or in connection with work, dies or suffers any of the specific major injuries or conditions, or where there is a dangerous occurrence, the responsible person shall:

- notify the enforcing authority straight away by the quickest practicable means
- within seven days, send a report about what has happened to the enforcing authority on a form approved for this purpose (Form 2508, see Figure 4.5).

Where a person at work is incapacitated for work of a kind that they might reasonably be expected to do, either under their contract of employment or, if there is no such contract, in the normal course of their work, for more than three consecutive days (excluding the day of the accident, but including any days that would not have been working days) because of an injury (other than a specified major injury) resulting from an accident at work, the responsible person shall, within seven days of the accident, send a report about this to the enforcing authority on the form approved for this purpose (Form 2508).

The duty to report the death of an employee (regulation 4)

Where an employee, as a result of an accident at work, has suffered a specified major injury or condition that is the cause of their death within one year of the date of the accident, the employer shall inform the enforcing authority in writing of this as soon as it comes to their knowledge, whether or not the accident had been reported previously.

The duty to report a case of disease (regulation 5)

Where a person at work suffers from a reportable disease, the responsible person shall send a report about it to the enforcing authority straight away on the form approved for this purpose (Form 2508A, see Figure 4.6). This requirement applies only if:

- in the case of an employee or a person undergoing training, the responsible person has received a written statement prepared by a registered medical practitioner diagnosing the disease as one of the reportable diseases
- in the case of a self-employed person, that person has been informed by a registered medical practitioner that they are suffering from the disease so specified.

The duty to keep records (regulation 7)

The responsible person shall keep a record of:

- any event that is required to be reported under regulation 3, that is a specified major injury or condition or dangerous occurrence
- any case of disease required to be reported under regulation 3.

The records shall be kept at the place where the work to which they relate is carried out or, if this is not reasonably practicable at the usual place of business of the responsible person. An entry in either of these records shall be kept for at least three years from the date on which it was made.

The responsible person shall send to the enforcing authority such extracts from the records required to be kept as the enforcing authority may, from time to time, require.

Health and Safety Executive
Health and Safety at Work etc Act 1974
Reporting of Injuries, Diseases and Dangerous Occurrences Regulations 1985

Spaces below are for office use only

Report of an injury or dangerous occurrence

- Full notes to help you complete this form are attached.
- This form is to be used to make a report to the enforcing authority under the requirements of Regulations 3 or 6.
- Completing and signing this form does not constitute an admission of liability of any kind, either by the person making the report or any other person.
- If more than one person was injured as a result of an accident, please complete a separate form for each person.

A Subject of report *(tick appropriate box or boxes) – see note 2*

Fatality ☐ 1 | Specified major injury or condition ☐ 2 | "Over three day" injury ☐ 3 | Dangerous occurrence ☐ 4 | Flammable gas incident (fatality or major injury or condition) ☐ 5 | Dangerous gas fitting ☐ 6

B Person or organisation making report (ie person obliged to report under the Regulations) – *see note 3*

Name and address –

Post code –

Name and telephone no. of person to contact –

Nature of trade, business or undertaking –

If in construction industry, state the total number of your employees –

and indicate the role of your company on site (*tick box*) –

Main site contractor ☐ 7 | Sub contractor ☐ 8 | Other ☐ 9

If in farming, are you reporting an injury to a member of your family? (*tick box*) ☐ Yes ☐ No

C Date, time and place of accident, dangerous occurrence or flammable gas incident – *see note 4*

Date ☐☐ 19☐ (*day month year*) Time –

Give the name and address if different from above –

Where on the premises or site –
and
Normal activity carried on there

ENV

Complete the following sections D, E, F & H if you have ticked boxes, 1, 2, 3 or 5 in Section A. Otherwise go straight to Sections G and H.

D The injured person – *see note 5*

Full name and address –

Age ☐ Sex ☐ (M or F)

Status (*tick box*) – Employee ☐ 10 | Self employed ☐ 11 | Trainee (YTS) ☐ 12 | Trainee (other) ☐ 13 | Any other person ☐ 14

Trade, occupation or job title –

Nature of injury or condition and the part of the body affected –

F2508 (rev 1/86)

continued overleaf

• FIG 4.5

E Kind of accident - *see note 6*

Indicate what kind of accident led to the injury or condition (*tick one box*) –

Contact with moving machinery or material being machined ☐ 1	Injured whilst handling lifting or carrying ☐ 5	Trapped by something collapsing or overturning ☐ 8	Exposure to an explosion ☐ 12
Struck by moving, including flying or falling, object. ☐ 2	Slip, trip or fall on same level ☐ 6	Drowning or asphyxiation ☐ 9	Contact with electricity or an electrical discharge ☐ 13
Struck by moving vehicle ☐ 3	Fall from a height* ☐ 7	Exposure to or contact with a harmful substance ☐ 10	Injured by an animal ☐ 14
Struck against something fixed or stationary ☐ 4	*Distance through which person fell ☐ (metres)	Exposure to fire ☐ 11	Other kind of accident (give details in Section H) ☐ 15

Spaces below are for office use only. ☐

F Agent(s) involved – *see note 7*

Indicate which, if any, of the categories of agent or factor below were involved (*tick one or more of the boxes*) –

Machinery/equipment for lifting and conveying ☐ 1	Process plant, pipework or bulk storage ☐ 5	Live animal ☐ 9	Ladder or scaffolding ☐ 13
Portable power or hand tools ☐ 2	Any material, substance or product being handled, used or stored. ☐ 6	Moveable container or package of any kind ☐ 10	Construction formwork, shuttering and falsework ☐ 14
Any vehicle or associated equipment/ machinery ☐ 3	Gas, vapour, dust, fume or oxygen deficient atmosphere ☐ 7	Floor, ground, stairs or any working surface ☐ 11	Electricity supply cable, wiring, apparatus or equipment ☐ 15
Otner machinery ☐ 4	Pathogen or infected material ☐ 8	Building, engineering structure or excavation/underground working ☐ 12	Entertainment or sporting facilities or equipment ☐ 16
			Any other agent ☐ 17

Describe briefly the agents or factors you have indicated –

☐

G Dangerous occurrence or dangerous gas fitting – *see notes 8 and 9*

Reference number of dangerous occurrence ☐ Reference number of dangerous gas fitting ☐

H Account of accident, dangerous occurrence or flammable gas incident - *see note 10*

Describe what happened and how. In the case of an accident state what the injured person was doing at the time –

☐

☐ ☐

Signature of person making report ☐ Date ☐

• **FIG 4.5 cont'd**

Health and Safety Executive
Health and Safety at Work etc Act 1974
Reporting of Injuries, Diseases and Dangerous Occurrences Regulations 1985

For HSE use

Report of a case of disease

- This form is to be used to make a report to the enforcing authority under the requirements of Regulation 5.
- Completing and signing this form does not constitute an admission of liability of any kind, either by the person making the report or any other person.

A Person or organisation making report
(ie person obliged to report under the Regulations)

Name and address

Post code

Name of person to contact for further inquiry

Tel. No.

Nature of trade, business or undertaking

B Details of the person affected

Surname ______ Forenames ______

Date of birth __ __ (*day*) __ __ (*month*) 1 9 __ __ (*year*) Sex (M or F) ☐

Occupation ______

Please indicate whether *(tick box)* Employee ☐ Other person ☐

If not an employee, what is the ill person's status?
(eg self-employed or trainee)

F2508A (1/86)

continued overleaf

• **FIG 4.6**

C Details of the disease which is being reported
(a full list of diseases which are reportable is given in the accompanying notes)

For HSE Use

Name or schedule number of the disease

Date of doctor's statement which first diagnosed the disease [day] [month] [19 year]

Doctor's name and address, if known

Post code

D Description of work giving rise to this report

Describe any work of the affected person which might be relevant to the onset of the disease. If the disease is thought to have been caused by the ill person's exposure to an agent at work (eg a specific chemical) please state what the suspected agent is.

ENV

E Any other relevant information

Signature of person making report

Date

4

• FIG 4.6 cont'd

In the case of an event that is required to be reported, the following particulars shall be kept in records of any event that is reportable under regulation 3:

- date and time of the accident or dangerous occurrence
- the following particulars of the person affected:
  - full name
  - occupation
  - nature of the injury or condition
- place where the accident or dangerous occurrence occurred
- a brief description of the circumstances.

In the case of a disease that it is required is reported, the following records shall be kept of instances of the diseases specified in Schedule 2 and reportable under regulation 5:

- date of diagnosis of the disease
- occupation of the person affected
- name and nature of the disease.

The defence in proceedings for an offence contravening the regulations (regulation 11)

It shall be a defence in proceedings against any person for an offence under these regulations for them to prove that they were not aware of the event requiring them to notify or send a report to the enforcing authority and that they had taken all reasonable steps to have all such events brought to their notice.

THE SAFETY REPRESENTATIVES AND SAFETY COMMITTEES REGULATIONS 1977

These regulations and the supporting ACOP and HSE Guidance Notes provide a basic framework within which each undertaking can develop effective relationships. The regulations are concerned with the appointment by recognized and independent trade unions of safety representatives, the functions of the representatives and the establishment of safety committees.

Interpretation (regulation 1)

The following definitions are important to these regulations:

- *recognized trade union* means an independent trade union, as defined in section 30(1) of the Trade Union and Labour Relations Act 1974, that the

employer concerned recognizes for the purpose of negotiations relating to or connected with one or more of the matters specified in section 29(1) of the Act regarding those employed by them or one that the Advisory, Conciliation and Arbitration Service has recommended be recognized under the Employment Act 1975, which is operative within the meaning of section 15 of the Act
- *safety representative* means a person appointed under regulation 3(1) of these regulations to be a safety representative
- *workplace* in relation to a safety representative means any place or places where the group or groups of employees they are appointed to represent are likely to frequent in the course of their employment or incidentally to it.

The appointment of safety representatives (regulation 3)

A recognized trade union may appoint safety representatives from among the employees in all cases where one or more employees are employed by an employer by whom it is recognized, except in the case of employees employed in a mine.

Each safety representative shall have functions as set out in regulation 4 and shall cease to be a safety representative when:

- their trade union notifies the employer in writing that their appointment has been terminated
- they cease to be employed at the workplace
- they resign.

A person appointed as a safety representative shall, so far as is reasonably practicable, either have been employed by their employer throughout the preceding two years or have had at least two years' experience in similar employment.

The functions of safety representatives (regulation 4)

In addition to their function under section (2)(4) of the HSWA to represent the employees in consultation with the employer under section 2(6) of the HSWA, each safety representative shall have the following functions:

- to investigate potential hazards and dangerous occurrences at the workplace and to examine the causes of accidents there
- to investigate complaints by an employee they represent relating to that employee's health, safety or welfare at work
- to make representations to the employer on matters arising from the investigations mentioned above
- to make representations to the employer on general matters affecting the health, safety or welfare at work of the employees at the workplace

- to carry out inspections
- to represent the employees they have been appointed to represent in consultations at the workplace with inspectors of the HSE and of any other enforcing authority
- to receive information from inspectors
- to attend meetings of safety committees in their capacity as a safety representative in connection with any of the above functions.

Any employer shall permit a safety representative to take such time off with pay during the employee's working hours as shall be necessary for the purpose of:

- performing their functions
- undergoing such training in aspects of these functions as may be reasonable in all the circumstances relating to any relevant provisions of a code of practice concerning time off for training approved, for the time being, by the HSC.

Here 'with pay' means in accordance with the Schedule to these regulations.

Inspections of the workplace (regulation 5)

Safety representatives shall be entitled to inspect the workplace or part of it if they have given the employer reasonable notice in writing of their intention to do so and have not inspected it, or that part of it, as the case may be, in the previous three months. They may, however, carry out more frequent inspections when this is agreed with the employer.

Where there has been a substantial change in the conditions of work (whether because of the introduction of new machinery or otherwise) or new information has been published by the HSC or HSE relevant to the hazards of the workplace since the last inspection, the safety representative, after consultation with the employer, shall be entitled to carry out a further inspection of the part of the workplace concerned, whether or not three months have not elapsed since the last inspection.

The employer shall provide such facilities and assistance as the safety representative may reasonably may require (including facilities for independent investigation by them and private discussion with the employees) for the purpose of carrying out an inspection, but this does not preclude the employer or their representative being present in the workplace during the inspection.

Inspections following notifiable accidents, occurrences and diseases (regulation 6)

Where there has been a notifiable accident or dangerous occurrence in a workplace or a notifiable disease has been contracted there and:

- it is safe for an inspection to be carried out

- the interests of employees in the group or groups that safety representatives are appointed to represent might be involved,

these safety representatives may carry out an inspection of the part of the workplace concerned and, so far as is necessary for the purpose of determining the cause, they may inspect any other part of the workplace. Where it is reasonably practicable to do so, they shall notify the employer or their representative of their intention to carry out the inspection.

The employer shall provide such facilities and assistance as the safety representatives may reasonably require (including facilities for independent investigation by them and private discussion with the employees) for the purpose of carrying out an inspection under this regulation, but this does not preclude the employer or their representative being present in the workplace during the inspection.

The inspection of documents and provision of information (regulation 7)

Safety representatives shall, if they have given the employer reasonable notice, be entitled to inspect and take copies of any document relevant to the workplace or to the employees the safety representatives represent that the employer is required to keep by virtue of any relevant statutory provisions except a document consisting of or relating to any health record of an identifiable individual.

An employer shall make available to a safety representative the information within the employer's knowledge necessary to enable them to fulfil their functions except:

- any information the disclosure of which would be against the interest of national security
- any information that they could not disclose without contravening a prohibition imposed by or under any enactment
- any information relating specifically to an individual, unless they have consented to its being disclosed
- any information the disclosure of which would, for reasons other than its effect on health, safety or welfare at work, cause substantial injury to the employer's undertaking or, where the information was supplied to them by some other person, to the undertaking of that other person
- any information obtained by the employer for the purpose of bringing, prosecuting or defending any legal proceedings.

Also, an employer is not required to produce or allow inspection of any document that is not related to health, safety or welfare.

Cases where safety representatives need not be employees (regulation 8)

Safety representatives need not be employees of the employer concerned in cases where the employees are members of the British Actors Equity Association or of the Musicians' Union.

Safety committees (regulation 9)

Any two safety representatives, at least, can request, in writing that, an employer establish a safety committee. Where an employer has received such a request they shall establish it in accordance with the following provisions:

- they shall consult with the safety representatives who made the request and with the representatives of recognized trade unions whose members work in any workplace the proposed committee is to oversee
- the employer shall post a notice stating the composition of the committee and the workplace or workplaces to be covered by it in a place where it may easily be read by the employees
- the committee shall be established not later than three months after the request for it has been made.

Provisions as to industrial tribunals (regulation 11)

A safety representative may present a complaint to an industrial tribunal that:

- the employer has failed to permit them to take time off in accordance with regulation 4(2)
- the employer has failed to pay them in accordance with regulation 4(2).

An industrial tribunal shall not consider such a complaint unless it is presented within three months of the date when the failure occurred or within such further period as the tribunal considers reasonable when it is satisfied that it was *not* reasonably practicable for the complaint to be presented within this period of time.

Where an industrial tribunal finds that a complaint regarding time off is well-founded, the tribunal shall make a declaration to this effect and may make an award of compensation to be paid by the employer to the employee. This shall be for an amount that the tribunal considers just equitable in all the circumstances, taking into account the employer's default in failing to permit time off to be taken by the employee and any loss sustained by the employee that is attributable to this.

Where, regarding a complaint pay, the industrial tribunal finds that the employer has failed to pay the employee the whole or part of the amount required to be paid under regulation 4(2), the tribunal shall order the employer to pay the employee the amount that it finds is due to them.

The schedule relating to regulation 4(2)

Pay for time off allowed to safety representatives

Where a safety representative is permitted to take time off, their employer shall pay them:

- where the safety representative's renumeration for the work they would ordinarily have been doing during this time does not vary with the amount of work done, as if they had been doing this work for the whole of this time
- where the safety representative's remuneration for this work varies with the amount of work done, an amount calculated by means of the average hourly earnings for that work.

These average hourly earnings are the average hourly earnings of the safety representative concerned or, if no fair estimate can be made of these earnings, the average hourly earnings for work of this description by people in comparable employment with the same employer or, if there is no one else doing this work, a figure of average hourly earnings that is reasonable in the circumstances.

THE SAFETY SIGNS REGULATIONS 1980

These regulations require that safety signs – other than those for fire fighting, rescue equipment and emergency exists – conform to a standard system with regard to colours and shapes.

Prohibition signs

These are to be circular with a red band enclosing a crossed-out symbol on a white background, such as 'No smoking'.

Warnings signs

These signs are to be triangular in shape with a yellow background and black borders, symbols and text, such as 'LPG – highly flammable'.

Mandatory signs

These are to be rectangular, incorporating a blue mandatory symbol and/or text on a white background, such as 'Wear face shield'.

Safe condition signs

These are to be indicated by a green square or rectangle with symbols and lettering in white, such as 'Emergency stop'.

BS 5378, 1976

A safety sign giving health or safety information must comply with Part 1 of BS 5378, 1976, as must any strip of alternate colours used to identify a hazard, such as 'tiger striping'.

Part 1 of BS 5378 describes the safety colours as red, yellow, blue and green:

- *red* is for stop or prohibition signs
- *yellow* is for caution or risk of danger signs
- *blue* is for mandatory signs
- *green* is for safe condition signs.

THE SIMPLE PRESSURE VESSELS (SAFETY) REGULATIONS 1991

These regulations apply to:

- simple pressure vessels, that is welded vessels made of certain types of steel or aluminium that are intended to contain air or nitrogen under pressure and manufactured in series
- relevant assemblies, that is any assembly incorporating a pressure vessel.

The regulations incorporate a number of definitions. In particular, note that:

- *safe* – means that, when a vessel is properly installed, maintained and used for the purpose for which it is intended, there is no risk (apart from one reduced to a minimum) of its being the cause or occasion of death, injury or damage to property (including domestic animals)
- *manufacturer's instructions* – are instructions issued by or on behalf of the manufacturer and include the following information:

  - the manufacturer's name or mark
  - the vessel type batch identification or other particulars identifying the vessel to which the instructions relate
  - particulars of maximum working pressure in bar, maximum and minimum working temperature in °C and capacity in litres
  - intended use of the vessel
  - maintenance and installation requirements for vessel safety

  and written in the official language of the member state accordingly
- *series manufacture* – means, where more than one vessel of the same type is manufactured during a given period by the same continuous manufacturing process, that it is in accordance with a common design
- *vessel* – means a simple pressure vessel, which is a welded vessel intended to contain air or nitrogen at a gauge pressure greater than 0.5 bar, not intended for exposure to flame, and having the following characteristics:

- the components and assemblies contributing to the strength of the vessel under pressure are made either of non-alloy-quality steel or of non-alloy aluminium or of non-age-hardening aluminium alloy
- the vessel consists of either:
  (i) a cylindrical component with a circular cross-section, closed at each end, each end being outwardly dished or flat and being also coaxial with the cylindrical component
  (ii) two coaxial outwardly dished ends
- the maximum working pressure (PS) is not more than 30 bar, and the PS.V (product of pressure and volume) not more than 10 000 bar litres
- the minimum working temperature is not lower than -50°C and the maximum working temperature is not higher than 300°C in the case of steel vessels and 100°C in the case of aluminium or aluminium alloy vessels.

The regulations apply only to vessels manufactured in series. They do not apply to:

- vessels designed specifically for nuclear use, where vessel failure might or would result in an emission of radioactivity
- vessels specifically intended for installation in, or for use as part of the propulsive system of, a ship or aircraft
- fire extinguishers.

The principal requirements of the regulations

Vessels with a stored energy of *over 50 bar litres* when supplied in the UK must:

- meet the essential safety requirements, that is with regard to materials used in construction, vessel design, manufacturing processes and placing in service of vessels
- have safety clearance, that is checks by an approved body
- bear the EC mark and other specified inscriptions
- be accompanied by manufacturer's instructions
- be safe (as defined above).

Vessels with a stored energy of *up to 50 bar litres* supplied in the UK must:

- be manufactured in accordance with engineering practice recognized as sound in the Community country
- bear specific inscriptions (but not the EC mark)
- be safe.

Similar requirements to these apply to such vessels when taken into service in the UK by a manufacturer or importer.

The regulations do *not* apply to exports to countries outside the EC or, for a transitional period, to the supply and taking into service in the UK of vessels that comply with existing UK safety requirements.

Failure to comply with these requirements:

- means that the vessels cannot be sold legally
- could result in penalties of a fine of up to £2000 or, in some cases, of imprisonment for up to 3 months, or both.

Categories of vessels

Different provisions are made for different categories of vessels depending on their stored energy expressed in terms of the product of the maximum working pressure in bar and its capacity in litres (PS.V).

Category A vessels

These are graded according to PS.V range thus:

- A.1 is 3000 to 10 000 bar litres
- A.2 is 200 to 3 000 bar litres
- A.3 is 50 to 200 bar litres.

Category B vessels

These are vessels with a PS.V of 50 bar litres or less.

For the safety requirements for Category A and Category B vessels, see under the principal requirements of the regulations, vessels with stored energy of over or up to 50 bar litres, above.

Safety clearance

A vessel in Category A has safety clearance once an approved body has issued an EC verification certificate or an EC certificate of conformity for such a vessel.

Approved bodies

These are bodies designated by member states, which, in the case of the UK, are those designated by the Secretary for Trade and Industry.

The EC mark and other specified inscriptions

Where an approved body has issued an EC verification certificate, it has responsibility for the application of the EC mark to every vessel covered by the certificate.

Where a manufacturer has obtained an EC certificate of conformity, they may apply the EC mark to any vessels covered by the certificate where they execute an EC declaration of conformity that they conform with a relevant national standard or the relevant prototype.

The EC mark must consist of the appropriate symbol, the last two digits of the year in which the mark is applied and, where appropriate, the distinguishing number assigned by the EC to the approved body responsible for EC verification or EC surveillance.

Other specified inscriptions to be applied to Category A and B vessels are:

- maximum working pressure in bar
- maximum working temperature in °C
- minimum working temperature in °C
- capacity of the vessel in litres
- name or mark of the manufacturer
- type and serial or batch identification of the vessel.

EC surveillance

This implies surveillance by the approved body that issued a certificate. The approved body has the following powers with respect to surveillance:

- powers of entry:
  - to take samples
  - to acquire information
  - t o require additional information
- to compile reports on surveillance operations
- to report to the Secretary of State cases of wrongful application, and failures by manufacturers to:
  - carry out their undertakings
  - authorize access
  - provide other facilities.

THE SOCIAL SECURITY (INDUSTRIAL INJURIES) (PRESCRIBED DISEASES) REGULATIONS 1985

These regulations list those diseases that are prescribed for the purpose of payment of disablement benefit. They were subject to minor amendments in 1987 and 1989.

A *prescribed disease* is defined in the Social Security Act 1975 as:

- a disease that ought to be treated, with regard to its causes, incidence and other relevant considerations, as a risk of occupation and not a risk common to everyone
- such that, in the absence of special circumstances, the attribution of particular cases to the nature of the employment can be established with reasonable certainty.

Schedule 1 to the regulations classifies prescribed diseases or injuries thus:

- conditions due to physical agents
- conditions due to biological agents
- conditions due to chemical agents
- miscellaneous conditions.

Within these four classifications, prescribed diseases or injuries are related to specific occupations. Each disease is numbered within the particular classification. The Schedule is very comprehensive and some examples of those listed in the four classifications are given in Table 4.1.

Table 4.1 Prescribed diseases

Prescribed disease or injury	*Occupation*
Conditions due to physical agents	Any occupation involving:
2 Heat cataract	frequent or prolonged exposure to rays from molten or red-hot material
5 Subcutaneous cellulitis of the hand (Beat hand)	manual labour causing severe or prolonged friction or pressure on the hand
9 Miner's nystagmus	work in or about a mine
Conditions due to biological agents	
1 Anthrax	contact with animals infected with anthrax or the handling (including the loading or unloading or transport) of animal products or residues
5 Tuberculosis	work in or about a mine
9 Infection by Streptococcus suis	contact with pigs infected with Streptococcus suis, or with the carcases, products or residues of pigs so infected
Conditions due to chemcial agents	
5 Poisoning by mercury or compound of mercury	the use or handling of, or exposure to, the fumes, dust or vapour of mercury or a compound of mercury or a substance containing mercury
21 (a) Localized new growth of the skin, papillomatous or keratotic (b) squamous-celled carcinoma of the skin	the use or handling of, or exposure to, arsenic, tar, pitch, bitumen, mineral oil (including paraffin), soot or any compound, product or residue of any of these substances, except quinone or hydroquinone

Prescribed disease or injury	*Occupation*
26 Damage to the liver or kidneys due to exposure to carbon tetrachloride	the use, or handling, of or exposure to the fumes of, or vapour containing, carbon tetrachloride
Miscellaneous conditions	
2 Byssinosis	work in any room where any process up to and including the weaving process is performed in a factory in which the spinning or manipulation of raw or waste cotton, or of flax, or the weaving of cotton or flax, is carried out
8 Primary carcinoma of the lung where there is accompanying evidence of one or both of the following (a) asbestosis (b) bilateral diffuse pleural thickening	a) the working or handling of asbestos or any admixture of asbestos (b) the manufacture or repair of asbestos textiles or other articles containing or composed of asbestos (c) the cleaning of any machinery or plant used in any of the foregoing operations and of any chambers, fixtures or appliance for the collection of asbestos dust (d) substantial exposure to the dust arising from any of the foregoing operations
10 Lung cancer	(a) work underground in a tin mine (b) exposure to bis (chloromethyl) ether produced during the manufacture of chloromethyl methyl ether (c) exposure to pure zinc chromate, calcium chromate or strontium chromate.

Under the regulations, pneumoconiosis, and the various causes of the disease, are treated separately.

THE WORKPLACE (HEALTH, SAFETY AND WELFARE) REGULATIONS 1992

Citation and commencement (regulation 1)

These regulations came into force on 1 January 1993.

Comment

These regulations come into effect in two stages. Workplaces that are used for the first time after 31 December 1992, and modifications, extensions and conversions started after this date, should comply as soon as they are in use. In existing workplaces (apart from any modifications) the regulations take effect on 1 January 1996 and the laws in Schedule 2 will continue to apply until that date. The majority of the requirements are of an absolute nature.

Interpretation (regulation)

The following definitions are important to the interpretation of the regulations:

- *new workplace* means a workplace used for the first time after 31 December 1992
- *traffic route* means a route for pedestrian traffic, vehicles or both and includes any stairs, staircases, fixed ladder, doorway, gateway, loading bay or ramp
- *workplace* means any premises or part of them that are not domestic premises and are made available to anyone as a place of work, including:
  - any place within the premises to which such a person has access while at work
  - any room, lobby, corridor, staircase, road or other place used as a means of access to or egress from the workplace or where facilities are provided for use in connection with the workplace other than a public road.

The application of these regulations (regulation 3)

The regulations apply to every workplace other than:

- a workplace that is, or is in or on, a ship
- a workplace where the only activities being undertaken are building operations or works of engineering construction
- a workplace where the only activities being undertaken are the exploration for or extraction of mineral resources
- a workplace that is situated in the immediate vicinity of another workplace or intended workplace where exploration for or extraction of mineral resources is being or will be undertaken, or where the only activities being undertaken are activities preparatory to, for the purposes of, or in connection with such exploration for or extraction of mineral resources at this other workplace.

When applied to *temporary work sites*, any requirement to ensure that a workplace complies with any of regulations 20–25 shall apply so far as is *reasonably practicable.*

The requirements of these regulations (regulation 4)

Every employer shall ensure that every workplace, modification, extension or conversion under their control and where any of their employees' work complies with any of the requirements of these regulations that:

- apply to these places
- are in force concerning them.

Everyone who has, to any extent, control of such places shall ensure that the places comply with any requirements of these regulations that:

- apply to these places
- are in force concerning them
- relate to matters within that person's control

Control here implies the control the person has in connection with the carrying out of a trade, business or other undertaking (whether for profit or not).

The maintenance of the workplace and of equipment, devices and systems (regulation 5)

The workplace and the equipment, devices and systems to which this regulation applis shall be maintained (which includes them being cleaned as appropriate) in *an efficient state, in efficient working order and in good repair.* They shall be subject to a suitable system of maintenance.

The equipment, devices and systems to which this regulation applies are:

- equipment and devices that if a fault occurred in them, would then be likely to fail to comply with any of these regulations
- mechanical ventilation systems provided pursuant to regulation 6.

Ventilation (regulation 6)

Effective and suitable provision shall be made to ensure that every enclosed workplace is ventilated by a sufficient quantity of fresh or purified air.

Any plant used in order to comply with this requirement shall include an effective device to give visible or audible warning of any failure of the plant, where necessary, for reasons of health or safety.

This regulation shall not apply to any confined space in a workplace.

The temperature in indoor workplaces (regulation 7)

During working hours, the temperature in all workplaces inside buildings shall be reasonable.

A method of heating or cooling shall not be used that results in the escape into the workplace of fumes, gas or vapour of such character and to such an extent that they are likely to be injurious or offensive to anyone.

A sufficient number of thermometers shall be provided to enable people at work to determine the temperature in any workplace inside a building.

Lighting (regulation 8)

Every workplace shall have suitable and sufficient lighting, which shall, so far as is reasonably practicable, be by natural light.

Suitable and sufficient emergency lighting shall be provided and maintained in any room in circumstances in which people at work are specially exposed to danger in the event of the failure of artificial lighting.

Cleanliness and waste materials (regulation 9)

Every workplace and the furniture, furnishings and fittings therein shall be kept sufficiently clean.

The surfaces of the floor, wall and ceiling of all workplaces inside buildings shall be capable of being kept sufficiently cleaned.

So far as is reasonably practicable, waste materials shall not be allowed to accumulate, except in suitable receptacles.

Room dimensions and space (regulation 10)

Every room where people work shall have sufficient floor area, height and unoccupied space for the purposes of health, safety and welfare.

This regulation shall be complied with sufficiently if any existing workplace was subject to the provisions of the Factories Act 1961 and it does not contravene Part 1 of Schedule 1 of the Act.

Workstations and seating (regulation 11)

Every workstation shall be so arranged that it is suitable both for anyone at work in the workplace who is likely to work at it and for any work of the undertaking that is likely to be done there.

Every workstation outdoors shall be so arranged that:

- so far as is reasonably practicable, it provides protection from adverse weather
- it enables anyone at the workstation to leave it swiftly or, as appropriate, to be assisted in the event of emergency
- it ensures that any person at the workstation cannot slip or fall.

A suitable seat shall be provided for everyone at work in the workplace whose work includes operations of a kind that the work (or a substantial part of it) can or must be done sitting.

A seat shall not be considered suitable unless:

- it is suitable for the person for whom it is provided as well as for the operations to be performed
- a suitable footrest is also provided, where necessary.

The condition of floors and traffic routes (regulation 12)

Every floor in a workplace and the surface of every traffic route in a workplace shall be of a construction that is suitable for the purpose for which it is used. In particular:

- the floor or surface of the traffic route shall have no hole or slope or be uneven or slippery so as, in each case, to expose anyone to a risk to their health or safety
- every floor shall have effective means of drainage, where necessary

So far as is reasonably practicable, every floor in a workplace and the surface of every traffic route in it shall be kept free from obstructions and from any article or substance that may cause a person to slip, trip or fall.

In considering whether or not a hole or slope exposes anyone to a risk to their health or safety:

- no account shall be taken of a hole where adequate measures have been taken to prevent a person falling
- account shall be taken of any handrail provided in connection with any slope.

Suitable and sufficient handrails and, if appropriate, guards shall be provided on all traffic routes that are staircases except in circumstances in which a handrail cannot be provided without obstructing the traffic route.

Falls or falling objects (regulation 13)

So far as is reasonably practicable, suitable and effective measures shall be taken to prevent any of the events specified below. Also, so far as is reasonably practicable, these measures shall be other than the provision of PPE information, instruction, training or supervision.

The events mentioned are:

- anyone falling a distance likely to cause personal injury
- anyone being struck by a falling object likely to cause personal injury

Any area where there is a risk to health or safety from any of these events shall be clearly indicated where appropriate.

So far as is reasonably practicable, every tank, pit or structure where there is a risk of a person in the workplace falling into a dangerous substance in the tank pit or structure, shall be securely covered or fenced.

Every traffic route over, across or in an uncovered tank, pit or structure shall be securely fenced. *Dangerous substance* here means:

- any substance likely to scald or burn
- any poisonous substance
- any corrosive substance
- any fume, gas or vapour likely to overcome a person
- any granular or free-flowing solid substance or any viscous substance that, in any case, is of a nature or quantity that is likely to cause danger to anyone

Windows and transparent or translucent doors, gates and walls (regulation 14)

Every window or other transparent or translucent surface in a wall or partition and every transparent or translucent surface in a door or gate shall, where necessary for reasons of health or safety:

- be of safety material or be protected against breakage of the material
- be appropriately marked or incorporate features that, in either case, make it apparent.

Windows, skylights and ventilators (regulation 15)

No window, skylight or ventilator capable of being opened shall be likely to be opened, closed or adjusted in a manner that exposes any person performing such an operation to a risk to their health or safety.

No window, skylight or ventilator shall be in a position that is likely to expose anyone in the workplace to a risk to their health or safety.

The ability to clean windows and so on safely (regulation 16)

All windows and skylights in a workplace shall be of a design or so constructed that they may be cleaned safely.

In considering whether or not a window or skylight is safe, account may be taken of equipment used in conjunction with the window or skylight or of devices fitted to the building.

The organization and control of traffic routes (regulation 17)

Every workplace shall be organized in such a way that pedestrians and vehicles can circulate in a safe manner.

Traffic routes shall be suitable for the people or vehicles using them, sufficient in number, in suitable positions and of sufficient size. They shall not satisfy these requirements unless suitable measures are taken to ensure that:

- pedestrians or, as the case may be, vehicles may use the traffic route without causing danger to the health or safety of people near it
- there is sufficient separation of traffic routes for vehicles from doors, gates and traffic routes of pedestrians that lead on to it
- where vehicles and pedestrians use the *same* traffic routes, there is sufficient separation between them.

All traffic routes shall be suitably indicated, where this is necessary for reasons of health or safety.

These requirements shall apply, so far as is reasonably practicable, to existing workplaces.

Doors and gates (regulation 18)

Doors and gates shall be suitably constructed (including being fitted with any necessary safety devices). They shall not comply with this requirement unless:

- any sliding door or gate has a device to prevent it coming off its track during use
- any upward-opening door or gate has a device to prevent it falling back
- any powered door or gate has suitable and effective features to prevent it causing injury by trapping somebody
- where necessary for reasons of health or safety, any powered door or gate can be operated manually, unless it opens automatically if the power fails
- any door or gate that is capable of opening by being pushed from either side is of such a construction as to provide, when closed, a clear view of the space close to both sides.

Escalators and moving walkways (regulation 19)

Escalators and moving walkways shall:

- function safely
- be equipped with any necessary safety devices
- be fitted with one or more emergency stop control that is easily identifiable and readily accessible.

Sanitary conveniences (regulation 20)

Suitable and sufficient sanitary conveniences shall be provided at readily accessible places and shall not be suitable unless:

- the rooms containing them are adequately ventilated and lit
- they, and the rooms containing them, are kept in a clean and orderly condition
- separate rooms containing conveniences are provided for men and

women, except where and so far as each convenience is in a separate room, the door of which can be secured from inside.

In existing factories, compliance with Part II of Schedule 1 shall be considered as sufficient compliance.

Washing facilities (regulation 21)

Suitable and sufficient washing facilities, including showers (if these are required by the nature of the work or for health reasons), shall be provided at readily accessible places.

Washing facilities shall not be considered suitable unless they:

- are provided in the immediate vicinity of every sanitary convenience, whether or not they are provided elsewhere as well
- are provided in the vicinity of any changing rooms required by these regulations, whether or not they are provided elsewhere as well
- they provide a supply of clean, hot and cold, or warm water (which shall be running water so far as is practicable)
- they include soap or other suitable means of cleaning
- they include towels or other suitable means of drying
- the rooms containing them are sufficiently ventilated and lit
- they and the rooms containing them are kept in a clean and orderly condition and are properly maintained
- separate facilities are provided for men and women, except where and so far as they are provided in a room the door of which is capable of being secured from inside and the facilities in each such room are intended to be used by only one person at a time.

This last point shall not apply to facilities that are used for washing only the hands, forearms and face.

Drinking water (regulation 22)

An adequate supply of wholesome drinking water shall be provided for all people at work in the workplace.

Every supply of drinking water shall:

- be readily accessible at suitable places
- be conspicuously marked by a suitable sign, where necessary, for reasons of health and safety.

Where a supply of drinking water is required, there shall also be provided a sufficient number of suitable cups or other drinking vessels, unless the supply of water is in a jet from which people can drink easily.

Accommodation for clothing (regulation 23)

Suitable and sufficient accommodation shall be provided:

- for anyone at work's own clothing that is not worn during working hours
- for special clothing that is worn by any person at work, but not taken home.

The accommodation shall not be considered suitable unless:

- where facilities to change clothing are required, it provides suitable security for clothes not worn
- where necessary to avoid risks to health or damage to the clothing, it includes separate accommodation for clothing worn at work and for other clothing
- so far as is reasonably practicable, it allows or includes facilities for drying clothing
- it is in a suitable location.

Facilities for changing clothing (regulation 24)

Suitable and sufficient facilities shall be provided for anyone at work in the workplace to change their clothing in all cases where:

- they have to wear special clothing for the purposes of their work
- they cannot, for reasons of health or propriety, be expected to change elsewhere.

These facilities shall not be considered suitable unless they include separate facilities for, or separate use of facilities by, men and women where necessary for reasons of propriety.

Facilities for rest and to eat meals (regulation 25)

Suitable and sufficient rest facilities shall be provided at readily accessible places. They shall:

- where necessary for reasons of health or safety include, in the case of a new workplace, extension or conversion, rest facilities provided in one or more rest rooms or, in other cases, in rest rooms or rest areas
- include suitable facilities to eat meals where food that is eaten in the workplace would otherwise be likely to become contaminated.

Rest rooms and rest areas shall include suitable arrangements to protect non-smokers from discomfort caused by tobacco smoke.

Suitable facilities shall be provided for anyone at work who is a pregnant woman or nursing mother to rest.

Suitable and sufficient facilities shall be provided for people at work to eat meals where meals are regularly eaten in the workplace.

Schedule 1, relating to regulations 10 and 20

The provisions applicable to factories that are not new workplaces, extensions or conversions

Part I: Space

No room in the workplace shall be so overcrowded as to risk the health or safety of people at work in it.

Without prejudice to the generality of this statement, the number of people employed at a time in any workroom shall not be such that the amount of cubic space allowed for each is less than 11 cubic metres.

In calculating, for the purposes of this last provision, the amount of cubic space in any room, no space more than 4.2 metres from the floor shall be taken into account and, where a room contains a gallery, the gallery shall be treated for the purposes of this Schedule as if it were partitioned off from the remainder of the room and formed a separate room.

Part II: Number of sanitary conveniences

In workplaces where *females* work, there shall be at least one suitable water closet for use by females only for every 25 females.

In workplaces where *males* work, there shall be at least one suitable water closet for use by males only for every 25 males.

In calculating the number of males or females who work in any workplace for the purposes of this Part of the Schedule, any number not itself divisible by 25 without resulting in a fraction or remainder shall be treated as the next number higher than it which is so divisible.

Schedule 2, relating to regulation 27

Part I: Repeals

These regulations repeal:

- sections 1–7, 18, 28, 29, 57–60 and 69 of the Factories Act 1961
- sections 4–16 of the Offices, Shops and Railway Premises Act 1963
- sections 3 and 5 and, in section 25, subsections (3) and (6) of the Agriculture (Safety, Health and Welfare Provisions) Act 1956.

Part II: Revocations

These regulations revoke, wholly or partly, a substantial number of Orders and regulations, in particular:

- the Sanitary Accommodation Regulations 1938
- the Washing Facilities Regulations 1964
- the Sanitary Conveniences Regulations 1964

and other Regulations dealing with safety, health and welfare in specific industries.

The ACOP and guidance notes

A very comprehensive ACOP and Guidance Notes accompany these regulations.

5

The principal cases

INTRODUCTION

The common law is based on cases recorded, in England and Wales, in the *Law Reports* and *All England Reports* (AER) and, in Scotland, the *Sessions Cases* (SC) and *Scots Law Times* (SLT). It is based on the doctrine of *precedent*, under which, in the vast majority of cases, a court must follow the earlier decisions of the courts at its own level and of superior courts – known as *binding precedent*. The doctrine of binding precedent is called *stare decisis*, which means 'keep to the decisions of past cases'. Other precedents established are of a *persuasive* nature, and are not binding. For the doctrine of *judicial precedent* to operate, it is necessary to know, first, the legal principle involved in a particular judgment (*ratio decidendi*) and, second, when a decision is binding and when it is persuasive.

The lower courts are bound by the higher courts and superior courts generally follow their own former decisions. In the lower courts, however, judgments are mainly concerned with questions of fact and so are not strict precedents.

THE FEATURES OF A JUDGMENT

Ratio decidendi

This means 'the reason for deciding', and is the legal principle behind a particular judgment, the actual finding on a particular fact. It is a propostion of law that decides the case in the light, or in the context, of the material facts. Whether or not it is binding will depend on the position in the hierarchy of the court that decided the case and of the court that is currently considering it. Thus, the *ratio decidendi* of a decision of the House of Lords binds all lower courts, whereas that of a Court of Appeal case binds the Court of Appeal and all the lower courts, but not the House of Lords.

Obiter dicta

These are 'comments by the way', such as a reference to what *could* have happened had the facts been different or a reference to an aspect of law that may not be specifically relevant to the case. *Obiter dicta* are persuasive, but not binding. However, the *obiter dicta* can be so persuasive that they may be integrated or incorporated into subsequent judgments and become part of the *ratio decidendi.*

THE PRINCIPAL CASES

The following cases form the basis for much of the current law on occupational health and safety and for its interpretation in the courts.

Donoghue v. *Stevenson* (1932) AC 562 – the duty to take reasonable care, or, the neighbour principle

The plaintiff purchased a bottle of ginger beer that had been manufactured by the defendant. The bottle was of dark glass so that its contents could not have been seen before they were poured out. The bottle was also sealed so that it could not have been tampered with until it reached the ultimate consumer. When the plaintiff poured out the ginger beer, the remains of a decomposed snail was seen floating in the ginger beer. Not unnaturally, she was taken ill, having already consumed part of the contents of the bottle.

This case established the fact that a manufacturer can be liable for negligence if they fail to take reasonable care in the manufacture or preparation of their products. Lord Atkin said 'a manufacturer of products, which he sells in such a form as to show that he intends them to reach the ultimate consumer in the form in which they left him with no reasonable possibility of intermediate inspection, and with the knowledge that the absence of reasonable care in the preparation or putting up of the products will result in an injury to the consumer's life or property, owes a duty to the consumer to take reasonable care'.

Lord Atkin's judgment went further:

> You must take reasonable care to avoid acts or omissions which you reasonably foresee would be likely to injur your neighbour , i.e. persons who are so closely and directly affected by your act so that you ought reasonably to have them in contemplating as being so affected ...

This has subsequently come to be known as *The Neighbour Principle.* It means that there must be a close and direct relationship between the defendant and plaintiff, such as that between employer and worker, occupier and visitor, shopkeeper and customer, and, second, the defendant must be able to foresee a real risk of injury to the plaintiff if they, the defendant, do not conduct their operations or manage their property with due care.

This case established the fact that a manufacturer can be liable for negligence for a defective product if it can be shown that they have failed to take reasonable care in the preparation and marketing of it and that a consumer of the product has suffered injury, damage or loss as a result.

Wilsons & Clyde Coal Co. Ltd v. *English* (1938) AC57, 2 AER 628 – the duties of employers at common law

At common law, employers owe a general duty towards their employees to take reasonable care so as to avoid injuries, disease and death at work. More specifically, employers must:

- provide a safe place of work with safe means of access to and egress from it
- provide and maintain safe appliances, equipment and plant for doing the work
- provide and maintain a safe system for doing work
- provide competent co-employees to carry out the work.

In this case, Lord Wright said that 'the whole course of authority consistently recognises a duty which rests on the employer, and which is personal to the employer, to take reasonable care for the safety of his workmen, whether the employer been an individual, a firm or company and whether or not the employer takes any share in the conduct of the operations'.

Edwards v. *National Coal Board* (1949) 1 AER 743 – 'reasonably practicable'

5

This case established the legal definition of the term 'reasonably practicable', a term that qualifies the duties of employers and others under the HSWA and many regulations. A duty qualified by 'so far as is reasonably practicable, as we saw in Chapter 4 implies a lesser level of duty than that qualified by the phrase 'so far as is practicable' (see *Adsett* v. *K. & L. Steelfounders and Engineers Ltd*).

In this case, Asquith, L.J., said ' "reasonably practicable" is a narrower term than "physically possible", and implies that a computation must be made in which the quantum of risk is placed in one scale and the sacrifice involved in the measures necessary for averting the risk (whether in money, time or trouble) is placed in the other, and that, if it be shown that there is a gross disproportion between them – the risk being insignificant in relation to the sacrifice – the defendants discharge the onus upon them'.

The burden of proof rests with the defendant to prove that the measures required were not 'reasonably practicable' in *all* the circumstances of the case.

Schwalb v. *Fass (H) & Son* (1946) 175 LT 345 – 'Practicable' in the light of current knowledge and invention

Where a statutory duty or obligation is qualified solely by the word 'practicable', this implies a higher level of duty than one qualified by 'reasonably practicable'. 'Practicable' means something other than physically possible, it means that the measures must be possible in the light of current knowledge and invention.

Paris v. *Stepney Borough Council* (1951) AC 367 – the Duty of care and the standard of care owed to vulnerable persons

This case involved a one-eyed workman employed in vehicle maintenance. The plaintiff was endeavouring to remove a bolt from the chassis of a vehicle and was using a hammer for this purpose. While hammering, a metal particle hit his good eye, resulting in total blindness. The plaintiff claimed damages from his employers for negligence on the basis that he had not been supplied with eye protection. The defendants showed in evidence that it was not standard practice to provide eye protection for activities of this nature, at least where employees had two good eyes.

The judge found for the plaintiff, but the Court of Appeal reversed the decisions on the grounds that the plaintiff's disability could be relevant *only* if it increased the risk, that is, that a one-eyed man was more likely to sustain eye injury than a two-eyed man. Having found that the risk was *not* increased, they allowed the appeal. However, the House of Lords reversed the decision and ruled that eye protection *should* have been provided for Mr Paris while undertaking work where there was a risk to his sound eye, even though the risk for a person with two sound eyes was relatively low.

Thus, an employer may owe a *higher* duty of care to an incapacitated employee than he does to an employee who is fit and has all his faculties.

Latimer v. *AEC Ltd* (1952) 2 AER 449 – the practicability of precautions and unreasonable precautions

The appellant was a milling machine operator employed by AEC Ltd. An area of a factory was flooded following a heavy storm and part of the floor was contaminated by an oily, slippery film. The floor was treated with sawdust following this event, but, owing to the very large area of floor involved, there was insufficient sawdust to cover the whole floor. The occupier of the factory was held not to be liable to an employee for injury sustained after he slipped on an untreated part of the floor.

It was held by the House of Lords that the respondents were not in breach of their statutory duty under section 25(1) of the Factories Act 1961 (for floors, steps and so on to be kept free of substances likely to cause people to slip and to be properly 'maintained'). This section referred to the general condition and soundness of construction of the floor, but did not include a 'transient and exceptional condition'. Second, it was held that the respondents had taken every reasonable step to obviate danger to the appellant and they were not liable for negligence at common law.

In this case, the practicability of the precautions was seen as appropriate in the circumstances. In the Court of Appeal, the point was put by Denning, L. J., thus: 'It is a matter of balancing the risk against the measures necessary to eliminate it'. In this situation, the cost to the defendant was too great in relation to the degree of harm that could arise.

Adsett v. *K & L Steelfounders & Engineers Ltd* (1953) 1 AER 97 and 2 AER 320 – the duties of employers with regard to dust and fume control and 'practicable' precautions

This case is one of a number of cases concerned with the interpretation of section 63(1) of the FA. This section states that, 'in every factory in which, in connection with the process carried on, there is given off any dust or fume or other impurity of such a character and to such an extent as to be likely to be injurious or offensive to the persons employed, or any substantial quantity of dust of any kind, all *practicable* measures shall be taken to protect persons employed against inhalation of dust or fumes or other impurity and to prevent it accumulating in any workroom and, in praticular, where the nature of the process makes it practicable, to provide and maintain exhaust appliances as near as possible to the point of origin of the dust, fume or other impurity, so as to prevent it entering the air of any workroom'.

The various cases have hinged on two conditions of this section, namely:

- 'dust or fumes or other impurity . . . as to be likely to be injurious or offensive to persons employed'
- 'any substantial quantity of dust of any kind'.

Where either of these two conditions is fulfilled, the occupier is under a duty to take the practicable measures detailed in the latter part of the section. The meaning of the word 'practicable' means more than 'physically possible' and imposes a stricter standard than that which is 'reasonably practicable'. The measures must be possible in the light of current knowledge and invention at the time.

Marshall v. *Gotham Co. Ltd* (1954) 1 AER 937 – 'practicable' and 'reasonably practicable'

In this case, the two levels of duty, that is those of a 'practicable' and 'reasonably practicable' nature were compared. In *Marshall* v. *Gotham Co. Ltd*, Lord Reid said, 'If a precaution is practicable it must be taken unless in the whole circumstances that would be unreasonable. And as men's lives may be at stake it should not lightly be held that to take a practicable precaution is unreasonable . . . .'

Richard Thomas & Baldwin v. *Cummings* (1955) AC 321 and 1 AER 285 – 'in motion' and 'in use' in relation to machinery

This case involved the machinery fencing requirements under the FA and the actual interpretation of machinery 'in motion or use'. The phrase includes motion *or* use in the mode or manner in which the machine operated and for the purpose for which it was used, not merely movement of any kind, and does not include movement of the parts by hand in the case of a power-driven machine.

Davie v. *New Merton Board Mills and Others* (1958) 1 AER 67 – defective work equipment

The plaintiff was employed by the defendants on a machine and, in the ordinary course of his employment, occasionally had to use a drift, that is a tapered bar about 30 centimetres long. When in use, the drift had to be struck with a hammer. The plaintiff had obtained a new drift from his employers and, although it appeared to be nearly new, at the second stroke of the hammer, the drift shattered and a piece of metal struck him in the eye, causing him to lose the sight of that eye.

The defendant established that he obtained his supply of drifts from another company who were well-established and reputable suppliers and who had, in turn, obtained them from toolmakers in Sheffield.

It was held that the employers had used reasonable care and skill in providing the tool and were not liable to the plaintiff for the injury.

Uddin v. *Associated Portland Cement Manufacturers Ltd* (1965) 1 AER 213 – dangerous machinery, disregard of danger and contributory negligence

The plaintiff was employed as a machine minder by the defendants in the packing plant in a cement factory. One day, in an attempt to catch a pigeon, he leaned across a revolving shaft in a place in which he was not authorized to be, losing an arm as a result. The shaft was part of some dust extraction equipment. However, his duties were concerned solely with the cement packing plant.

He brought an action for damages against his employer, alleging that the shaft was a dangerous part of machinery that should be fenced in accordance with section 14(1) of the FA 1937.

It was held by the Court of Appeal that the defendants were in breach of their obligations under the above section and that the plaintiff, who, at the time of the injury,

- was performing an act wholly outside the scope of his employment
- for his own benefit
- at a place to which he knew he was not authorized to go,

was not totally debarred from recovering damages. The responsibility, therefore, was apportioned on the basis of 20 per cent to the defendants and 80 per cent to the plaintiff.

John Summers & Sons Ltd v. *Frost* (1955) 1 AER 870 – the absolute duty to ensure secure fencing of machinery, reasonable forseeability and breach of statutory duty

The respondent was employed by the appellants at their steelworks as a maintenance fitter. While grinding a piece of metal on a power-driven grinder, he was injured when his thumb came into contact with the revolving grindstone. The machine was fitted with an efficient guard and the only part of the revolving grindstone exposed was an arc of approximately 18 centimetres long. There was a gap of approximately 1 centimetre between the guard and the grindstone.

It was held by the House of Lords that, as the grindstone was a dangerous part of machinery within section 14(1) of the FA 1937, there was an absolute obligation in that subsection that it should be securely fenced to prevent such injury as is *reasonably foreseeable*, regardless of whether or not the operator using the machine is careless or inattentive. In this case, the machine was not 'securely fenced' and the appellants were in breach of their statutory duty under the FA, even though the outcome of securely fencing such a machine would render it unusable.

Kilgollan v. *Cooke & Co. Ltd* (1956) 1 AER 294 – the breach of statutory duty and the 'double-barrelled' action

This case also involved the fencing requirements for machinery under the FA 1937. Here, an employee was injured as a result of his employer's failure to comply with the fencing requirements of the FA.

In this 'double-barrelled' action, the employee sued the employer for damages in two specific actions: first, for negligence, and, second, for breach of a statutory duty.

It should be noted that this legal right of an injured party to take a 'double-barrelled' action was, to some extent, excluded as a result of section 47 of the HSWA. Thus:

- a breach of any of the general duties in sections 2 to 8 *will not* give rise to civil liability
- breach of any duty contained in health and safety regulations made under the HSWA *will* give rise to civil liability, unless the regulations state otherwise.

Close v. *Steel Company of Wales Ltd* (1961) 2 AER 953 – the breach of statutory duty

The appellant was operating an electric drilling machine when the drill bit shattered and a piece struck him in the eye. He claimed damages for breach of statutory duty under section 14(1) of the FA. There was no indication that this type of accident had happened previously, although bits had shattered occasionally in the past.

It was held by the House of Lords that:

- the respondents were not in breach of duty under the section because danger from the use of the bit in the drill was not a reasonably foreseeable danger as the section required
- the duty to fence dangerous parts of machinery as required by section 14(1) was a requirement that the dangerous parts be so fenced only so as to prevent the operator's body coming into contact with the machinery
- the obligation was to fence the machinery in and not to prevent fragments

of it, or the material being worked, from flying out of the machine
- if, in a factory, there is a machine that it is known from experience has a tendency to emit parts of the machine itself or of the material being worked, so as to be a danger to the operator, the absence of a guard to protect them may well give the injured person a cause for action at common law.

Dewhurst v. *Coventry Corporation* (*The Times*, 22 April 1969) – due diligence under the OSRPA 1963 and cleaning of machinery by young people

A bacon slicer was used by staff at one of Dewhurst's shops in Coventry. There were only two employees: a manager and a boy aged 16. The machine was manually operated by turning a handle that caused the cutting blade to rotate. The blade was guarded when in use and had to be removed in order to clean the machine properly.

It transpired that there were two ways of cleaning the blade, either by:

- removing the blade from the machine and wiping it
- by cleaning it in position by drawing a cloth across half the blade and then turning the handle to expose the other half and wiping it.

No locking device was fitted to prevent the blade turning. When the boy was first employed, he was instructed to use the second of these two methods, but not to turn the handle after getting the blade into position for cleaning.

The boy was, on one occasion, told to clean the machine. He removed the gate holding the bacon and the guard to the blade. While cleaning the blade, he turned the handle and the blade rotated, cutting the tip off his left index finger. He had used this method on several occasions previously as it was quicker than the first method, but not in the presence of his manager.

The company was prosecuted and convicted for a breach of section 18(1) of the OSRPA, which requires that 'no young person employed to work in premises to which this Act applies shall clean any machinery used as, or forming part of the equipment of the premises if doing so exposes him to risk of injury from a moving part of that or any adjacent machinery'.

Dewhurst appealed to the Divisional Court of the Queen's Bench, but the appeal was dismissed on the basis that section 18(1) of the Act imposed an absolute prohibition, subject to the defence in section 67, which provided that there was no liability if *all due diligence* had been used to prevent this event. The only escape from liability was to show that no reasonable care could have prevented the injury and the company had failed in their duty because they must have foreseen that, using their method, it was intended that the handle should be used and was used, at a time, when, clearly, the boy was near the blade.

Lister v. *Romford Ice and Cold Storage Ltd* (1957) 1 AER 125 – vicarious liability, the duty to non-employees and breach of contract

This case involved a lorry driver, employed by the defendants, who negligently reversed the company's vehicle into another employee (actually his father). This employee was awarded damages to be paid by the company under the doctrine of *vicarious liability*. The defendants held insurance cover for this form of liability and the insurance company paid the damages. The insurance company subsequently sued the lorry driver in the name of the company to recover what they had paid out.

It was held unanimously in the House of Lords that the lorry driver, as a servant of the company, owed them a duty to perform his tasks with reasonable care and skill, and that a servant who involves his master in vicarious liability by reason of negligence is liable in damages to the master for breach of contract. The damages in such a case amount to a complete indemnity with regard to the amount that the employer has been held vicariously liable to pay the injured plaintiff.

White v. *Pressed Steel Fisher Ltd* (1980) IRLR 176 – the training of trade union safety representatives

Under section 2(2)(c) of the HSWA, an employer must provide information, instruction and training for their employees. This case drew the distinction, however, between the health and safety training that an employer must provide, so far as is reasonably practicable, for all their employees, which includes trade union-appointed safety representatives, and the specialist training required for a safety representative in trade union aspects of their work as a representative of the union's members. 5

Thus, the training of safety representatives must be viewed by employers as being different to that required for other trade union officials who, by virtue of section 27 of the EPCA, must be approved by the TUC.

Thompson, Gray, Nicholson v. *Smiths Ship Repairers (North Shields) Ltd* (1984) IRLR 93–116 – occupational deafness and the apportionment of liability

This was one of several cases involving a claim for occupational deafness by an employee who had been exposed to noise in a number of former employments. Former cases had established the view that the last employer was specifically liable for damages. However, it was recognized that much occupational deafness occurs during the early years of exposure, and that previous employers could have been subject to a similar claim.

The outcome of this case is the tendency of the courts to apportion liability between the various employers, all of whom, through exposing the individual to various levels of noise, have contributed to the hearing loss and subsequent occupational deafness.

R. v. *Swan Hunter Shipbuilders Ltd* (1982) 1 AER 264 – the provision of safety instructions to both employees and non-employees

This case was brought by the HSE following the deaths of eight workmen on board HMS Glasgow in 1976, which was being fitted out in Swan Hunter's shipyard in Newcastle-upon-Tyne at that time.

Oxygen had leaked for several hours from a hose on a higher deck that passed down through a hatch and a cable duct into a compartment on the lowest deck. The last known user of the oxygen hose most likely to have been the source of the leak was an employee of Telemeter Installations, a firm of subcontractors.

The fire burned extremely rapidly and fiercely because the original flame was ignited in a confined space in an atmosphere heavily enriched with oxygen. Minutes before, four workers had tried to smoke cigarettes, but had found that these had rapidly burned away as soon as they were lit, a classic indication of oxygen enrichment.

Swan Hunter Shipbuilders Ltd were charged with the following breaches of the HSWA:

- under section 2(2)(a), the failure to provide and maintain a safe system of work
- under section 2(2)(c), the failure to provide information and instruction for their own employees
- under section 3(1), the failure to conduct their undertaking in such a way as to ensure that those *not* in their employ were not exposed to risks.

Swan Hunter submitted that it was not their responsibility to inform and instruct employees working on the ship who were not their own employees. It was this last submission that the trial judge turned down and whose decision the Court of Appeal agreed with.

Lord Justice Dunn said that Swan Hunter's had a strict duty 'to ensure, so far as was reasonably practicable', the health, safety and welfare of all their employees. If the provision of a safe system of work for the benefit of an employer's own employees involves informing and instructing those other than their own employees concerning the potential dangers, then the employer is under a duty to provide such information and instruction. Only if this was outside the bounds of reasonable practicability could there be any answer to a charge.

This case fundamentally emphasizes the duty of an employer to train others. In this case, it included a duty to provide subcontractors' employees with information about the dangers of oxygen enrichment in confined spaces and such instruction as was necessary to ensure the safety of *all* the workers on the vessel.

The outcome of this case was that the subcontractors, Telemeters Ltd, was fined £15 000 and the main contractor, Swan Hunter Ltd, £3000.

***British Railways Board* v. *Herrington* (1972) AC 877 – injuries to trespassing children**

In this case, the House of Lords adopted a more humane approach and softened its ruling, dating back to 1929, that an occupier owed virtually no duty of care to a trespasser even when that person was a child. The reason was based on a change in the climate of opinion as to the acceptable distribution of risks between occupiers and those injured on their premises.

Thus, an occupier may even owe a duty to trespassers in certain circumstances and must act with humane consideration. Public bodies, of course, take out public liability insurance to cover these types of claim.

Ebbs v. *James Whitson & Co. Ltd* (1952) 2 AER 192 – dermatitis from wood dust

The plaintiff was employed by the defendants as a coach builder. His job involved him in scraping and sanding monsonia wood, a species of West African walnut. The plaintiff contracted dermatitis as a result of exposure to the wood dust and claimed damages for breach of statutory duty under section 4(1) and section 47(1) of the FA 1937 (now sections 4 and 63 of the FA 1961).

It was held by the Court of Appeal that:

- there had been no breach of section 4(1) as this section related only to ventilation, not to other methods of rendering dust harmless
- the dust was not of such a character and given off to such an extent as to be injurious or offensive to those employed and, accordingly, there had been no breach of section 47(1) either.

CONCLUSION

Case law is an important source of law and goes back hundreds of years. It contains the principles and rules of common law based on the decisions of courts and reported in the various law reports. As such, common law is accumulated case law and supported by the doctrine of precedent.

In many cases, the decisions of courts based on the common law are written into statutes, to become the written law of the land.

Bibliography and further reading

Chapter 1

Department of Trade and Industry, *The Single Market: The Facts* (1990)

Dewis, M., and J. Stranks, *The Health and Safety at Work Handbook* (Tolley Publishing Co. Ltd, 1990)

Keenan, D. S., and L. Crabtree, *Essentials of Industrial Law* (Pitman Publishing 1970)

Stranks, J., *The Health and Safety at Work Handbook* (Pitman Publishing, 1994)

Zander, M., *The Law-making Process* (Weidenfeld & Nicolson, 1985)

Chapter 2

Dewis, M., and J. Stranks, *The Health and Safety at Work Handbook* (Tolley Publishing Co. Ltd, 1990)

Munkman, J., *Employer's Liability at Common Law* (Butterworths, 1979)

Chapter 3

Broadhurst, V. A., *The Health and Safety at Work Act in Practice* (Heyden, London, 1978)

Dewis, M., and J. Stranks, *Fire Prevention and Regulations Handbook* (Royal Society for the Prevention of Accidents, Birmingham, 1988)

Fife, I., and E. A. Machin, *Redgrave's Health and Safety in Factories* (Butterworths, 1988)

Home Office and Scottish Home and Health Department, *Guides to the Fire Precautions Act 1971* (HMSO, 1977)

Zander, M., *The Law-making Process* (Weidenfeld & Nicolson, 1985)

Chapter 4

Health and Safety Commission, *First Aid at Work: Health and Safety (Frist Aid) Regulations 1981: Approved code of practice* (HMSO, 1990)

Health and Safety Commission, *Management of Health and Safety at Work: Approved code of practice* (HMSO, 1992)

Health and Safety Commission, *Safety of Pressure Systems: Approved code of practice* (HMSO, 1990)

Health and Safety Commission, *Safety Representatives and Safety Committees* (HMSO, 1978)

Health and Safety Commission, *Workplace Health, Safety and Welfare: Approved code of practice* (HMSO, 1992)

Health and Safety Executive, *A Guide to the Pressure Systems and Transportable Gas Containers Regulations 1989* (HMSO, 1990)

Health and Safety Executive, *Control of Asbestos at Work: The Control of Asbestos at Work Regulations 1987* (HMSO, 1988)

Health and Safety Executive, *Control of Lead at Work: Approved code of practice* (HMSO, 1980)

Health and Safety Executive, *Control of Major Industrial Accident Hazards Regulations 1984 (CIMAHR): Further guidance on emergency plans* (HMSO, 1985)

Health and Safety Executive, *Control of Substances Hazardous to Health: Approved codes of practice* (HMSO, 1989)

Health and Safety Executive, *Display Screen Equipment Work: Guidance on regulations* (HMSO, 1992)

Health and Safety Executive, *Ionising Radiations Regulations 1985* (HMSO, 1985)

Health and Safety Executive, *Manual Handling: Guidance on regulations* (HMSO, 1992)

Health and Safety Executive, *Personal Protective Equipment at Work: Guidance on regulations* (HMSO, 1992)

Health and Safety Executive, *The Reporting of Injuries, Diseases and Dangerous Occurrences* (HMSO, 1986)

Health and Safety Executive, *Work Equipment: Guidance on regulations* (HMSO, 1992)

Chapter 5

Dewis, M., and J. Stranks, *The Health and Safety at Work Handbook* (Tolley Publishing Co. Ltd, 1990)

Fife, I., and E. A. Machin, *Health and Safety in Factories*, (Butterworths, 1988)

Munkman, J., *Employer's Liability at Common Law* (Butterworths, 1979)

Index